Integrative Therapy

Darrell Smith

BAKER BOOK HOUSE
Grand Rapids, Michigan 49516

Library of Congress Cataloging-in-Publication Data

Smith, Darrell.
   Integrative therapy/Darrell Smith.
   p.   cm.
   Includes bibliographical references and index.
   ISBN 0-8010-8308-7
     1. Pastoral counseling. 2. Psychotherapy—Religious aspects—Christianity. 3. Pastoral psychology. I. Title.
BV4012.2.S56 1991
253.5'2—dc20   90-37790
                                                               CIP

Printed in the United Stated of America

Contents

Preface

This book began when I wrote a paper on counseling theory in a graduate course more than twenty years ago. Instead of shelving the paper, as students usually do, I continued to expand and refine the ideas I presented in it. Eventually I developed the concepts, principles, and methods into a personal approach to counseling, published as a monograph, *Integrative Counseling and Psychotherapy* (Smith 1975). Due to the philosophical preferences of a secular publisher and the page limit imposed by a monograph, I did not integrate Christian principles as much as I had hoped to. Since then the themes of integrative counseling and psychotherapy have been at the center of my professional life as a trainer of counseling psychologists, a researcher, and a part-time psychological counselor.

I have always wanted to develop my concept of counseling and psychotherapy fully and offer it in book form as *Integrative Therapy*. Another author (Urban 1978, 1981) has published his work under this major title, but he writes from a non-Christian perspective. Since Urban and I have different readers in mind, I feel comfortable using the same title. Also, I published my thoughts on integrative therapy several years before he did.

This book is my attempt to formulate an approach that responds both to the current theoretical openness in counseling and psychotherapy and to the interest prevalent among Christian counselors and therapists. I have sought to create a counseling approach that is theologically sound, theoretically open, and methodologically rich and varied. At the same time, I have aimed for an outlook that is disciplined, systematic, and true to evangelical Christian faith.

No single theory encompasses the complete truth about human personality and therapeutic change. Rather, a comprehensive approach to counseling and psychotherapy integrates biblical concepts and principles with unique, complementary elements carefully derived from many theories and methods of psychotherapy. Throughout my crafting of this integrative approach, I have worked with the attitude Koteskey (1980) communicated when he wrote, "This book is not an attempt to point out what is unchristian about various [theories of counseling and psychotherapy], but an attempt to take what is consistent with Christianity and show how it fits into the perspective presented here" (31).

Integrative Therapy is a model for synthesizing insights of various theories and methods into an integrated approach to counseling and psychotherapy. I hope it will prove helpful as a guide for colleagues, students, and trainees who wish to follow an integrative path to the understanding and practice of psychotherapy. It is not intended to represent a new system or school of psychotherapy.

I have tried to write in a way that will appeal to both Christians and non-Christians. I honor both the evangelical world view and the defining criteria of good counseling theory. The book may serve either as a reference for practicing Christian counselors and therapists, on the one hand, or as a text for courses in counseling, psychotherapy, counseling psychology, clinical psychology, and psychiatry at seminaries, theological schools, and Christian colleges and universities, on the other. It also could prove useful as a supplemental text or recommended reading resource for clinical and counseling psychology, counselor education, and psychiatric social work in secular training programs, particularly for professors and students with a Christian world view.

Many people have helped, either directly or indirectly, to make this book a reality. Foremost are my seminary professors, who gave me a greater understanding of the Scriptures and their relevance to all of life's questions and issues. My counseling and psychology professors, especially Bruce Shertzer, Shelley Stone, and Joseph Rychlak, encouraged me to write and modeled the task of building plausible frameworks to understand and change human behavior.

Thanks are due to my many students, who have challenged me over the years to clarify my perspective on psychotherapy. Seminars that I have conducted on the various aspects of counseling and psychotherapy have provided a laboratory in which to examine, debate, analyze, and synthesize the contributions of all major orientations to psychotherapy.

I would be remiss not to express my sincere gratitude to my clients, who have provided an ongoing opportunity to test my integrative approach empirically through its application to their lives and problems. They have made my philosophy, theory, and methodology become concrete.

Finally, I want to express appreciation for David Benner's support and encouragement during the writing and production of this book.

Prologue

Psychotherapy is part of American culture. The process by which psychotherapy emerged and developed as a profession, first in Europe and later in America, is in some aspects analogous to the origin and development of our national heritage. Therefore, I offer here a recasting of Abraham Lincoln's Gettysburg Address as an opening statement in my discussion of counseling and psychotherapy.

Four score and some years ago a man of great genius brought forth a new psychological system conceived in the treatment of hysteria and neuroses and founded on the assumptions that all behavior is biologically, culturally, and psychically determined and that Christianity—or all religion, for that matter—is the neurosis of all humanity.

Since the founding of Freudian psychoanalysis, many other European and American psychotherapies have emerged and engaged in a civil war contesting whether that system or any system established on such nontheistic and deterministic premises can adequately account for the development of the whole human being and positive change in human behavior. We are now met on the philosophical and theoretical battlefield of that feud between conflicting systems of counseling and psychotherapy. We have come as integrationists to explore the many approaches to psychotherapy and to provide a resting place for the complementary principles, concepts, and methods derived from the works of those theorists who have invested their time and talent in order that psychotherapy might be well established and advanced as a profession. It is altogether fitting and proper that we should do this integrative work to bring together the best elements extracted from psychotherapy systems and harmonize them with the truths found in the Judeo-Christian Scriptures.

We humbly acknowledge that we cannot create, we cannot formulate, we cannot initiate a new system of psychotherapy. The creative and pioneering individuals, living and dead, Christian and non-Christian, who struggled in the development and evolution of this profession, have been productive far beyond our meager ability to add or detract. The world of counseling and psychotherapy will little note nor long remember what we say here, but it can never forget what our predecessors have contributed to this still-emerg-

9

ing profession. It is for us to be dedicated to the God of the Scriptures and to the unfinished work that previous framers of psychotherapies have thus far advanced. It is for us to be devoted to the great task of integrating compatible components of the many psychotherapies with the truths found in the Bible rather than merely perpetuating the conflict between them. It is time to bury the polemic hatchet and to begin to build unitedly and wisely upon the foundations of Scripture and the scientific bases of counseling and psychotherapy already laid.

Let us finally resolve that no one system presents the total truth regarding human beings and psychotherapeutic change, nor is any system devoid of some truth, but each system contains certain aspects of the complete truth about human behavior and its change. Let us work to give counseling and psychotherapy a new sense of vitality, openness, and unity. Let us build a psychotherapy that is concerned with the well-being of the whole person made in the likeness of a living and personal God, rather than founding, promoting, and defending proprietary schools of counseling and psychotherapy. Let us build a psychotherapy that accommodates the growth needs, hurts, and concerns of all people, rather than fostering systems that cater to the needs of select or elite clientele. Let us build a psychotherapy that honors both God and the scientific objectivity that should underlie counseling and psychotherapy, a psychotherapy that need not perish from but may flourish on the earth.

Introduction

Meaning

Integrative Therapy is a comprehensive, multidimensional approach to counseling and psychotherapy that unifies biblical truths with complementary psychological concepts, principles, and methods derived from a variety of theoretical orientations. While disciplined and systematic, it is open to all sources of truth regarding human personality and behavior and is loyal to the tenets of evangelical Christianity.

Background

My initial exposure to psychotherapy was as a client being helped by a therapist who practiced Freudian psychoanalysis. I was impressed by the insight I gained through my therapist's use of nonjudgmental free association, dream analysis, and interpretation. Such impressions commonly linger in one's memory and influence later perceptions; they did in my experience.

When I began my training in the late 1960s, Rogerian therapy was stressed as the preferred approach in counseling and psychotherapy. I welcomed the warmth, openness, and interpersonal genuineness characteristic of client-centered therapy and assimilated them into my philosophy of life. Many of the concepts—particularly the emphasis on a caring interpersonal relationship between counselor and client and a reflective, nonjudgmental style—were compatible with my Christian values. In fact, my relationships with most Christians had been more harsh and judgmental than the attitudes I saw in Carl Rogers and his kind. The new experience was like a psychological rebirth that provided an experiential outlook with an emotional expression to augment my spiritual life, which had been restricted by an excessively cognitive viewpoint or "intellectual Christianity" filled with too many dos and don'ts.

My earliest personal counseling orientation was a loosely framed hybrid of Freudian and Rogerian approaches. In my counselor-client relationships, I sought to give clients insight through reflective, interpretive, and supportive interventions. The approach worked well with clients suffering from interpersonal conflicts, poor communication patterns, difficulties with self-concept and identity, and the typical personal and social struggles. But this laid-back approach did not work so well with antisocial adolescents who had trouble with the law or adults battling with serious sexual dysfunction, substance abuse, and similar problems. I had to look further.

In my next stage of theory building, I combined a little of Freud, some of Rogers, and a variety of behavioral strategies that I fitted, not very systematically, into a Christian world view. My first written attempt to describe my eclectic approach to personal counseling was a paper prepared in a graduate course on counseling theory.

I read everything I could get on eclectic counseling and therapy and sought out advocates of this orientation. While the approach appeared to be a good idea to many therapists, including me, many others said that eclecticism was a lazy person's bag of tricks. I had no desire to be called lazy, so I sought a better name for my personal orientation. I found it in the works of Frederick Thorne. Although he considered himself an eclectic, Thorne used the terms *integrative, integrate,* and *integration* repeatedly in his writing. His *Integrative Psychology* (1967) and *Psychological Case Handling* (1968) led me to adopt *integrative* as the name for my therapeutic approach. My first published statement on integration was an article (Smith 1974) in which I addressed the methodological limits of Rogerian relationship therapy and proposed to combine Rogerian and behavioral approaches to counselor training and practice in order to provide greater accountability in counseling and psychotherapy. I gave virtually no attention in the article to specific biblical truths or principles.

In 1974 Bruce Shertzer and Shelley Stone invited me to prepare a monograph on Rational-Emotive Therapy (RET) as part of the Houghton Mifflin Guidance Monograph Series. I told them that writing a monograph on RET had little or no appeal to me but that I would be delighted to write about my own concept of counseling and psychotherapy. They welcomed that, and *Integrative Counseling and Psychotherapy* was published in 1975. Ever since then I have wanted to write about my ideas more fully in book form.

Many authors who propound integrative counseling and psychotherapy emerged in the 1970s and 1980s. Most, I surmise, are evangelical Christians. I have developed most of my ideas apart from their influence, but I do try to incorporate in this work the truths they have discovered. Many fine works exist, but those by Gary Collins (1977) and Ronald Koteskey (1980, 1983) have been especially valuable in refining my integrative approach.

Content

Knowledge of Self

Since counseling and psychotherapy is a skilled interpersonal process, Integrative Therapy sees thorough self-knowledge as the beginning of the development of a personal approach to therapy. Self-exploration and discovery engender an awareness of one's values, needs, attitudes, interests, priorities, capabilities, limits, and motives as they relate to pursuing psychotherapy as a profession. Just as "not many . . . should presume to be teachers" (James 3:1), not many should seek to be counselors and therapists. Accurate self-knowledge is necessary for both deciding on psychotherapy as a career and functioning effectively as a counselor or a therapist. Among the ways of obtaining self-knowledge are involvement in experiential learning that provides feedback regarding personal qualities, interpersonal effectiveness, openness to growth, and similar factors; evaluative feedback from mature, experienced mentors or professionals; test data gathered from carefully selected batteries of psychological assessment devices; voluntary or paid work in helping relationships; and enrollment in academic courses like supervised clinical practica and group process.

Knowledge of Psychotherapy

Effective psychotherapists must be informed scientist-practitioners who not only know their own orientation to therapy but also can articulate the tenets of other systems. Chapter 1 presents a careful but brief survey of the historical background of professional counseling and psychotherapy and the scientific presuppositions that relate to framing Integrative Therapy.

Philosophy of Life

Inextricably bound to a therapist's knowledge of self and psychotherapy is an articulate philosophy of life. A well-rounded philosophy of life includes a concept of the essential nature of the human person fitted into a larger set of assumptions that can be described as a personal cosmology or world view. Various conceptions of the nature of human beings and possible world views are the focus of chapter 2. The person in the likeness of God who inhabits a universe with a personal-theistic design is a central theme of this book.

Psychology of Human Development and Behavior

Strategic to Integrative Therapy is a broad psychology of human development and behavior. A theory of the healthy personality, including the role of the Holy Spirit in human growth and development, is presented in chapter 3.

Personality disorders, problematic behaviors, and problems in living versus mental illness and psychopathology are the subjects of chapter 4. How sin enters the etiology of problems in living is part of that discussion.

In chapter 5 I develop a realistic, holistic, and optimistic theory of behavior change. I consider the role of the Holy Spirit in behavior change an integral factor.

Therapy Process and Procedures

The philosophical, theoretical, and methodological dimensions of Integrative Therapy take on functional reality through a network of therapeutic processes and procedures described in chapters 6–10.

Therapeutic relationship. Chapter 6 develops the art of building and maintaining a facilitative relationship between therapist and client. The emphasis is on the well-researched central core of empathy, positive regard, nonpossessive warmth, and personal genuineness. These relationship conditions are communicated in Integrative Therapy as specific expressions of love. Transference and physical touch in the therapy process are treated as special facets of the therapist/client relationship. In chapter 6 I delineate the moral, ethical, and legal guidelines that dictate the professional limits and conduct of the integrative therapist.

Problem analysis and goals for therapy. A multimodal approach to diagnosis that stays clear of the mental-illness paradigm is the subject of chapter 7. The discussion is augmented by an identification of the criteria to be used in establishing outcome goals for the therapy process.

Modes of therapy. An extensive storehouse of complementary methods of therapeutic intervention gives Integrative Therapy methodological diversity, versatility, and richness. Chapters 8 and 9 identify, explain, and illustrate methods and techniques derived from a wide array of theoretical orientations. The strategies and methods are both complementary to one another and compatible with the philosophical, theological, and theoretical tenets of Integrative Therapy. Each method also makes a unique contribution to the storehouse of interventional modes. My objective is to demonstrate that a truly comprehensive Christian approach to therapy requires creative use of a diversity of methods and that so-called secular methods can be adapted to a solid Judeo-Christian theoretical foundation.

Chapters 8 and 9 also provide guidelines for integrative therapists in selecting and using different counseling methods and strategies for specific interventions.

Integrative Therapy in practice. Just as the proof of the pudding is in the eating, the effectiveness of Integrative Therapy is shown in its applicability to individuals, couples, families, and groups of clients in their surroundings (chap. 10). Chapter 10 also treats assessing therapy success, terminating therapy, and follow-up.

A unique feature of Integrative Therapy is its commitment to community in action. Chapter 10 concludes with a portrayal of Integrative Therapy as therapeutic teamwork in the individual's total environment that seeks an interdisciplinary approach to human development and adjustment in a psycho-socio-spiritual system. This perspective is seen as harmonious with the biblical teaching that the Christian community should live and function as an interdependent body of caring and supporting members.

Integrative Process

Several specific and essential processes are involved in crafting an integrative approach to counseling and psychotherapy.

Exploration and Observation

An open and inquisitive mind marks the integrative theory builder in the quest of truth. This intellectual and theoretical openness most likely will take the investigator into anthropology, sociology, biblical theology, psychology, and many systems of psychotherapy in the search for data descriptive of human personality and behavior and therapeutic change. Christian integrationists dare not depend solely on their own understanding in scientific inquiry, but must trust the Holy Spirit to give intellectual guidance in the pursuit of truth (Prov. 3:5–6).

Selection and Assimilation

Exploring and observing only disclose the building blocks of Integrative Therapy. The next scientific procedure consists of careful selection of appropriate data and systematic assimilation of the truth parts. Compatibility, complementarity, and internal consistency of concepts, principles, and methods are paramount concerns. Success at this stage hinges on accurate self-knowledge and a defensible world view around which a psychology of human development and behavior can be erected. This theoretical basis must be combined with a tentative approach to therapy that includes facilitative relationship skills, a diagnostic schema, ability to set basic goals for therapy, and a variety of intervention strategies.

Experimentation

The tentative formulation made at the selection and assimilation stage is hardly more than an untested hypothesis as an approach to therapy. While its parts might look good theoretically, they are not therapy until proven in

Content

Self-Knowledge
Values
Attitudes
Needs
Interests
Priorities
Capabilities
Limitations
Motives

Philosophy of Life
View of the Person
Personal World View

Psychology of Human Development and Behavior
Theory of Healthy Personality
Theory of Problems in Living
Theory of Therapeutic Personality Gain or Change

Complementary Modes of Intervention
Complementarity
Compatibility
Uniqueness of Contribution

Therapy Process and Procedures
Ethics
Relationship
Diagnosis
Goals
Methods
Outcomes
Follow-up

Community Focus
Socio-spiritual System
Therapeutic Teamwork in Total Environment
Interdisciplinary Sharing and Caring

All Truth Is God's Truth

Primary Stages

Observation and Exploration
An open and inquisitive mind actively searches for evidence of truth wherever it might be found, with a firm and consistent commitment to the premise that all truth is God's truth.

Selection and Assimilation
The truth parts are carefully selected and systematically arranged to form a tentative approach to therapy that is marked by internal consistency of concepts, principles, procedures, and methods.

Experimentation
The tentative formulation of the therapy approach is put to expirical test in clinical practice to evaluate it for proper fit of truth parts, over-all consistency, and practical effectiveness.

Integration
The cumulative results of observation, exploration, selection, assimilation, and experimentation combine to form an integrative therapy that is systematic, comprehensive, internally consistent, unified, personalized, and effective.

The Human Mind Guided by the Holy Spirit

practice. They must be tested empirically in order to determine the enduring compatibility between personal, philosophical, theological, and theoretical tenets, on the one hand, and the technical and procedural aspects, over-all consistency, and practical effectiveness, on the other.

The experimental phase discussed here has particular relevance to the training, supervisory, and pre-service stage in professional development and preparation. However, the same empirical attitude should hold true throughout the therapist's life.

Integration

The combined results of the exploratory, observational, selective, assimilative, and experimental steps form an integrated and well-articulated approach to counseling and psychotherapy. The approach is comprehensive and multidimensional; it is open, yet systematic, consistent, and empirically sound; it is a well-defined position that is flexible and fits the personality and world view of the counselor or therapist.

Figure 1

The Contents and Processes of Integrative Therapy Summarized Schematically

Repeated Testing in Practice

An integrative approach to counseling and psychotherapy that is open, yet systematic, comprehensive, unified, and empirically sound is repeatedly tested in ongoing clinical application to the problems of a diversity of clients in the real world. The repeated practice of the approach leads to further refinement of the truth parts and their harmonization both with one another and with personality and modus operendi of the therapist. Practice in the real world is the crucible in which integrative therapy is forged into formality and internal consistency and kept from inflexibility and stuffiness.

Conformity to Revealed Truth

Neo-Integration

Integrative therapy never claims to represent the final truth in counseling and psychotherapy. Instead, it is persistently open to new truth to be integrated in the ever-temporary and ever-growing approach to therapy. An empirical attitude and commitment to the unity of truth are perpetually operative.

Progressive

"Then you will know the truth, and the truth will set you free. . . [and] if the Son sets you free, you will be free indeed." [John 8:32, 36]

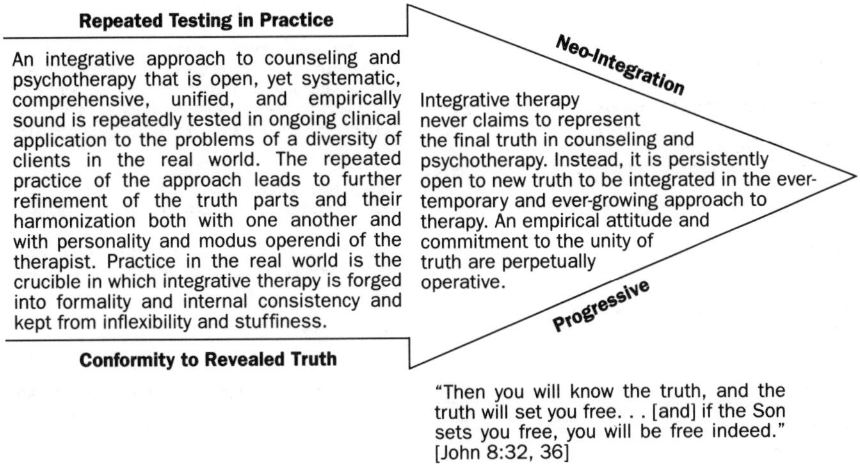

Application

Integrative Therapy proves itself by its consistent effectiveness in clients' lives. Repeated application and testing of the approach reveal the need for continual revision, updating, and modification to insure a truly scientific posture and an openness to new growth. The nitty-gritty of practical experience is the crucible in which an authentic integrative therapy is forged into formality and internal consistency.

Neo-Integration

Although the truths, particularly the steadfast biblical principles, that constitute integrative therapy are timeless, the approach itself is always temporary. Integrative therapists never presume that their approach represents the final truth. Rather, they seek new truths—concepts, principles, methods—to integrate into the ever-emerging approach. In essence, building a genuinely integrative therapy is a life-long process, and the approach will be only as dynamic and progressive as is the therapist who crafts it.

The essential contents and formative processes of Integrative Therapy are summarized schematically in figure 1.

Part 1

Foundations
of Integrative Therapy

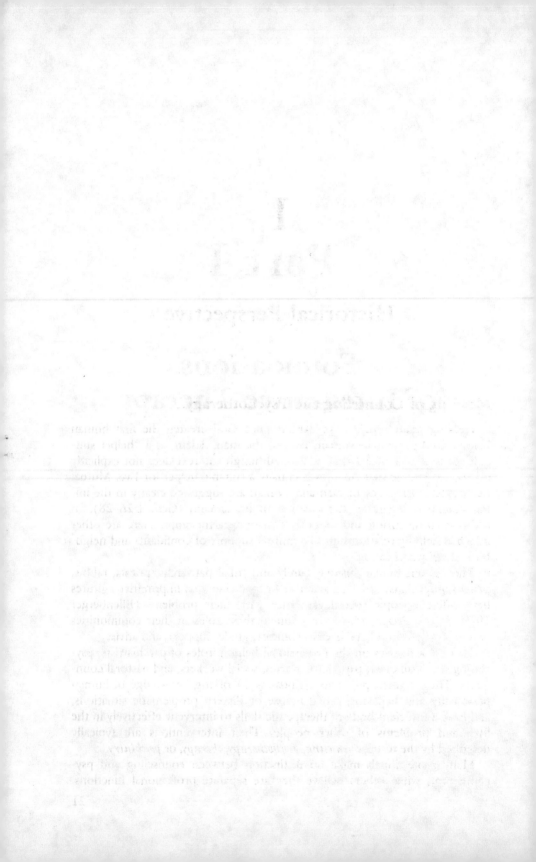

1

Historical Perspective

Meaning of Counseling and Psychotherapy

Helping relationships have existed since God created the first human beings. God presented woman, Eve, to the man, Adam, as a "helper suitable for him" (Gen. 2:18; cf. v. 20). Although the text does not explicitly say so, we assume that Adam was equally a suitable helper for Eve. Mutual helping and coregency of man and woman are suggested clearly in the initial statement regarding the creation of humankind (Gen. 1:26–28). In addition to nurturing and supportive marital partnerships, there are other informal helping relationships like mutual support of confidants and neighborly sharing and caring.

Throughout human history, family and tribal patriarchs, priests, rabbis, pastors, physicians, and even shamans or medicine men in primitive cultures have offered people special assistance with their problems (Ellenberger 1970, 3–52). People who have assumed these roles in their communities have intervened in others' lives to comfort, guide, support, and advise.

This book focuses on the professional helping roles of psychiatrists, psychologists, counselors, psychiatric nurses, social workers, and pastoral counselors. These trained professionals possess a working knowledge of human personality and behavior, can diagnose or discern problematic situations, and have a sufficient body of therapeutic skills to intervene effectively in the lives and problems of other people. Their interventions are typically described by the terms *counseling, psychotherapy, therapy,* or *psychiatry*.

Many professionals make no distinction between counseling and psychotherapy, while others believe they are separate professional functions.

Those who differentiate the two usually focus on the degree of the client's personality disturbance. In counseling, clients are viewed as normally functioning individuals who need help developing their potential. In psychotherapy, they are viewed as persons who present neuroticism or some more serious psychopathology and require remedial help with their psychological disturbance (Vance & Volsky 1962).

Patterson suggests a reasonable attitude toward the two concepts:

> There seems to be agreement that both counseling and psychotherapy are processes involving a special kind of relationship between a person who asks for help with a psychological problem (the client or the patient) and a person who is trained to provide that help (the counselor or the therapist). The nature of the relationship is essentially the same, if not identical, in both counseling and psychotherapy. The process that occurs does not seem to differ from one to the other. Nor do there seem to be any distinct techniques or group of techniques that separate counseling and psychotherapy. When objectives are considered . . . there may appear to be some differences . . . [But] it is concluded that there are no essential differences between counseling and psychotherapy in the nature of the relationship, in the process, in the methods or techniques, in goals or outcomes (broadly conceived), or even in the kinds of clients involved. [1986, xvii, xix]

On the basis of the etymology of the two terms, I prefer *psychotherapy* (healing or strengthening of the soul, mind, or life) to the term *counseling* (consulting or giving advice). Yet the practical and vernacular aspects of their usage do not allow for such an easy choice. In this book, counseling and psychotherapy are viewed as arbitrary and overlapping segments on a continuum with no clear indication where counseling ends and psychotherapy begins, if such ending and beginning even exist. Thus the words *counseling* and *psychotherapy* are used interchangeably. Furthermore, the term *therapy*, in this book, has a meaning identical to that of *psychotherapy*, being an abbreviated form of the longer word.

Psychiatry can be defined as the practice of counseling or psychotherapy by a psychiatrist, a professional individual who holds a doctor of medicine degree and may write medical prescriptions as adjunctive treatment. Other practitioners of counseling and psychotherapy typically have earned either a master's degree (e.g., M.S., M.A., M.S.W.) or a doctoral degree (e.g., Ph.D., Psy.D., Ed.D.) in counseling or clinical psychology, nursing, or social work. Nonmedical counselors and therapists usually do not write prescriptions for their clients or patients, but they are actively seeking this privilege.

A Brief History of Counseling and Psychotherapy

Ellenberger (1970) cites the year 1775 as the date of "the emergence of dynamic psychiatry . . . [when there] was a clash between the physician

[Franz Anton] Mesmer [1734–1815] and the exorcist [Johann Joseph] Gassner [a member of the clergy]. . . [This was] the fateful turning point from exorcism to dynamic psychotherapy" (53, 57).

Psychotherapy as a formal and systematic practice has its roots in the late 1800s and early 1900s, when considerable attention was directed toward personality theory and the treatment of personality problems (Corsini 1984, 8). Contemporary counseling or psychotherapy owes its existence, in a large measure, to the seminal work of Sigmund Freud (1856–1939), but it would be erroneous to give him sole credit for founding the profession. Ellenberger (1970) affirms that Pierre Janet (1859–1947) was "the first person to found a new system of dynamic psychiatry" (331); Janet in turn had been trained by the most renowned neurologist at that time, Jean-Martin Charcot (1825–1893). Freud himself studied with Charcot. Thus, from a mentoring point of view, it could be concluded that Charcot was an indirect founder of psychotherapy. At least he had a tremendous influence on its development.

Josef Breuer (1842–1925), in the opinion of Arlow (1984), originated psychoanalytic therapy proper through his sharing with Freud the hypnotic procedure he used to cure a female hysteric. Breuer and Freud subsequently collaborated in their Vienna practices from about 1883 to 1900 and published their classic work, *Studies of Hysteria*, in 1895. Freud and Breuer soon began to part company due to conflicting theories regarding the etiology of hysteria and neuroses. At the turn of the twentieth century Freud launched his own system of psychological thought.

While acknowledging the contributions of Freud's mentors and associates, I concur with Rychlak (1981, 41) that the publication of his two great initial works, *The Interpretation of Dreams* and *The Psychopathology of Everyday Life* in 1900 through 1901 marked Freud's beginnings as the father of psychoanalysis and, indeed, as the father of modern personality theory. These works and other professional productivity identify Freud as the father of modern psychotherapy as well.

In 1902, Freud invited a number of colleagues in the Vienna community to meet with him to discuss personality theory and treatment. Among that group were independent thinkers such as Alfred Adler (1870–1937), Carl Jung (1875–1961), Otto Rank (1884–1939), Wilhelm Reich (1897–1957), Paul Federn (1871–1950), and Ernest Jones (1879–1958). Some of these men, particularly Adler and Jung, had formulated many of their major concepts prior to associating with Freud. Freud was unable to hold the friendship and collegial loyalty of these equally ambitious men, who rather quickly abandoned the psychoanalytic coterie to promote their own systems of thought.

Psychotherapy systems developed by Freud, Adler, Jung, and the so-called neo-Freudians became dominant in both Europe and the United States, with Freudian psychoanalysis gaining the upper hand. The practice of psychotherapy prior to World War II was restricted largely to psychiatrists who adhered to psychoanalytic treatment or some variant of neo-Freudianism. The number of nonmedical therapists was small, and even those few were relegated primarily to psychometric tasks, often in support and assistance of psychiatrists who had little or no testing skills.

The status of psychologists changed dramatically during and after World War II. Psychiatrists were too few and inadequately skilled to meet all the assessment, placement, and psychotherapy needs in society. Special efforts were made to recruit and train psychologists to help primarily with military personnel needs. This increased role and function of clinical psychologists led to greater opportunities for other mental-health professionals. Psychologists, social workers, and other professional groups began to assume some of the same counseling and psychotherapy responsibilities once reserved for psychiatrists.

Virtually all counseling and psychotherapy until the late 1940s followed either a psychoanalytic or a directive model that reflected strong medical influences in terms of psychopathology and preferred modes of treatment. Carl Rogers (1942, 1951, 1957, 1961, 1979).undeniably revolutionized counseling and psychotherapy through his introduction of nondirective or client-centered therapy (renamed person-centered therapy in the 1970s).

About the same time that Rogers was confronting the established world of psychotherapy with an easygoing and gentle client-centered approach, behavior therapy began to emerge as a major option through the influence of Eysenck (1952, 1960), Skinner (1938, 1953), Wolpe (1958), and to lesser degrees the earlier contributions of Thorndike (1913) and Watson (1919, 1920, 1925). Wolpe made one of the first efforts to present a systematic and thorough approach to the practice of behavior therapy that was based largely on the classical paradigm. However, the emphasis on operant conditioning originated by Skinner became the central paradigm in the further development and expansion of behavioral approaches to counseling and psychotherapy.

The late 1950s and early 1960s saw rapid growth in the number of systems of counseling and psychotherapy. Most emerged from what has been labeled "third force psychology" that emphasized human potential, freedom, and self-actualization. Major among these new approaches, in addition to Rogerian person-centered therapy, were Gestalt therapy and Transactional Analysis.

Psychotherapy of the individual was the modus operandi until the mid-1950s, when group therapy began to emerge. Sensitivity training, encounter group therapy, and group process—all with an experiential base—became widespread phenomena. Psychodynamic group therapy settled out as the major approach.

An increased interest in family and marital therapy was also manifested in the 1950s and 1960s, with Nathan Ackerman (1958), John Bell (1961), and Don Jackson (1960, 1968) stressing the molding dynamics of family relationships. An important event was the cooperation of Ackerman and Jackson in 1962 to found the journal *Family Process* to give the family therapy movement an official voice. Many, but certainly not all, of the professionals involved in psychodynamic group therapy were also leaders in the marital and family therapy movement.

The 1970s and 1980s gave rise to cognitive behavior therapy, general systems theory, health psychology, and continued development of marital and family therapy. Family systems theory and cognitive behavioral emphases in particular have gained substantially in interest and influence.

Schools of Counseling and Psychotherapy

There has been a proliferation of therapy systems since Freud's psychoanalytic orientation was born less than a century ago. Following is a representative sample of schools of psychotherapy that have emerged since Freudian psychoanalysis, with the name of a founder of each system: Individual Psychology (Alfred Adler), Analytical Psychology (Carl Jung), Will Therapy (Otto Rank), Relaxation Therapy (Sandor Ferenczi), Active Analytic Psychotherapy (William Stekel), Orgone Therapy (Wilhelm Reich), Character Analysis (Karen Horney), Psychobiologic Therapy (Adolf Meyer), Interpersonal Psychotherapy (Harry Stack Sullivan), Dynamic Psychotherapy (Franz Alexander), Socio-Psychological Analysis (Eric Fromm), *Daseinanalyse* or Existential Analysis (Medard Boss), Logotherapy (Viktor Frankl), Conditioned Reflex Therapy (Andrew Salter), Psychodrama (Jacob Moreno), Personal Construct Therapy (George Kelly), Gestalt Therapy (Fritz Perls), Family Therapy (Nathan Ackerman), Behavior Therapy (Joseph Wolpe), Rational-Emotive Therapy (Albert Ellis), Transactional Analysis (Eric Berne), Reality Therapy (William Glasser), Encounter Therapy (William Schutz), Primal Therapy (Arthur Janov), Cognitive Behavior Therapy (Donald Meichenbaum), and Multimodal Therapy (Arnold Lazarus).

To illustrate that this is a mere sampling of systems of counseling and psychotherapy, let me point out that Corsini (1981) features in one huge volume "authoritative . . . account[s] of 64 major innovative approaches to psychotherapy in *current* use" (ix). In the same volume, Corsini identifies a total of 250 schools or systems of counseling and psychotherapy and remarks that this is only a partial listing of all the approaches in existence (x).

Each of the "new" systems of psychotherapy has faulted, to some degree, its predecessors and claimed superiority to them in conceptualizing the nature of the person and human behavior, the etiology and diagnosis of problems in living, the desired goal(s) of therapy, appropriate therapeutic procedures and methods, or some combination of these factors.

The assumed newness of these theories, or any psychological theory, is debatable. Boring has applied the wisdom of Solomon that "there is nothing new under the sun" (Eccles. 1:9) to the notion of originality in psychological schools of knowledge:

> I have tried to show for psychology . . . that nothing which is supposed to be new is ever really new. . . . Careful scrutiny of a creative imagination seems to reveal little that is brand-new. The ideas occur as the result of individual thinking, or the facts are found as the result of experiment, both are put forward, and nothing much happens. Then, perhaps many years later, someone comes along, sees relationships, puts things together and formulates a great theory or founds a great movement. . . . Often the formulator or founder is not even the compounder, but some other [person], who because of his personality or because of the times in which he speaks, has the capacity for gaining attention. So he originates . . . a new step in progress, lending his name to a theory or school. [1929, 114]

It is interesting to observe that the same kinds of parochialism, exclusiveness, and redundancy that characterize Christian denominationalism in churches prevail in many of the systems of counseling and psychotherapy. Stein has noticed that

> each school was founded by a charismatic leader who attracted loyal disciples. They, with their students, worked in partisan-like fashion to demonstrate the value and validity of their orientation. . . . Freudians, Jungians, Adlerians, Sullivanians, Rogerians [,] . . . each group having little, if any, communication with the others. At times, one gets the impression that there is much duplication of effort and wasted energy in these groups as they go about rediscovering each other's principles and. . . coining new terms for theories and techniques that are practically synonymous with or special cases of already existing ones. [1961, 5–6]

Others have called attention to the religiosity that surrounds exclusive schools of psychotherapy. Di Loreto asserts that

> adherence to any of these theoretical views was [is] based on faith, conviction, and personal satisfaction; and loyalties were [are] maintained and perpetuated by identification with a particular set of esoteric rituals. . . . With little more than faith and the sheer force of opinion to back their untested propositions and doctrinaire assertions, it is not surprising that these so-called coteries or "schools" of psychotherapy are based as much, if not more, on faith and dogma as on comparatively derived research findings. By worshipping their flimsy hypotheses into truth and then selecting "research" to bolster their already well developed personal convictions, these schools become implacable and categorically indestructible. [1971, 2, 7]

Wolberg (1954) has observed that the parochial bias in psychotherapy "usually takes the form of a flaunting of one's special brand of therapy as superior or 'best' . . . [and individuals] wedded to a specific school of psychotherapeutic thinking, espouse their theories with as great vehemence as they denounce and depreciate those of other schools" (106).

Ford and Urban (1963) state that "some zealots . . . give the status of fact to what originally were offered frankly as hypotheses. They . . . convert into dogma what was originally offered as theory to be tested and revised . . . [and] polemics sometimes have been the avenues chosen to settle [their] theoretical disputes" (15). Thorne (1973) has been brash enough to ascribe the term *cultist* to individuals who affiliate with a single school of psychotherapy.

No doubt there have been both good and bad motives involved in the prolific founding of psychotherapy systems. Some might have been promoted by eager aspirants who wished to achieve recognition and find their place in the sun. Also, any profession must have its share of prima donnas. Yet many of the schools of psychotherapy were developed out of unpretentious and altruistic motivations. One plausible reason for the proliferation of apparently diverse systems of psychotherapy, suggested by both Maskin (1960) and Stein (1961), is the difference in the types of clients or patients on which the founders of the different schools based their initial observations and made their therapeutic interventions.

Even with the overlap of theory and techniques, each system of counseling and psychotherapy, in most instances, has offered some innovative or unique contribution. Certainly the need for innovative counseling and psychotherapy concepts and methods will always exist, whether or not the needs warrant the introduction of "new" schools.

Ambiguity exists regarding the status of therapy systems. Both Brammer (1969) and Patterson (1974) once claimed that the days of specific schools in counseling and psychotherapy surely were drawing to a close. Just a few years later Brammer acknowledged that although their emphasis had diminished, schools of therapy still prevailed (Brammer & Shostrom 1977), while Patterson (1980) thinks he erred in his early judgment and now believes that there is even greater divergence among systems of therapy. Even though the number of psychotherapists who identify with the psychoanalytic orientation has steadily decreased over time (Kelly 1961; Garfield & Kurtz 1974; Smith 1982), the fact that psychoanalysis is the sixth most recent division (Division 39) of the American Psychological Association suggests that psychoanalytic therapy is far from its demise. Other systems of psychotherapy are equally alive today.

We cannot agree with Ivey (1980) that the final gasp of the claims of exclusive schools of therapy will soon be heard, but the findings of survey research (Garfield & Kurtz 1974, 1977; Prochaska & Norcross 1983; Smith 1982) do indicate that the heyday of schools of psychotherapy is past and that other options are desired by counselors and therapists.

Eclecticism and Beyond

Although adherence to a particular school of psychotherapy often appears to be most appropriate, and perhaps more prestigious, many counselors and therapists have shown a consistent disenchantment with exclusive systems of psychotherapy and a preference for an eclectic orientation (Garfield & Kurtz 1974, 1976, 1977; Kelly, Goldberg, Fiske & Kokowski 1978; Prochaska & Norcross 1983; Smith 1982; Swan & McDonald 1978).

The English word *eclectic* transliterates the compound Greek word *eklego,* which means literally "to pick, select, or choose." Eclecticism typically emphasizes the practice of choosing what appears best from the concepts, principles, and methods of systems developed by others. English and English (1958) define eclecticism as follows:

> Eclecticism . . . in theoretical system building, has reference to the selection and orderly combination of compatible features from diverse sources, sometimes from otherwise incompatible theories and systems; the effort to find valid elements in all . . . theories and to combine them into a harmonious whole. The resulting system is open to constant revision even in its major outlines. . . . Eclecticism is to be distinguished from unsystematic and uncritical combination, for which the name is syncretism. . . . The eclectic . . . a systematizer . . . seeks as much consistency and order as is currently possible, but . . . is unwilling to sacrifice conceptualizations that put meaning into a wide range of facts for the sake of what . . . is apt to [be considered] as a premature and unworkable over-all systematization. [168]

Theoretical eclecticism is not a new phenomenon in either psychology or psychotherapy. William James (1842–1910), the psychologist turned philosopher, sought to bring together the thoughts of tender-minded rationalists and tough-minded empiricists through the pragmatic method (1907). He considered pragmatism a mediator and reconciler that eschewed fixed principles, rigid dogma, pretense of finality in truth, and closed systems. He viewed it as marked by openness and a flexible empiricist attitude that invited the application of any and all principles, concepts, and methods that could be assimilated, validated, corroborated, and verified in reality.

Woodworth (1931, 1948, 1964) referred to himself as a "middle-of-the-roader" who saw some good in every school of psychology and believed that none of them was ideal. He maintained that each school or system makes its special contribution to the whole of psychological knowledge but no single one possesses the final answer. For a half-century Woodworth encouraged rapprochement of overtly competitive factions.

Gordon W. Allport (1964, 1968) was a self-described "polemic-eclectic" —theoretically open, yet prepared to challenge any psychological idol. His concept of a theoretical system was "one that allows for truth wherever found, one that encompasses the totality of human experience and does full justice to the nature of man" (1968, 406). Allport consistently argued for the open system in the study of personality and supported a reasoned eclecticism.

Adrian van Kaam (1966, 1968) has proposed that the existential outlook provides both the attitude and the foundation for a comprehensive theory of human beings and their behavior. He sees this psychological viewpoint as one that is open to all that is true about human nature and subscribes to the need for a continual multiplication of methods and principles. To achieve a unified theory of behavior from the isolated profiles that exist in the many particularized theories, there must be an integration of these differential constructs. The vehicle of integration is an open and ongoing dialogue between the envisioned whole and the isolated parts. The integrationist must be able to tolerate ambiguity in the process of looking for unifying principles.

Numerous eclectic approaches to psychotherapy have been developed in the last three-quarters of a century. Janet (1924, 1925), an open-minded synthesizer, attempted perhaps the first eclectic approach to psychotherapy, in which he sought to develop a comprehensive theory of personality that would allow the use of a wide range of techniques like hypnotic suggestion, automatic writing, automatic talking, corrective emotional release, moral re-education, and religious instruction.

The psychobiologic therapy or common sense psychiatry developed by Adolf Meyer (Lief 1948) represents another early eclectic option in psychotherapy. Meyer wanted an integration of the psychological, sociological, and biological dimensions of human behavior. He insisted on a comprehensiveness that included the life history of the individual, a thorough diagnosis of the clinical situation, and the application of a variety of techniques that fitted the person and the presenting problem.

Dollard and Miller (1950) endeavored, in their classic *Personality and Psychotherapy,* to integrate the psychoanalytic concepts of Freud, principles of learning theory, and cultural influences. Their stated aim was "to combine the vitality of psychoanalysis, the vigor of the natural science laboratory, and the facts of culture" (3).

Wolberg (1954) made an initial effort to extract methods from the fields of psychoanalysis, psychobiology, psychiatric interviewing, and therapeutic counseling, and to blend these extractions into an eclectic system of methodology. He has broadened the scope of the inclusions in subsequent editions of *The Technique of Psychotherapy.*

For more than thirty years Frederick Thorne advocated eclecticism in psychotherapy so ardently that he could have been recognized as the "prince of the eclectics." He wrote prolifically on eclecticism (e.g., 1955, 1961, 1967, 1968), and each of his works was encyclopedic. A quote from his *Psychological Case Handling* illustrates his position:

... to collect and integrate all known methods of personality counseling and psychotherapy into an eclectic system which might form the basis of standardized practice ... to be rigidly scientific ... [with] no priority given to any theoretical viewpoint or school ... [but] to analyze the contributions of all existing schools and fit them together into an integrated system ... [that] combines the best features of all methods. [1968, 1:vi]

Therapeutic Psychology by Brammer and Shostrom, published in 1960 and now available in the fourth edition, is a landmark in the evolution of eclectic counseling and psychotherapy. They used the term *emerging eclecticism* to define their efforts to develop a comprehensive and dynamic perspective on personality structure and change as a basis for clinical practice. They assimilated extractions from psychoanalytic, humanistic, existential-phenomenological, and behavioral approaches to form a multidimensional system of therapy.

Shostrom (1976), in developing his *Actualizing Therapy*, went at least one step beyond where he and Brammer left off in *Therapeutic Psychology*. In it he expressed dissatisfaction with eclecticism per se and stressed what he called a "creative synthesis." He used a strong humanistic base to support a theory of personality and behavior change that centers on the self-actualizing of human potential.

Another substantial work on eclectic therapy, *Beyond Counseling and Psychotherapy* (Carkhuff & Berenson 1967), featured a central core of facilitative conditions around which was built an armory of clinical methods judged compatible both with the central core and with one another. The methods were derived from client-centered, existential, behavioral, trait-factor, and psychoanalytic orientations.

In one of the latest efforts to craft an eclectic psychotherapy, Arnold Lazarus (1976, 1981) espouses a technical rather than a theoretical emphasis with his multimodal therapy. Starting with social learning theory and behavioral principles, Lazarus develops a broad-spectrum system that focuses on personality, diagnosis, and intervention in addressing the client's behavior, affect, sensations, imagery, cognitions, interpersonal relationships, and experiences with mood-modifying activities and substances like physical exercise and drugs.

Hart (1983), building on the functional psychology of William James and its application to psychotherapy by Pierre Janet, Trigant Burrow, Jessie Taft, and Frederick Thorne, has fashioned an approach that he calls "a functional orientation to counseling and psychotherapy." His modern eclectic stance employs James's pragmatic method in meshing a variety of techniques within a metatheoretical framework that uses a plurality of role models.

Several other psychotherapies with eclectic themes have appeared, exhibiting various breadths in content and levels of integration. A sample of titles and their authors includes *Developmental Counseling* (Blocher 1966, 1974), *Psychological Counseling* (Bordin 1968), *Strategies in Counseling for*

Behavior Change (Osipow & Walsh 1970), *Psychobehavioral Counseling and Therapy* (Woody 1971), *Action Counseling* (Dustin & George 1973), *Psychotherapy: An Eclectic Approach* (Garfield 1980), *A Primer of Eclectic Psychotherapy* (Palmer 1980), *Integrative Therapy: Foundations for Holistic and Self-Healing* (Urban 1978, 1981), and *Eclectic Psychotherapy: A Systematic Approach* (Beutler 1983).

A mixed audience exists regarding eclecticism in counseling and psychotherapy. On the one hand, there are those who hold that eclecticism is essential for a psychotherapy that is open, comprehensive, flexible, and truly responsive to the unique needs of clients and their gamut of problems in living (Carkhuff & Berenson 1967; Lazarus 1967; Thorne 1968; Wolberg 1954). On the other hand, some therapists—including those who endorse the eclectic attitude—believe that it is sometimes the theoretical preference of lazy, inept, and irresponsible individuals who opt for an undisciplined and poorly integrated collection of concepts and a grab bag of tricks (Brammer 1969; Hart 1983; Ivey 1980). Patterson addressed the problems with eclecticism most lucidly:

> It is difficult to know just what eclecticism means. While most eclectics may not be antitheoretical, they appear to be atheoretical. They seem to have little in common; they do not subscribe to any common principles or systems. Thus there seem to be as many eclectic approaches as there are eclectic therapists. Each operates out of his or her unique bag of techniques; on the basis of his or her particular background of training, experience, and biases; and case by case, with no general theory or set of principles for guidance. Essentially, it amounts to flying by the seat of one's pants. [1986, 460]

Counselors and therapists who consider single-theory orientations too provincial both in theory and in methodology and seek an eclectic alternative that promises the possibility of a comprehensive psychotherapy run the risk of being disappointed. Rejecting an exclusive school of therapy and adopting an eclectic stance does not necessarily fulfill the therapist's theoretical and methodological needs and interests.

It appears that many eclectic approaches can be more appropriately called syncretism (undisciplined subjectivity and poor systematization)—the very situation that English and English cautioned against in their definitional statement. This particular weakness in eclectic theory building has led many current counselors and therapists to turn away from eclecticism and strive instead for masterful integration, creative synthesis, and disciplined systematization.

Although the larger proportion of counselors and therapists continues to identify with eclecticism, there are indications that this number possibly could be decreasing (Garfield & Kurtz 1977; Prochaska & Norcross 1983; Smith 1982; Swan & MacDonald 1978). Clearly, neither exclusive schools of psychotherapy nor mediocre eclectic approaches provide what really satisfies counselors and psychotherapists. They are looking beyond both of these options for comprehensiveness and unity in psychotherapeutic truth.

The Scientific Bias in Psychology and Psychotherapy

Investigation of the human being in terms of essential nature, composition of personality, motivation, origin, and relationship to the cosmos has long been an academic pursuit of scholarly minds. Until the Renaissance and the Age of Enlightenment, and particularly during the sixteenth through the eighteenth centuries, which gave birth to modern science, researchers assumed a unified approach in studying the person. Data derived from both physical and metaphysical domains were equally acceptable in the search for a better understanding of humankind. For example, the works of Aristotle (384–322 B.C.) reveal that he did not "need to distinguish between rationalistic and empirical methods" (Boring 1950, 157) and was impartial regarding the source of knowledge or truth, whether it emerged from what might be classified as science, philosophy, psychology, or theology.

Before the emergence of science in the seventeenth century, people "were primarily concerned with the saving of their immortal souls and were perpetually seeking authority through revelation in order that they might discover truth. . . . [But during] the Renaissance, the problems of living became more important than the problems of eternity and the scientific method replaced [biblical and ecclesiastical] authority as the avenue to truth" (Boring 1950, 158–59). The empirical method of René Descartes (1596–1650) moved psychological thought, at least in France, toward materialism and helped to free both philosophy and psychology from the controlling influence of theology and religious doctrine. Boring (1950) views Descartes's work as marking "the actual beginning of modern psychology" (160).

Empiricism, the search for knowledge by direct observation of nature itself, was advanced in Britain by men like John Locke (1632–1704) and David Hume (1711–1776). Each advancement in the establishment of empiricism tended to take psychology and philosophy further from traditional values and the Christian world view.

Charles Darwin (1809–1882) used the empirical method to provide the data base for his revolutionary theory of evolution. His work, especially *The Origin of Species,* not only challenged the biblical account of theistic creation but also allowed for human beings without souls and a psychology that eventually refused to differentiate qualitatively between animals and humans.

Psychology as a discipline so named did not exist until Wilhelm Wundt (1832–1920) founded the first formal psychological laboratory in 1879 in Leipzig. His objective was to make psychology a distinct and independent science that vigorously applied the empirical method.

The central core of the scientific ideology on which both modern psychology and psychotherapy were built consists of a firm belief in empiricism, determinism, relativism, reductionism, and naturalism (Collins 1977). Thus the founders of most systems of psychology and psychotherapy worked with a mindset that assumed that "science apprehends the truth by a method involving only sense contacts, [and] anything that can be apprehended by sense contacts is natural, [and] there is no truth except scientific truth, [and] there is no truth except natural truth; therefore, there is no supernatural" (Bube 1971, 113).

Freud's frontal attack on religion and Christianity in *Totem and Taboo* (1913/1946) and *The Future of an Illusion* (1928/1955) is a classic example of the scientific bias prevalent in psychology and psychotherapy. Freud purported to trace the origin of religion to primitive cultures in which human beings conjured up animal gods to meet their needs and to protect them against violent forces of nature. The gods were to exorcise the terrors of nature, to reconcile people to the cruelty of their fate, particularly death, and to make amends for the sufferings and privations that culture imposed on them. Freud argued that human beings, as they progressed in enlightenment, created an anthropomorphic or human-like god because they needed a "father figure" whom they both admired and feared. Contrary to the Genesis account of human beings created in the image of God, Freud posited a god made in the image of human beings. Thus Freud's concept of God is nothing more than a deified hypothetical/psychological construct. The ambivalence that exists in the father-child relationship, Freud reasoned, is imprinted on all religions, whose repressive doctrines serve to create a cultural neurosis.

Freud proceeded to describe religious belief as an illusion that has wish-fulfillment as a prominent factor for its motivation. He believed that all religious beliefs or doctrines, especially belief in an exalted and paternalistic God, are premised on wish-fulfillment; therefore, all religious beliefs, indeed all religions, are illusions. Such unreal religious concoctions produce infantile dependency in human beings that prevents their growth to maturity, both in the individual and in all society. As a result, religion becomes the neurosis of all humankind. He advocated that all nations remove religions from their citizens so that the human race could come to maturity. He stood convinced that the answer to the massive neurotic condition is the application of science, which is no illusion.

It is obvious that Freud, in essence, declared war on religion and Christianity. The same type of world view has characterized psychotherapy throughout most of its history. For example, Albert Ellis (1975) echoed the themes of Freud in "The Case Against Religion: A Psychotherapist's View." It is logical that systems of psychology and psychotherapy based on naturalistic presuppositions would be explicitly or implicitly hostile toward Christianity. Even many who began their pursuit of psychological training with some degree of religious or Christian commitment (e.g., Carl Jung,

William James, Carl Rogers, Rollo May, and Erich Fromm) renounced or diminished the significance of their former religious beliefs (Vitz 1985).

The Emergence of Christian Psychotheology

The Christian world view and the scientific method need not be seen as either opposed or contradictory to each other. In fact, some of the leading figures in the development of modern science were both devout Christians and thorough scientists. Among the many that could be identified are Copernicus, Galileo, Newton, Pascal, and Mendel.

As was true before skepticism, agnosticism, and atheism colored scientific investigation, the Christian mind is committed to "unity of truth" (Holmes 1977). This attitude assumes that God is the author of all truth, whether it is found in the Bible or in nature, whether it is the content of theology, anthropology, biology, geology, mathematics, philosophy, or psychology.

During the last several decades a scattered handful of Christian psychologists and psychotherapists has communicated a psychological message that reflects traditional Judeo-Christian beliefs and values (e.g., Paul Tournier 1957, 1962; William Hulme 1956; Paul Meehl 1958; Clyde Narramore 1960; Don Tweedie 1961; John Drakeford 1967; James Dobson 1970; Larry Crabb 1975, 1977; Gary Collins 1969, 1976, 1980). Scores of evangelical authors could now be listed, indicating a surge of interest in the role of Christian values in psychology and psychotherapy. Since the 1970s there has been a rapidly expanding movement among psychologists and psychotherapists who hold to traditional values, especially evangelical Christians, to integrate psychology and theology into what might be called "psychotheology."

That Christian psychologists and therapists are serious about reframing psychological truth is evidenced by several organizational indices. The founding of the *Journal of Psychology and Theology,* under the leadership of Bruce Narramore, to serve as an evangelical forum for the integration of psychology and theology stands out as a landmark. Another visible sign is the international affiliation of Christian counselors, therapists, psychiatrists, and psychologists in the Christian Association for Psychological Studies (CAPS). The *CAPS Bulletin,* now the *Journal of Psychology and Christianity,* is a second evangelical forum for interchange among Christian professionals in mental-health work. Somewhat less evangelical but just as serious about religious values are members of Psychologists Interested in Religious Issues (Division 36 of the American Psychological Association).

From a book publishing perspective, both religious and secular publishers have been producing a phenomenal number of books dealing with psychological themes from a Christian perspective. The production of such books appears to be increasing in terms of the number of publishers and the quantity of titles.

Two clinical psychology training programs housed in evangelical institutions, Fuller Theological Seminary and Rosemead School of Professional Psychology (now the graduate division of Biola University), have been granted full accreditation by the American Psychological Association. Numerous other evangelical colleges, universities, and seminaries are developing graduate training programs in counseling and in clinical and pastoral psychology.

Christian counselors, therapists, and psychologists are seeking a modified scientific foundation on which to build approaches to psychology and psychotherapy that truly integrate the best of psychology with biblical truth in a credible manner (Carter & Narramore 1979). I addressed previously some of the scientific issues that concern evangelical Christians (Clements & Smith 1973; Smith 1975, 1978, 1979). I desire here to draw on the creative efforts of other Christian therapists and scholars, whom I highly respect, in order to lay a workable foundation for another approach to psychotherapy with a distinct Judeo-Christian base.

Bube articulated the central element of the Christian perspective on scientific investigation:

> Science apprehends the truth by a method involving only sense contacts. [While] anything that can be apprehended by sense contacts is natural, [it] may well have a supernatural interpretation. The manifestation of the supernatural in the natural can be apprehended by science, [but] any manifestation of the supernatural in a manner not apprehendable through sense contacts will be out of the domain of science. [Therefore] science is only one way of obtaining truth, [because] the whole truth always requires more than the scientific perspective. [1971, 113]

Gary Collins (1977, 137–54) goes further to provide an expanded set of assumptions that allow for a scientific foundation that is sufficient for building evangelical approaches to counseling, psychotherapy, and psychology. I have followed rather closely the statements offered by Collins but have made some minor modifications.

First, there must be an *expanded empiricism* that is open to gathering data through both sense contacts and other avenues to truth. A theistic empiricism allows for sense experience, intuition (e.g., awareness of the influence of the Holy Spirit's presence in an individual's life), and truth revealed in the Bible.

Second, there must be a *flexible determinism* that allows for genuine and God-influenced personal choices by individuals. The fact that supernatural influence is a working assumption does not reduce the realness of individual decisions and the acceptance of personal responsibility for one's choices. An absolute and rigid determinism precludes real human choices.

Third, the idea of relativism needs to be replaced with *biblical absolutism or imperativeness* in order to have sure and normative guidelines for personal value systems and decisions of a moral and ethical nature.

Fourth, a *balanced holism* must be substituted for reductionism so that the human being, personality, and behavior can be examined in their wholeness rather in an atomized fashion. A balanced holism does not rule out studying parts of the whole, but it does guard against both the fragmentation of the individual and the reduction of the person to mere material substance.

Fifth, a *Christian supernaturalism* prohibits any thought of nontheistic naturalism. This presupposition holds that a personal and sovereign God created the universe and superintends the laws and principles that give order to the cosmos.

Finally, a *biblical anthropology* based on the affirmation that human beings exist in the image of God is another central assumption in the Christian perspective on scientific investigation. Biblical anthropology addresses the impact that the misuse of freedom has had on humankind, including the state of moral and spiritual alienation from God as a result of the original decision to depart from God's will.

In summary, the essential scientific base for developing a credible approach to Christian counseling and psychotherapy consists of these dimensions:

1. The unity of truth: God exists personally and
   is the source of all truth.
2. Corollary: Human beings exist in the image of God and
   can discover and know the truth.
3. A scientific search for truth assumes:
   a. expanded empiricism;
   b. flexible determinism with freedom of choice;
   c. biblical absolutism or imperativeness;
   d. balanced holism;
   e. Christian supernaturalism;
   f. biblical anthropology.

The outline of the history of counseling and psychotherapy and the reframed scientific model serve as the background and foundation, respectively, against and on which Integrative Therapy is developed.

2

The Person in a Judeo-Christian World View

Definitive positions on the essential nature of human beings and the world in which they reside are theoretical pillars in the framework of an approach to counseling and psychotherapy. Therapists' assumptions about these two issues provide the philosophical tenor of their orientation to psychotherapy (Smith 1980) and influence procedures such as the selection of clients, establishment of counseling goals, topics of exploration, and the methods used in the therapy process (Lowe 1976). Also, descriptive data about human beings and their world serve as the warp and woof of a personal world view. The professional psychotherapist has a responsibility to be articulate about these issues.

The following are descriptions of competitive basic world views and concepts of the person, followed by a clear statement of the world view and anthropological model that form the philosophical center of Integrative Therapy.

Meaning and Components of a World View

A world view consists of the presuppositions or assumptions people hold about the makeup of their world (Sire 1976). It is a way of looking at life in terms of origin, purpose, boundaries of proper conduct, ultimate relationships, and destiny. These assumptions may be held either explicitly or implicitly and may be either fully in people's consciousness or, at times, operative but outside of their immediate awareness.

A bona fide world view includes thoughtful answers to a number of basic questions. The first question asks about the nature of ultimate reality or, more specifically, the existence and character of God or the supernatural. When questioned about the nature of God, some assert that God is a personal being; others that God is an impersonal force or principle permeating nature; others that there is no God—the only power is natural law; and still others that there is insufficient evidence for either believing or disbelieving in God.

The second question asks about the nature of the universe or cosmos. Is the cosmos a vast mechanical device that produced itself through a random arrangement of atoms and molecules over millions, perhaps billions, of years? Or is it the splendid design of an infinitely intelligent and powerful Creator?

The third question in formulating a world view asks about the nature of humankind. Are human beings malleable, unformed protoplasm passively shaped by environmental determinants, or persons with dignity and nobility created in the image of God, or something else?

The fourth question asks what basis there is for ethics and morality. Some people propose that moral and ethical behaviors stem from human experience, need, and interest and that they are autonomous, environmentally conditioned, totally situational, and have no need for any theological sanction (Kurtz & Wilson 1973; Skinner 1971, 1974). Yet the universal presence of the idea of right behavior, fair play, decency, or morality might not be a mere concept about human behavior or something humankind has created; it might derive from something above and beyond the natural sphere of human behavior (Lewis 1952).

The fifth question asked by a well-rounded world view is about death and dying. What happens to human beings at death? Are they merely complex systems of physical molecules that survive only through their progeny and in the memory of survivors (Kurtz & Wilson 1973)? Do they go through a series of existences and reincarnations until perfect oneness with the cosmos is realized? Do they survive death of the body via resurrection to live eternally either in the blissful presence of God or in painful separation from God? Or . . . ?

Finally, a complete world view asks about the meaning of human history. At one end of the spectrum are those who consider human history nothing more than a random series of cause-and-effect events with no plan or purpose. At the other end are individuals who view history as a meaningful unfolding of God's purposes for humankind, both individually and collectively.

Profiles of Basic World Views

As James Sire (1976) has remarked, the sum of extant personal world views equals the number of conscious inhabitants of the universe at any one time. From an informal perspective, this observation is probably true. But the number of formalized assumptions about the makeup of the world is substantially smaller than this sum, because authentic world views don't just happen. Rather, a personal world view becomes a formal reality through learning experiences, observation, scrutiny, debate, and deliberation. Regardless of the actual count, it is possible to identify the tenets of any given world view as essentially atheistic, agnostic, deistic, or theistic. The basic assumptions that characterize these world views can be subsumed under each of these headings.

Agnosticism

The agnostic world view maintains that metaphysical questions regarding the origin of the human species, the ontology of the universe, and the existence of God or a Supreme Being are purely speculative. There is no way of knowing or finding the answers, and even if we knew them, they would affect the quality of life little, if at all. God might or might not exist. There is insufficient evidence for either believing or disbelieving in God. There appears to be some intelligent force at work in the universe, but it need not be supernatural. The physical world and all its phenomena can be explained satisfactorily by the laws of natural science.

Human beings are either amoral or basically good and self-determining. They are enlightened and self-sufficient enough to manage their own affairs without help from any transcendent Supreme Being.

Evidence is lacking to support belief either that the human being has a separate soul or that there is life after the death of the body. To engage in speculation about such improbabilities diverts people from self-actualization and the modification of social injustices.

Moral values and ethics arise from human experience. Social relationships and culture are the significant elements in people's lives, and the big concern is to build a society characterized by justice, equality, and philanthropy.

Human history has purpose and significance simply because creative human beings give it meaning. Focusing attention on present and future possibilities and trusting in the unlimited potential of the human being serve more valuable ends than reflecting on either the past achievements of humankind or the illusion of personal salvation and immortality in the future.

Atheism

Both agnosticism and atheism subscribe to naturalism, the assumption that all phenomena in the universe can be accounted for by the laws of natural science. Perhaps the expressions *soft* and *strict* naturalism can be applied appropriately to the agnostic and atheistic viewpoints, respectively.

Strict naturalism, or atheism, denies the existence of God or any form of a supernatural being. There is no need for a God, since natural law accounts adequately for everything.

The universe is a vast, mechanical device that has resulted from forces of cause-and-effect determinism operating over millions or billions of years on particles of self-existing matter or energy. Phenomena that can be apprehended by sense contacts and validated by the rigors of the scientific method are the sum of reality.

The human species emerged from the evolutionary process and reflects the highest form of randomly arranged molecules and cells on earth. The human being is a purely physical entity whose present condition is completely determined by environmental contingencies of survival and reinforcement. Driven by biological instincts and drives, people differ from animals primarily in their capacity for rationality and self-consciousness.

Human beings become extinct as persons when their bodies die. They survive bodily death only through their progeny, tangible contributions to culture, and in the memory of survivors, particularly in how they influence others in the culture.

Ethics and morality are manmade and are derived totally from human experience. Contingencies of reinforcement shape moral and ethical values into cultural norms and practices.

The human race exists without divine purpose or providence. Therefore, history is merely a series of cause-and-effect events that emerge at the social level according to the same evolutionary forces that regulate organic evolution.

Deism

Deism stresses the supremacy of human reason and represents a world view that is at least one full step removed from Judeo-Christian theism.

God is best understood as a transcendent force or energy that created the universe and subsequently abandoned it totally and permanently. God has no personal relationship to the world, which is a vast uniformity of cause and effect in a closed system. God neither loves nor cares for humankind. The only remaining semblance of God is impersonal law that operates throughout the universe but is indifferent to human beings. Knowledge of God is limited to empirical observation of natural phenomena.

The human being is part of the clockwork of the universe but possesses intelligence, a sense of morality, and the capacity for community and creativity. The ideas of human freedom and transcendence are closer to illusion than reality. The person is made up of body, mind, and soul, but only soul and mind survive the body's death.

Ethics stems from a sense of rightness inherent in nature. Natural law is normative and always discloses what is right.

The events of human history were determined at the time of creation, and they happen in accordance with the divine law resident in nature.

Judeo-Christian Theism

The term *theism* depicts belief in a god or gods of any kind and includes varieties like monotheism, polytheism, and pantheism. For the purposes of this book, use of the term is limited to Judeo-Christian theism or belief in the personal God revealed in the Hebraic-Christian Scriptures.

This world view conceives of the universe as the magnificent design of an omniscient, omnipotent, omnipresent, and eternally self-existing Creator who is personal, approachable, and knowable. God is distinct from the physical universe and transcends it, yet is personally and immanently involved in guiding it according to the laws, principles, and goals built into a master plan. God is both Creator and Sustainer of the total cosmos and its inhabitants (Col. 1:15–17).

Humankind exists in the image of God and shares, in limited degrees, God-like attributes such as creative intelligence, moral consciousness, intrinsic worth and dignity, capacity for purposeful emotional expression, and ability to make informed choices. The human being is a unity of mind, body, soul, and spirit.

Every human being has an immortal soul and an immortal spirit and survives death of the body via resurrection. The promise of eternal life and belief in the resurrection of the body are distinguishing tenets of biblical theism.

Ethics and moral values are transcendent and are derived ultimately from the morally perfect, or righteous and just, essence of God. While a sense of morality and rightness has a theistic origin, value systems are developed and transmitted with unique nuances that define particular cultures or subcultures.

History has meaning and all events are leading toward the fulfillment of God's purposes for humankind and all creation.

Diverse Views of the Human Being

Paralleling the four basic categories of world views outlined are four distinct categories of views of the human being. These four categories were suggested by Donald Tweedie (1961).

Humans Are Mechanical

This view, based on naturalistic premises, originated in pre-Socratic thought but is current today. It considers the human being as a purely physical entity whose existence stems from the chance linkage of physical particles that make up the atomic universe. Thus, the human being is solely physical substance or protoplasm (Watson 1928), and it is useless to look inside the person to discover anything that differs qualitatively from what is observable outwardly. It is nonsense to think that a soul and a spirit, distinct from the physical body, give uniqueness, dignity, and nobility to persons (Skinner 1971).

The human being is an organized body of systemic matter among an innumerable quantity of more or less similar material bodies. The individual is essentially a machine whose behavior conforms to the general laws of nature and the rigors of empirical science. Skinner (1969) described the human being as such in the article "The Machine That Is Man." Aspects of behavior that lack empirical validation are considered spurious and must be rejected. As Allport (1962), a critic of the mechanical view of human beings, has observed, this model reduces the human being to a reactive organism no different in kind from a monkey, dog, or pigeon whose behavior is to be studied biologically, behaviorally, and mathematically in predictable terms.

The mechanical view of the person treats the individual like a living robot (Ford & Urban 1963) whose present situation is completely determined and controlled by the environmental contingencies of reinforcement and survival. The environment determines even which innate genetic characteristics have hereditary value for the survival of the human species.

The mechanical model of the human being is espoused by psychologists and psychotherapists who adhere to a strict behavioral orientation and focus largely on the animal-like attributes of humans.

Humans Are Phylogenetic

This naturalistic model views the human being as a complex biological organism who, through the evolutionary process, emerged from inanimate matter. Humankind, examined according to the rules and principles of physical science, is an inexplicable enigma among both living and nonliving matter.

The phylogenetic view of the person, popularized by Darwin, ascribes to human beings a regal position over the kingdom of all living things because of their rationality and self-consciousness. However, even the noblest and most creative human aspirations and achievements can be attributed to mere cellular activity. Social behavior and rationality are accidental or chance results of biological instincts, needs, motives, and drives. Speculations about an immortal human soul and spirit are just as spurious in the phylogenetic model as in the mechanical concept of persons.

The human being is a reactive being motivated primarily by internal drives, needs, and impulses and differs from the mechanical person primarily in the focus on determinism (Allport 1962). In the mechanical view, humans are shaped and determined by their external environment; in the phylogenetic model, they are determined by the internal environment as well.

The phylogenetic perspective on humankind has served as the anthropological model of Freudian psychoanalysis, which applied the rigidly deterministic principles of Darwinian theory to the evolution of the human psyche. Carl Jung's analytical psychology was based on a softer determinism, but he also assumed a phylogenetic model of human beings. Therapists who work from a biomedical model versus a sociopsychological model tend to view the phylogenetic paradigm as most plausible. Even humanistic therapists (e.g., Carl Rogers and Fritz Perls), who adhere to existential and self-determining tenets, usually reflect a phylogenetic outlook, especially on the physical aspects of the human being.

Humans Are Rational Animals

The rational, or classical, view of humans has its roots in the thought of Socrates, Plato, and Aristotle. Human beings are unique in the animal world due to their rational faculties. The capacity for reason and rationality—the mind—in the human being is the unifying principle and is identified with the creative and ordering principle of the universe. This creative intelligence in humans reflects what might be called God or the Primary Cause of the universe.

Historically, the classical or rational model has described the human being as a dual entity in which an essentially good rational and immortal soul or mind is imprisoned in a physical body plagued by base passions and drives. Humans express their true nature or essence only when they are thinking to attain rational ends. Defects and problems in human behavior stem from ignorance, gullibility, and irrationality. Solutions to human problems come only through rational thinking.

The modern scientific viewpoint tends to rule out the metaphysical concepts of an immortal soul or mind, limiting the study of human beings to empirically derived data. The most obvious emphasis of the model among current systems of counseling and psychotherapy undoubtedly is observed in the Rational-Emotive Therapy of Albert Ellis. Ellis, an avowed atheist, does not view the body as base but maintains that all human beings are genetically predisposed to psychopathology and are born with sizeable holes in their heads (Ellis 1977, 178).

Humans Are Bearers of God's Image

The Judeo-Christian view of the human being conceives of the person as the unique creation of a personal God and, in definite but limited ways, existing in the very image of God. The human being, a creature of God, is a unity of mind, soul, spirit, and body.

Koteskey (1980) has stated succinctly and clearly the Christian concept of human beings: "humans are a composite unity of spirit and matter created in the image of God. They are rational beings capable of personal communication and fellowship with God . . . " (17).

The person as bearer of the image of God is a central theme of all bona

fide Christian approaches to counseling and psychotherapy. Although sometimes not explicitly stated, many so-called secular systems of psychotherapy
(e.g., Jungian, Rogerian, Adlerian) reflect the nuances of the Judeo-
Christian view of and respect for the person, especially in their views of
human freedom and the counselor-client relationship. For example, Harold
Mosak (1984), one of the foremost Adlerian psychotherapists, has remarked, "These factors, variations on the Christian virtues of faith, hope,
and love, appear to be necessary, but not sufficient, conditions of effective
therapy" (73). The works of Jung, such as his *Modern Man in Search of a
Soul* (1933), touch repeatedly on themes characteristic of Judeo-Christian
anthropology.

We will return to this theme, which is indispensable to Integrative
Therapy, in the last section of this chapter.

The World View Intrinsic to Integrative Therapy

God

Focal in my concept of the universe is a God who exists eternally and
without cause (Ps. 90:2) as a unity of three co-equal but distinct persons
(Matt. 3:16–17; 28:19).

Although God, in all three persons of Father, Son, and Holy Spirit, is
identified in the Bible and by Jesus Christ during his earthly ministry as
masculine, the Scriptures also reveal that God sometimes relates to his creation with a feminine or motherly touch (Ps. 36:7; Luke 13:34). Thus I use
masculine pronouns in talking to and about God but understand him to be
androgynous in nature or at least in his treatment of human beings.

God possesses infinite intelligence and power, yet he is kind, gentle, mer-
ciful, and compassionate. While he is characterized by absolute goodness,
God has the capacity to express constructive anger. His being personal, having all the attributes of personality at the level of perfection, makes interpersonal I–Thou relationships between God and human beings both feasible
and desirable. Relationships with God are established on the same bases as
are all other person-to-person relationships—love, trust, and commitment.

As Creator, God is the ultimate source of everything that exists. He sus-
tains, rules, and guides all of creation supremely and absolutely. His
sovereignty is universal and cannot be limited or transcended by any power,
authority, or law. God is separate from his creation and is not subject to its
natural order, yet his presence permeates the whole universe, and he is personally involved in world events and human affairs.

The Cosmos

I consider the universe, the habitat of humankind and all living things, to
be the best of all possible cosmic systems. It has been designed, formed,

established, and sustained by the infinite genius of God. The cosmos is engineered for maximal beauty and efficiency. From the moment of creation the universe was complete (Gen. 1:31–2:2), yet filled with mysteries and secrets (Job 9:9–10; 38:1–40:2) enough to challenge the curious and creative mind of human beings for countless millennia.

Not only is the universe of a definite design, but also it exists for a purpose—much like the purpose for which you and I design and build a home or some other creative project: to express the character of and give pleasure to the Creator and to give enjoyment to all who share or experience it. The universe declares the glory of God (Ps. 19:1) while supplying all of the life needs of human beings.

Human beings are focal to both the design and the purpose of the universe. The universe, the earth in particular, was fashioned for people to use, rule, and enjoy. The laws and principles built into the cosmos, rather than being forces that determine human beings, exist for people to discover and use ingeniously to make the world more productive for them and to enhance their existence. When God demonstrated his creative power in forming a universe ex nihilo, he included in the overall design ample provision for people to be self-actualizing. Thus the universe as a planned system does not suggest, as many critics of the theistic model are prone to argue, a willful despot or puppeteer making all the decisions and reducing individuals to the status of robot or puppet. Instead, it is the best of all possible designs in which people can be fully human and maximize their God-given potential and talent. This is in stark contrast to the presuppositions of the naturalistic world views on which most psychotherapy approaches are based.

The Person

Holding a Judeo-Christian world view that presupposes that people are created in the image of God implies an inclusive rather than an exclusive concept of the person. The unique contributions of the views regarding humans that were reviewed earlier in our discussion are needed in the construction of a complete anthropology.

The human being, as a creature of God, exists and functions as a holistic organism. In 1 Thessalonians 5:23, this whole person is identified as a unity of *soma* (body), *psyche* (soul or subjective mind), and *pneuma* (spirit). Personal holism includes also, among other qualities, the *nous* (reason or objective mind) that is stressed in scriptural contexts such as Deuteronomy 6:5, Ephesians 4:23, and Matthew 22:37.

Physically or somatically, the human being is essentially animal and functions like much of the animal kingdom, especially the nonhuman primates. While distinctions exist between human and animal flesh (1 Cor. 15:39), in biological functioning humans are basically one with nature. Even elemental and programmed learning phenomena are similar in animals and humans.

When we focus on the higher mental or psychic functioning and the spiritual dimension, we observe phenomena unique to human beings. Among all biological creatures, only humans have an objective mind *(nous)* and a spirit *(pneuma)*. Humans are creatures of nature and might occupy the status of most advanced species in the phylogenetic spectrum, but they are very much more than mere biological organisms. Humans are unique, indeed, because they are intelligent and spiritual beings made in God's image. As Berkouwer (1962) has stated so colorfully, the human being is a "microtheos," a child of a Father who created him or her in his very likeness.

When God created man and woman, he endowed them, in finite proportions, with his attributes of intelligence, power, volition, creativeness, nobility, dignity, freedom, immortality, capacity for transcendence, moral goodness, capacity for community and fellowship, and personhood. Thus, human personhood is derived directly and exclusively from the personhood of God.

God endowed human beings with freedom and ability to plan, to decide, to act, and to become within the permissive confines of his sovereignty. There are genetic and environmental limitations that human beings must struggle with and accept, but the real choices, not illusions, that they can make determine, more than anything else, the quality of their present and future lives.

In endowing human beings with freedom of choice, God made them "free moral agents capable of personal departure from [his] will. Through misuse of [their] freedom, humans have fallen into a state of moral and spiritual alienation from God and social alienation from one another, a state from which there is recovery only through the redemption that is in Jesus Christ" (Koteskey 1980, 17).

Even in their fallen and alienated state, human beings retain—intrinsically and indelibly, however tarnished—their unique personhood marked by God-like characteristics. Alienated human beings need to respond to the redemptive love of God through a personal faith relationship with Jesus Christ in order to be reconciled to God and experience newness of life (2 Cor. 5:14–21).

Death

A painful and universal consequence of the willful transgression of God's will by human beings is physical and spiritual death (Gen. 2:17; 3:1–4:8; 5:1–5; Rom. 5:12–14). The transgression of God's will led first to the alienation of humans from fellowship with God (Gen. 3:8; Rom. 1:18–3:23). This state of personal alienation or separation is best described as spiritual death. Physical death or the separation of the human soul and spirit from the physical body is a logical and observable consequence of spiritual death.

The state of alienation and spiritual death in the human being can be changed to that of eternal spiritual life by personally accepting God's offer of salvation (Rom. 5:1–21). An acceptance of God's provision results in both a joyful, peaceful, loving fellowship with God and a living hope regarding the future. The person who has been restored to fellowship with God views physical death, though a lamentable event in human experience, as a temporary and necessary stage in the unfolding of God's plans for the human race. Furthermore, holding firmly to the Bible's claims of the immortality of the human soul and spirit and the clear promise of the resurrection of the body, persons at peace with God have no fear of death (1 Cor. 15:12–57). Rather, they courageously anticipate physical death, believing that it brings them into the actual presence of their Lord forever (2 Cor. 5:1–8; Phil. 1:21–23; 1 Thess. 4:13–18; Rev. 21:1–7).

Even though there need be no horrifying fear of death and dying, the brevity of life and the certainty of death should serve as positive motivators for pursuing meaningful and productive lives. Moses expressed the matter this way: "The length of our days is seventy years—or eighty, if we have strength . . . for they quickly pass, and we fly away. . . . Teach us [therefore] to number our days aright, that we may gain a heart of wisdom" (Ps. 90:10, 12).

A rejection of God's offer of reconciliation and restoration to fellowship perpetuates the spiritual death and alienation of human beings. The ultimate consequence is their being eternally separated, physically and spiritually, from God (Rev. 20:11–15; 21:8).

Death phenomena, from both the physical and spiritual domains, have powerful relevance to counseling and psychotherapy. Few topics warrant as much attention as death and dying. Yet most systems of psychology and psychotherapy have tended to omit open discussion of these issues. I surmise that the omission has resulted largely from discomfort with the metaphysical nuances inherent in death phenomena.

Moral and Ethical Values

All persons depend on morality, or conformity to the principles or ideals of right human conduct, to order their individual life styles and their participation in society. It is the responsibility of the shapers of culture—parents, teachers, ministers, counselors, legislators—to provide opportunities for individuals to develop effective moral judgment and to establish ethical principles to guide both personal and professional conduct. The development of moral judgment and systems of ethical values follows sequential learning and growth stages just as do cognitive development and physical maturation (e.g., Kohlberg 1981).

Forming and transmitting specific moral and ethical values are tasks of the educational process in any culture or subculture. Yet the ideals of right human conduct transcend the boundaries of natural science and all cultures.

The moral law of God is universal and is communicated through codes of law (Exod. 20:1–17), the person and teaching of Jesus Christ (Matt. 5:1–7:28), nature (Rom. 1:18–20), the human conscience (Rom. 2:14–15), and human government (Rom. 13:1–5).

The essential nature of morality and ethics is more theological than scientific. The principles and ideals of moral living and ethical practice have their origin in the just and perfect nature of God. Thus, the revealed moral law of God that reflects his essence is the ultimate standard for all moral and ethical codes.

History

Human beings, creatures of time and space, have a distinct position in history. The Old and New Testaments of the Bible tell the redemptive story of God's creating human beings and fulfilling his plans for their salvation after they chose to abandon his will. From the opening statement regarding the creation of the universe and humankind (Gen. 1–2) to the concluding disclosure about the renewing of creation (Rev. 21–22), men and women are foremost in the will and plan of God.

God is the sovereign ruler in human history, and all events are leading to the climactic end when he judges individuals and nations, sentences unbelieving angels and people to exist forever in tormented alienation from him (Rev. 19–20), and makes a new heaven and earth to be occupied eternally by himself and his people. The citizens of the renovated earth will be persons who have accepted God's offer of salvation and entered fellowship with him through the mediation of Jesus Christ.

Even most of secular history is measured by the advent of Jesus of Nazareth (e.g., dating historical events as B.C. or A.D.). "But when the time had fully come, God sent his Son, born of a woman . . . to redeem . . . " (Gal. 4:4). This Jesus, the God-man, is the central figure of history. The world and history have not been and cannot be the same since his coming to reclaim people for God.

History, when seen from the perspective of the unfolding drama of God's redemptive love for human beings, therefore has a strategic relevance to counseling and psychotherapy.

Part 2

Human Development and Behavior

3

Personality

This chapter further develops a major theme of the preceding one: the innate nature of the human being. Simply identifying the intrinsic character of the person is an insufficient anthropological base for an approach to counseling and psychotherapy. A plausible theory of personality is essential to an informed and credible psychotherapy. Here we will develop an integrated personality theory that includes a definition, the structure, the development, and the dynamics of personality.

Definition

Our frequently used terms *person* and *personality* stem from the Latin *persona,* which referred initially to the mask worn by a theatrical player in ancient Roman drama. The *persona* at first represented the particular role or character the player assumed in a dramatic performance. In time, the concept took on the additional meanings of the outward appearance of the player and, eventually, the actual self or total identity of the player. The English word *personality* has gone through a similar evolution in meaning (Allport 1937).

A typical dictionary definition of personality assumes the term to describe an individual's distinguishing behavioral, emotional, and attitudinal tendencies, character traits, and habits. These organized characteristics are the ones by which the person is recognized by self and others as unique.

Personality may be viewed as a mosaic of both visible and invisible factors, of conscious learning experiences and unconscious processes, and of innate and acquired qualities, features, and attributes. The mosaic is holistic

51

and ever changing as the individual or person grows and actualizes. Thus, personality is the person *being* and *becoming* himself or herself holistically and uniquely in day-to-day experiences.

Building on Lazarus's (1976) multimodal and pragmatic perspective, Integrative Therapy assumes that information about salient behaviors, affective processes, sensory reactions, imagery, cognitions, interpersonal relationships, particularized habits, and spiritual values provides an integrated and workable definition of personality.

Structure of Personality

While human beings are holistic organisms, they are not monolithic. The person is fundamentally a complex integration of physical and nonphysical dimensions and attributes. In the functioning of the human organism, the two domains are indivisible and nondualistic. Though the physical (body) and nonphysical (mind, soul, and spirit) aspects of personality are organismically bonded, the rational, psychic, and spiritual dimensions are distinguishable from the body per se but are manifested holistically through the medium of the body. Similarly, just as the somatic and nonsomatic aspects are united but distinguishable, so are mind, soul, and spirit.

I concur with Rychlak (1981) that one of the questions to be answered in personality theory is, "What is the essential structure of personality? Or, if structure is to be disregarded, what are we to substitute?" (31). Following is an outline of a structural framework for comprehending personality.

The Physical Person

The starting point in seeking a structure of personality is the most obvious element, the *primus locus* of personhood, the body. Without the physical body, there is no person so identified during this mortal phase of human existence. Even though the body as we know it is temporary and inferior to our promised spiritual bodies (1 Cor. 15:42–53; 2 Cor. 5:1–10), it remains the foundational component of personality. The Genesis account of creation presents the physical body as the initial component of the human being (Gen. 2:7, 21–23).

Allport (1955) has observed that the first aspect an individual encounters or experiences is the body. Young children have no awareness of any personal beingness other than their bodies. Gestalt theorists maintain that human beings don't *have* bodies, they *are* their bodies (Perls 1969).

Our physical senses, sensorimotor activities, internal sensations, and body image combine to form the basis for conceiving of ourselves as persons. Simply stated, our bodies are the bio-psycho-spiritual spaces that give us tangible existence and are the sensorimotor vehicles by which we experience reality and actualize ourselves.

The Spiritual Person

From a Judeo-Christian perspective, soul and spirit are two absolutely necessary components of human personality. They are nonphysical and immortal realities that are innate in human beings.

After forming the physical body of man from the dust of the ground, the Lord God breathed into his nostrils the breath of life and man became a living soul (Gen. 2:7). The Hebrew *nephesh* and Greek *psyche* are translated *soul* in English and are understood to refer to the life principle, self, or personal existence of the individual.

God by nature is spirit, *ruah* (Gen. 1:2) or *pneuma* (John 4:24), and he created human beings with this same quality of personality. The spirit reflects the more elegant or God-like characteristics in human personality (e.g., see Rom. 8:16) and is concerned with love, justice, truth, beauty, meaning, relationships, values, righteousness, benevolence, and eternality. Thus, the human soul and spirit, the spirit in particular, are the personality components that distinguish persons from animals and express their likeness to God.

The Sensory Person

The capacities for seeing, tasting, touching, hearing, and smelling are the individual's sensory windows and gates to the external world. Variations in the use of these marvelous senses and the diversity of perceptual nuances among human beings allow for unique personal experiences and interpretations of the phenomenal world. Someone's using one of the senses as the predominant way of experiencing the world leads to the formation of a "primary representational system" (Dilts, Grinder, Bandler, & De Lozier 1980; Grinder & Bandler, 1976). For example, some people depend predominantly on visual cues and stimuli. Their primary representational system and particular body of organized, or mapped, sensory experiences reflect a sense orientation to life that strongly influences their personality.

Responses to external stimuli are only one set of sensory experiences that characterize human personality. Various internal sensations that might have very little or no connection to the external environment also shape people's identities.

The Feeling Person

Closely related to bodily sensations and sensory responses is a wide range of psychological phenomena that can be described as the experiences of the feeling person. These human experiences include emotions, feelings, desires, moods, affections, and sentiments. The Scriptures vividly describe the emotions of both God and human beings. Most often the heart (*leb* in Hebrew and *kardia* in Greek), which is the center of both physical life and consciousness, is identified as the source of all feelings and emotions (e.g., Gen. 6:5–6; Rom. 9:2).

The feeling person can be associated, but not too closely, with Freud's concept of the Id that seeks to invest emotional or instinctual energy in love objects and to experience pleasure and avoid pain. The feeling person also reflects the same dimension of personality that Berne, in Transactional Analysis, envisioned in the Child ego state, which expresses the emotional or felt concept of life. The feeling person also is somewhat synonymous to Rogers's idea of the sensory and visceral "experiencing organism" in that both concepts center on the emotionality associated with intra-, inter-, and extrapersonal experiences.

The Thinking Person

A characterizing feature of the human being is the capacity for creative reasoning and rational thinking. This faculty of the personality can be described best as active mind or intelligence. While thinking or reasoning is associated primarily with the functioning of the brain, the thinking and reasoning process appears to be more organismic than mere brain-centered activity.

The word *nous* was used by ancient Greek scholars and the writers of the New Testament to identify the highest level of rational and intelligent functioning in the human being (e.g., Rom. 7:23; 12:2). However, a central connotation of *soul* or *psyche* is mind or mental functioning. Thus, *soul* or *psyche* is also used to express the rational or reasoning faculty of the human personality (Prov. 23:7, Hebrew). Reference also is made to the heart as a seat of reason and intelligent processing (Dan. 2:30, Hebrew; Matt. 13:15).

The thinking person in Integrative Therapy suggests Freud's concept of Ego or reality principle, which is based on the secondary process or rational thinking; Berne's Adult ego state, which has reference to the "thought concept of life"; and Ellis's rational thinker.

The Valuing Person

The individual's valuing capacity is still another dimension of personality. Reason, emotion, and spirituality all interact to effect the valuing person.

The innate sense of moral rightness is the logical starting point to understand the valuing person. In Judeo-Christian anthropology, this innate moral awareness is called the conscience. The conscience exists and functions universally in all human beings apart from any codified system of moral or religious principles (Rom. 2:12–15). Both the Greek and the Latin root terms, *syneidesis* and *conscientia*, respectively, are composite words that mean "co-knowledge" or "knowing together." We suggest that this "knowing together" refers to an agreement between learned values and one's inner moral beingness. Thus, an intrinsic moral awareness is supplemented by learned values to generate the valuing person.

The valuing person is similar in function to the Superego posited by

Freudian psychoanalysis as people's value systems received from their same-sex parents, the Parent ego state of Transactional Analysis that depicts the "taught or acquired concept of life," and the "responsible individual," who, according to William Glasser's reality therapy, lives in harmony with a personal standard of right and wrong behavior.

The Deciding Person

In addition to feeling, thinking, and valuing, people can act decisively. The human capacity to decide or make choices is frequently referred to as either volition or conation.

Three central verbs are used in the New Testament to denote the act of deciding. *Boulomai* expresses the ability to will or engage in the deliberate exercise of volition (2 Cor. 1:15–17). *Thelō* has to do with the power to pursue a personal desire or wish (Eph. 2:3). *Krinō* refers to the capacity to decide, choose, or make critical judgment (Acts 16:4). The ability to decide is the component of personality that is marked by the potential to make deliberate choices and the power to execute or actualize what is purposed or intended.

Existential psychologists and therapists—Rogers, May, Frankl, and Maslow—describe the decisive dimension of personality through their stress on personal freedom, will to meaning, intentionality, and self-actualizing potential.

The Acting Person

The composite of an individual's actions or behaviors portrays the most observable aspect of personality. The acting person's behaviors consist of performances or deeds ranging on a continuum "from simple motor skills (grooming, walking, eating, smiling) to more complex reactions (playing the guitar, drawing, speaking a foreign language, solving puzzles) all the way to the highly refined nuances of personal perceptiveness and sensitivity (as exemplified perhaps by the best poets and writers) and numerous occupational skills (from surgery to bridge-building)" (Lazarus 1976, 32).

Particular or peculiar habits, behavioral repertoires, and either excesses or deficits in behavioral repertoire are specific nuances that add to the uniqueness of an individual's personality.

The Social Person

The capacity for interpersonal communication, reciprocal companionship, and creating nurturing social systems is another characterizing quality of human personality. An individual personality is distinguished in part by the person's idiosyncratic style of relating and communicating interpersonally. Also, the capacity for intimacy, degree to which social interest has been developed, and ability to assume productive roles in society are manifestations of the maturity of the social person. The social maturity and interpersonal style might indicate that someone is a recluse, a leader with charisma, a loner, a social star, a manipulator, or a philanthropist.

The Loving Person

Unselfish caring for others and devotion to their welfare are the most elegant functions of the human personality. In authentic love, human beings realize experiential contact with God. God is love (1 John 4:8, 16), human beings are made in the likeness of God (Gen. 1:26), and the more loving and kind they are in relationships with both themselves and others, the more like God they are in their personal conduct. Thus, loving people know God experientially (1 John 4:7–8) and exhibit a personality that reflects the very essence of God.

The Self-Conscious Person

The sum of the preceding dimensions and functions of an individual represents a person, and this representation is his or her personality. The unique integration of body image and related phenomena, thoughts, feelings, values, decisions, spiritual realities, social life style, and sensory orientation to the external world leads each person to an awareness that *This is I.* This self-consciousness of personhood or selfhood gives the individual an identity. The acknowledged Self, Ego, or I serves as the personal center of personality.

The Development of Personality

Human infants possess at birth, barring congenital or organic defects and impairments, the potential to become self-actualizing individuals. The kind of person infants eventually will become depends largely on postnatal experiences. In this section we will survey the variables involved in forming a personal identity or acquiring individuality as a unique person.

The Experiencing Person in a Phenomenal Universe

From the moment of birth, each developing human being is an experiencing person located, relative to self, at the center of a universe of physical, social, psychological, and spiritual phenomena. The experiencing occurs both within the individual (inner-personal level) and through interactions with the total external environment (perceptual-motor level). The experiencing person (thinking, feeling, acting, perceiving) and the surrounding environment are reciprocal or interdependent regions of the individual's life space (Lewin 1935). This life space represents the whole social, psychological, and spiritual reality peculiar to the individual. Furthermore, the continuous reciprocal interaction between people's inner experiences, their overt behavior, and their surrounding environments (Bandura 1977) generates a world of experience or learning that is private or exclusive to each person. This personal set of experiences may be viewed as the individual's "phenomenal field." Within this matrix of an experiencing person dynamically involved in a universe of life-influencing phenomena, a unique personality develops.

Due to the lack of verbal symbols to label, define, and interpret experiences, most learning in the very early years is recorded primarily at the feeling level with relatively little cognitive apprehension. The individual's phenomenal field changes and expands continually. Each new contact with the external world or universe of phenomena adds another element—be it conscious or unconscious emotional learning—to the individual's private view of the world. As individuals extend themselves into the external environment, they accept and assimilate selected parts of the environment. Continuous interaction with their environment leads to their forming concepts, attitudes, and feelings about themselves, the universe, and relationships with the universe, especially relationships with other people. Individuals learn to perceive the world (realm of objective-external reality) and themselves (realm of subjective-internal reality) in terms of how the world treats them. These perceptions constitute their subjective-normative reality. Sometime during the first five years of life, children recognize a portion of their total phenomenal field as their unique possession. They know what and who belong to them, can recognize themselves in a mirror or photograph, realize that their names have significance, and know their likes and dislikes. This differentiated portion of the phenomenal field constitutes each individual's self-concept (Rogers 1959). This is the "I," "me," "my," "mine," or "myself," and it includes the fused perceptions and evaluations of both what is intrinsic to the individual and what is external to him or her. Figure 2 displays the differentiated self of the experiencing person in the phenomenal universe.

Social Learning Theory and Personality Development

I agree with Albert Bandura (1977) that "most human behavior is learned observationally through modeling. . . . [F]rom observing others one forms an idea of how new behaviors are performed, and on later occasions this coded information [i.e., acquired symbolic representations of the modeled activities] serves as a guide for action" (22). People in general and children in particular observe the behaviors of parents and significant others and later imitate what they observe. The influence of social and spiritual modeling and imitative learning on life styles is emphasized in the Bible, especially in the writings of the apostle Paul. Paul directly challenged those who knew him to imitate (from the Greek verb *mimeomai,* which means "to mimic or imitate") the various behaviors and attitudes he modeled before them (e.g., 1 Cor. 4:16; 11:1). Social modeling and observational or imitative learning influence the learning of values and behaviors that range from basic table manners to elaborate cultural practices and customs like

Figure 2

The Experiencing Person in the Phenomenal World*

*The basic motif of my personal and professional logo symbolizes the four-dimensional person in this figure. The "IX" are the initials for Ἰησοῦς Χριστός (Jesus Christ), who is the center of the fully balanced and integrated person.

courtship and marriage, dress and grooming, and specific styles of public worship.

Ability to think and act independently, to engage in self-regulatory psychological processes, to use cognitive, imaginal, and verbal symbols to organize experiences and communicate with others, and to analyze and assimilate the effects of the mutual interactions between intrapsychic processes, overt behaviors, and external factors is essential to personality development.

When people see that their responses or performances are approved by their parents or other social models and are positively reinforced or rewarded, they are likely to incorporate this experience favorably into their self-concept (Rogers 1959; Bandura 1977). However, they are likely to avoid responses that are punished or unrewarded and to exclude them from their conscious sense of self, or assimilate them in a way that lowers their self-esteem.

The Role of the Holy Spirit in Personality Development

Intrapersonal dynamics and environmental influences are the primary but not the exclusive developmental determinants of personality. The Holy Spirit works in Christian believers to give them new natures (John 3:1–8; 2 Cor. 5:17; Titus 3:5) and renewed minds (Rom. 12:2; Eph. 4:23). He enables them to progressively exhibit personalities and characters that are more God-like (2 Cor. 3:18).

Developmental Stages

The human being is a living, learning, and growing organism. "Anything that grows has a ground plan, and out of this ground plan the parts arise, each part having its time of special ascendancy, until all parts have arisen to form a functioning whole" (Erikson 1980, 52). Integrative Therapy adopts Erikson's epigenetic principle and its developmental paradigm as the framework for tracing personality growth and development.

A number of basic assumptions underlie the developmental model followed here: (1) The life cycle consists of eight psychosocial stages of personality growth in which people must establish new orientations to themselves and the social world. (2) Personality development continues all through life. (3) Each stage or phase of the life cycle is characterized by a specific developmental task or group of tasks to be accomplished (e.g., Havighurst [1972] identifies several tasks for each developmental stage). (4) Each of the eight component stages is systematically related to all others and each depends on the successful development in the proper sequence of each prior component. (5) Each component exists in some elemental form before its decisive and critical time normally arrives.

Infancy

The infant's first major psychological task is learning to trust or distrust the external world and other people. Motor behavior is quite limited, but the senses are very much alive, active and reactive, especially the senses of sight, hearing, and touch. Experiential data gained through these sensory avenues influence a baby's first decisions about life and the world.

Sometime during the first twelve to eighteen months after birth, infants make personal judgments either that the world is safe and can be trusted or that it is unsafe and cannot be trusted. Granted, the concepts infants hold are nonverbal or precognitive; still, the emotional encoding serves as guiding principles for the valuing process. Infants' decisions are based on whether their parents or caretakers are loving, comforting, caring, and nurturing, or rejecting, punitive, noncaring, and hurtful. The quality of the social interaction between infants and their parents or caretakers results in either close emotional bonding or emotional distancing and leaves a lasting effect on their personality. If basic trust and emotional bonding become the reality, then a secure and socially courageous self is in the making. But if basic mistrust and emotional distance predominate, an insecure and anxious person is most likely to emerge.

Early childhood

During the second and third years of life, young children experience a pronounced development in verbal and language skills, increased amounts and varieties of motor behavior, and the challenges that come with learning how to feed themselves and control elimination. They need to learn to be proud of themselves as they seek to become autonomous, and the approval of significant others is very important to them. At this stage, youngsters begin to discriminate between good and bad behaviors as determined by their caretakers' patterns of offering rewards and administering punishment (Kohlberg 1981).

If parents or caretakers provide sufficient freedom and are generous with positive reinforcement, children will achieve a sense of personal autonomy and a feeling of "I'm OK." Should caretakers be too demanding, overprotective, too permissive, too critical, or too punitive, children will learn to have doubts about themselves, feelings of shame and "I'm not OK."

Although children have by this time developed some cognitive ability, much of their learning is still at the emotional or prelogical level.

Middle childhood

By age four or five, children usually have substantial control over their bodies, possess a fair command of language and verbal skills, and exhibit a vivid imagination and rich fantasy life. While children of this age usually identify with their parents and fantasize being or becoming like them, they desire to do things for themselves and follow their own initiative. They also learn to distinguish between right and wrong and develop a functional conscience.

Children's inquisitive minds are filled with questions at this stage of development. If parents give permission and provide opportunities for self-initiated play and exploration, respect their children's questions, answer them openly and honestly, and respond positively to their fantasy and creative behaviors, then their children's initiative is reinforced. But excessive parental control and criticism, or derision, will lead to children's acquiring a sense of guilt and intensified "Not OKness."

By age five, children have laid down a basic "life style" (Adler 1956) or "life script" (Berne 1961) that is a decision about themselves, the world, and people. The life style frames the meaning of existence and shapes personal goals. Children who have achieved a basic trust toward life, feel autonomous, and possess self-initiative are then able to experience a sense of OKness and a "good me" and come at life in a creative, honest, and spontaneous style. In contrast, children who have a basic mistrust toward life and feel ashamed, guilty, or stupid are well on the way to an emotionally handicapped personality marked by an increasing sense of Not OKness and either a "bad me" or "not me." Thus, at age five, they are already living out, consciously and unconsciously, a learned concept of self and life.

Late childhood

During the juvenile or elementary-school years, ages six to twelve, children develop mental capacity for concrete thinking, deductive reasoning, and adult-like logic. Special focus and energy are directed toward learning skills necessary for social and competitive games, learning to cooperate and play according to rules, learning appropriate social roles as sexual beings, achieving greater personal autonomy, and developing basic skills in reading, writing, and calculating.

Children at this age seek approval of authority figures and both need and desire their acceptance. Late childhood is marked also by learning to live with codes and rules that define good and bad or right and wrong conduct.

Six- to twelve-year-olds want to feel useful. They need to know that they can design, build, and do things well. It is important to them how parents, teachers, and peers view their performance. If they receive praise and encouragement in response to creative and industrious efforts, they feel adequate and competent. But if they are chided about their attempts at physical, social, and educational achievement, they develop a sense of inadequacy and inferiority. Thus, at the conclusion of this phase of growth in personality, either an enhancing quality or a crippling attitude is added to the evolving image of self.

Adolescence

Adolescence, roughly ages thirteen to eighteen, is a period of physiological, psychological, spiritual, and social revolution in young persons' lives. Rapid body growth, physical sexual maturity, increased mental capacity, and a multitude of new feelings, sensations, and desires combine concurrently to create psychological turbulence in teenagers. Sometimes it appears to adolescents that past learning, prior experiences, and former relationships have lost their relevance—there is no sense of continuity.

As they stand on the threshold of adulthood, adolescents must struggle with a variety of concerns. There is the constant challenge to accept a rapidly changing physique. The body image is so important to sexual identity and social desirability that achieving a satisfying social role in terms of masculinity or femininity is often problematic and painful. Moving from chumships with people of their own sex to intimacy with people of the opposite sex can be difficult, even to the point of alienation and loneliness.

Establishing emotional independence of parents and other significant adults can be disconcerting. Questioning family values, beliefs, and moral standards in their search for their own personal values is part of their struggle for independence. Usually teenagers must deal with a conflict between their families' values and those advocated by peer groups and other competitive forces in society. Choosing social norms for their personal lives is another challenge for adolescents.

During late adolescence, special attention and energy must be directed to educational and career goals in the pursuit of economic independence. At the same time, adolescents must develop intellectual and social skills at a level that makes them effective in interpersonal relationships and communication.

Essential to success in this stage of personality development is a sense of psychosocial identity or "a persistent sameness within oneself and a persistent sharing of some kind of essential character with others" (Erikson 1980, 102). To achieve such a stable sense of self or identity, there must first be a realization of trust, autonomy, initiative, adequacy, and OKness. This requires integrating all previous learning, experiences, images, and identifications into a harmonious whole. Teenagers who achieve this have a genuine awareness of who they are and a realistic philosophy of life. They have a success identity (Glasser 1965). Those who reach late adolescence with a sense of mistrust, shame, doubt, inadequacy, inferiority, and general Not OKness will suffer identity confusion. They will lack both an awareness of who they really are, and where and to whom they belong, and a clearly defined orientation to life. They are likely to see themselves as failures (Glasser 1965).

Young adulthood

The period that spans the ages nineteen through thirty is characterized largely by social relationships like courtship, marriage, marital adjustment, child rearing, engagement in productive work, assuming civic responsibilities, and seeking membership in social or religious groups. At this age people tend to be concerned for individual rights and living according to moral and ethical principles at both personal and professional levels.

A basic need of young adults is to experience intimacy with spouse and friends of both sexes. Intimacy with the spouse involves social, emotional, spiritual, and sexual sharing in a context of mutual commitment in a union or a partnership. Personal fulfillment in social relationships extends beyond the marital union to friends and associates. Young adults need to be part of a network of individuals who nurture and support one another through a variety of social interactions. Only after a wholesome identity as a unique individual has been achieved can true intimacy with either a spouse or a friend occur. Thus, emerging from adolescence with a solid psychosocial identity is a prerequisite for experiencing true friendship, mature love, and authentic intimacy.

Young adults without a wholesome self-concept or a capacity for emotional intimacy will tend toward isolation. Their social relationships most likely will be marked by an excessive tendency to follow one of three movements in life (Horney 1945): movement *toward* people in order to secure love and affection, usually through some form of symbiotic attachment without mature love and authentic union (Fromm 1963); movement *away* from people to gain independence and a sense of self-sufficiency in an emotionally barren existence; or movement *against* people for the purpose of attaining power, prestige, recognition, and mastery. Isolated persons, regardless of basic interpersonal style, are typically egocentric, manipulative, exploitive, and possessive.

Middle age

Middle age, roughly ages thirty to sixty, can be either the most rewarding or the most disappointing stage in life. Middle-aged adults are interested in adopting a personal and carefully articulated body of ethical and
moral principles that shape their total lives. Morally and ethically sensitive
middle-aged persons are characteristically concerned with achieving a sense
of productivity as responsible members of their community, being effective
parents, experiencing fulfillment in creative and productive work, providing
well for their families, fostering a satisfying relationship with the spouse,
enjoying creative leisure, adjusting to the physiological and other changes
unique to middle age, and deepening religious or spiritual life.

If the middle-age years are preceded by a solid psychosocial identity and
the attainment of personal intimacy, then an individual at mid-life stands a
good chance of becoming thoroughly productive, altruistic, and self-actualizing. People who have failed to form a wholesome sense of self and lack
the capacity for genuine intimacy are likely to become self-absorbed in middle age. Instead of becoming socially expansive, altruistic, and fully productive, self-absorbed middle-aged individuals experience stagnation, boredom,
and frustration and, to compensate for the lack of intimacy and personal fulfillment, become preoccupied with self-gratification. Possible avenues for
resolving frustrations experiencing gratification are the use or abuse of
drugs and alcohol, increased sexual activity with several partners, increased
membership in clubs and social groups, spending more time on the job,
divorce and remarriage, securing new and "better" material possessions, and
a change in career.

Late adulthood

At sixty or over, people are faced with life issues like decreasing physical
strength, declining health, retirement, changes in income, incapacitation or
death of a spouse, sustaining affiliation with a body of friends or confidants,
coping with the geographical remoteness of children and grandchildren,
and maintaining a sense of social and professional significance.

Older adults realize that their major efforts or contributions are nearing
completion. This realization is likely to result in a sense of either personal
accomplishment or despair. If people who reach late adulthood can review
their lives with personal satisfaction, believing that they have fulfilled their
plans and intentions and can see meaningful continuity between the phases
of their existence, then they will experience feelings of personal worth, significance, usefulness, and success. In contrast, people who see their lives as a
series of failures, disappointments, missed opportunities, and wrong decisions and who are unable to meaningfully integrate their past experiences,
their present situations in life, and their future possibilities tend to resign
from authentic living to await remorsefully the certainty of death.

People who have a dynamic spiritual life find that their relationship with

God is a source of strength and encouragement as they face late adulthood. Moses appears to have been focusing on the concerns of this period of life when he wrote, "The length of our days is seventy years—or eighty, if we have the strength. . . . Teach us to number our days aright, that we may gain a heart of wisdom. . . . May the favor of the Lord our God rest upon us; establish the work of our hands for us—yes, establish the work of our hands" (Ps. 90:10, 12, 17).

Motivation in Personality and Human Behavior

Human personality and behavior are dynamic rather than static. Some factors prompt people toward specific goals or objectives. Thus, human behavior is intentional and purposive, or teleological. Frequently used expressions to identify the prompting dynamics in human personality and behavior are instincts, drives, stimulus responses, cues, impulses, and motives. Each of these labels can be used appropriately at various times to describe the cause of people's actions and reactions. However, the terms *motive* and *motivation* are used here to describe the dynamic causality in human behavior.

Fulfillment of Needs Through Gestalt Formation

Motivation, as used in Integrative Therapy, refers to the factors that serve both to energize people to function in a particular manner at a specific time and to direct or guide their behavior. The most plausible way to understand motivation in human behavior is to observe how people strive to fulfill their needs. As discussed earlier in this chapter, the relationships and interactions between persons and their environment form their phenomenal field. "The phenomenal [field] is organized by the needs of the individual. Needs energize behavior and organize it on [both] the subjective-perceptual . . . and . . . the objective-motor level[s]. The individual [perceives a need or needs and] then carries out the necessary [motoric] activities in order to satisfy the needs" (Wallen 1971, 9). In the words of Fritz Perls (1973), "Formulating this principle in terms of Gestalt psychology, we can say that the dominant need of the [human] organism, at any time, becomes the foreground figure, and the other needs recede, at least temporarily, into the background. The foreground is that need which presses most sharply for satisfaction" (8).

Combining the Gestalt principle with Maslow's (1967, 1970) hierarchy of needs provides a remarkable model for comprehending the motivational process. Each person has a hierarchy of needs that are continually and serially becoming figural in Gestalt formations (i.e., becoming dominant life concerns) and, upon completion or fulfillment, disappearing into the background. In the case of a well-adjusted or integrated individual, the process goes on constantly without interruption. When one need is satisfied it is "destroyed" or ceases to be figural and becomes part of the background in the individual's experience, allowing the next most urgent or prepotent need on the hierarchy to become the figural motivator or energizer of behavior. Thus, life can be viewed dynamically as the process of forming and destroying Gestalts—moving from one fulfilled need to another.

Hierarchy of Needs

The needs that motivate human behavior, as proposed by Maslow and accepted with modification by Integrative Therapy, are arranged hierarchically. The hierarchy suggests the order in which needs are most likely to become energizing figures in human experience. Thus the needs are arranged from the lowest to the highest, indicating that people proceed up the hierarchy of needs once lower needs have become figures in experiential Gestalts, have been completed or destroyed, and have receded into the background of experience.

Physiological needs

Everyone needs food, drink, warmth, rest, and sleep in order to maintain bodily homeostasis or stability and to avoid the pain of hunger, thirst, freezing, fatigue, and sleepiness. Among other physiological needs are sexual desire and physical exercise. These needs motivate the human being both to survive and to be free of pain, tension, and discomfort.

This multi-motive is likely to be identified by Freudians as the "pleasure principle," by Rogerians as the "enhancement of the organism," by Jungians as "striving for balance," and by Gestaltists as "organismic homeostasis." However we define the motive, until people experience sufficient physiological well-being they ordinarily will be organismically uninterested in attending to higher-order needs.

Safety needs

Not far removed from the physiological motivators of behavior are the needs for safety and security. People require and seek an orderly and trusted environment that can provide a personal sense of social, economic, physical, psychological, and spiritual well-being. Any environmental factor or variable that threatens their personal security becomes figural, making all else background. Authentic progress in meeting all other needs is thwarted until this Gestalt is completed.

Love needs

"The deepest need of [human beings]," says Fromm (1963), "is to overcome [their] separateness, to leave the prison of [their] aloneness, [their] disunited existence . . . to reach out, unite [themselves] in some form or another with [other persons] . . . to achieve union" (7, 8). Humans have a deep need for relatedness, the need to belong, to share, to give and receive mature love and care. Virtually all developmental psychologists and psychotherapists agree that love is one of the indispensable needs of the person. For example, encouraging and caring love is a central theme of Adler's, Glasser's, and Rogers's psychotherapies.

Both biblical data (1 Cor. 13) and research findings (e.g., Spitz 1949; Harlow 1958, 1971) affirm and confirm that "love is the principal developer of one's capacities for being human . . . and the only thing on earth that can produce the sense of belongingness and relatedness to the world of humanity" (Montagu 1970, 467). The degree to which the individual's love needs are satisfied affects behavior and personality as much as any other motivating factor, if not more.

Esteem needs.

Another basic psychological need of the individual is to have a feeling or sense of personal worth. Glasser (1965) maintains, and I agree, that being respected by both self and others is essential to successful identity. In order to have the feelings of self-confidence, personal worth, strength, capability, and adequacy there first must be the satisfaction of the self-esteem, self-respect, and self-regard needs (Rogers 1959).

A song once popular declared, "I can't be right for someone else if I'm not right for me." The need to feel good and right about oneself is a strong motivating force in personality and behavior. If it is unmet, life can become miserable and distorted.

Self-actualization needs

Needs can be either growth-motivated or deficiency-motivated. Self-actualization has reference to people's desire to develop, use, and fully experience their potentials, talents, gifts, and capacities; they are motivated to become everything they are capable of becoming. Perhaps it would be more accurate to say that the motive to self-actualize stems more from people's desire to grow than from a need per se.

The motivation for self-actualization is synonymous with Rogers's (1961) idea of the individual becoming a "fully functioning person," Landsman's (1968) notion of human growth toward the "beautiful and noble person," and the biblical concept of the spiritually mature person whose life style is characteristically Spirit-filled and Christ-like. The evangelical sage Vernon Grounds (1984) sums it up this way: "God is in the business of building Christians up, maximizing their talents and fulfilling their potential . . . [and increasing] selfhood. . . . Selfhood is what you and I are as human beings created in God's image . . . [for] ultimate conformity to Jesus" (40).

Cognitive needs

People, rational and intelligent beings, are motivated by the need or desire to know, to explore, and to explain the unknown; to satisfy personal curiosity about the mysterious; to discover new truth through experiment; to give system and order to chaos; and to master bodies of knowledge.

Fulfillment of cognitive needs is inseparable from self-actualization. When the more basic human needs have been satisfied and people are unable to fulfill their cognitive needs and interests, they become bored, intellectually stagnant, and frustrated.

Philosophical-spiritual needs

As spiritual beings, people seek to find meaning in life and give meaning to it. Their striving to find meaning in life or to have a set of values and ideals that frames their existence is a potent motivational force (Allport 1968; Frankl 1962, 1969). Even some so-called secular psychotherapies recognize people's spiritual needs. "Although Adler alluded to the *spiritual,* he never specifically named it. . . . But each of us must deal with the [spiritual] problem of defining the nature of [the] universe, the existence and nature of God, and how one relates to these concepts" (Mosak 1984, 59). Maslow (1971) believed that people have just as great a need and hunger for a philosophy of life as they do for vitamins and minerals and that persons without a system of religious, spiritual, or moral values—a philosophy of life—are likely to be psychologically unhealthy.

Aesthetic needs

Humans have both the capacity and the desire to experience the true, the good, and the beautiful. People define themselves in part by how they pursue and satisfy their needs and desires for beauty, design, harmony, symmetry, unity, order, structure, creativity, and orchestration. Fulfilling aesthetic needs and desires is related to the self-actualizing process just as is fulfilling the cognitive and philosophical-spiritual quests.

The Motivating Influence of the Holy Spirit

A Christian or spiritually-minded therapist would be remiss to discuss motivation in human personality and behavior without addressing the influence of God, especially the Holy Spirit, in people's lives. The Scriptures teach that the Holy Spirit is the dynamic agent who causes men and women to seek a relationship with God, prompts people to desire and perform what God intends for them, stimulates and enables believers to live lovingly, joyfully, and peacefully (Gal. 5:22–23) and makes it possible for the followers of Jesus Christ to acknowledge him authentically as "Lord" (1 Cor. 12:3).

Integrative Therapy presupposes that the involvement of the Holy Spirit in human experience is essential both to the fulfillment of foundational spiritual needs like entering a genuine faith relationship with God and to full self-actualization.

4

Problems in Living

Counselors and therapists of all orientations acknowledge that there are psychological problems in people's lives, but they disagree about the causes and nature of these problems. Typical generic names for the mental, emotional, and behavioral difficulties with which people must cope include abnormality, maladjustment, mental disorder, emotional disturbance, maladaptive behavior, mental illness, personality dysfunction, psychopathology, problematic behavior, and problems in living. The choice of a particular nomenclature to define or describe human suffering reflects to some degree the theoretical bias of the therapist. The task of this chapter is to examine the primary models for thinking about human problems and to provide a theory of personality dysfunction that is compatible with the other theoretical tenets of Integrative Therapy. Specifically, we need to know what interrupts and disturbs personal maturation so much that people seek counseling and psychotherapy for remedial or developmental help.

Basic Models for Comprehending Maladjustment

Several models have been advanced for comprehending the cause and nature of personality dysfunction and problematic behavior. It is possible, however, to address the central nuances of these various perspectives under four headings: biomedical, biosocial, sociopsychological, and moral.

Biomedical Model

The biomedical model emphasizes genetic and physiological factors underlying mental and emotional problems. The assumed direct or indirect influence of biochemical processes on personality dysfunction leads logically to equating such disturbance with illness or disease. Thus, personality dysfunction is virtually synonymous with mental illness. Furthermore, since a mental illness or mental disorder usually has some amount of genetic and organic basis, it is necessarily a medical disorder. This has been the model advocated consistently by the psychiatric establishment, a fact reflected in the activities of the American Psychiatric Association. Psychiatrists who hold either a psychoanalytic or a neurobiological theory of personality appear to be the principal but not exclusive endorsers of the biomedical model of mental illness.

Advocates of the biomedical model clearly differentiate, both qualitatively and quantitatively, between what is considered normal personality functioning and conditions diagnosed as mental disorders.

Biosocial Model

The biosocial model considers social and environmental factors to be just as important as genetic and biological factors in the development of maladjusted life styles (e.g., Adler 1981; Sim 1983). Exponents of the biosocial model restrict the use of *illness* and *disease* to conditions that affect only the physical body. Thus, they think it a misnomer to refer to a mental or emotional disorder as mental illness. Szasz (1960, 1974), a psychiatrist and ardent advocate of the biosocial perspective, has been persistent in his claims that the expression *mental illness* is a metaphor and myth that is inappropriately used to describe nonmedical conditions in order to keep psychiatric problems within the conceptual framework of medicine and under the control of medical psychiatry. He holds firmly to the position that mental illnesses do not exist in a strict or literal sense and that psychiatrists who adhere to the disease theory of mental disorder and other like-minded psychotherapists are actually helping individuals deal with personal, social, and ethical problems in living, not curing them of disease. Other psychiatrists (e.g., Alfred Adler, Eric Berne, William Glasser, Carl Jung, Fritz Perls, Joseph Wolpe) also have rejected the idea of mental illness per se and have favored alternative explanations for human maladjustment. There are nonmedical psychotherapists, especially clinical psychologists and psychiatric nurses, who also find the biosocial model the most plausible model for understanding problems in living.

Advocates of the biosocial model do make distinctions between so-called normal people and those who suffer from some type of personality dysfunction, but they are less rigid in their differentiation than are the biomedical practitioners.

Sociopsychological Model

The majority of counseling psychologists, most professional counselors and social workers, and many clinical psychologists adhere to the sociopsychological model of maladaptive behavior and personality. This model locates the predominant body of etiological factors in the social milieu of the individual. Particular attention is given to the impact that opportunities for needs fulfillment, family-of-origin experiences, learning conditions, perceptions, and social relationships have on human growth and development. It is generally assumed that the learning of maladaptive behaviors follows the same principles as does the learning of adaptive behaviors. Personality and behavior conditions that might be considered either normal or maladaptive are viewed as points on a continuum rather than separate diagnostic categories. Many advocates of the sociopsychological model prefer to avoid the systematic classification of clients or patients as if they were suffering medical diseases (e.g., George Albee, Arnold Lazarus, Harold Mosak, Carl Rogers).

The tendency of systems adherents to locate maladjustment or dysfunction within the family or a social system instead of the individual needs to be pointed out as an exception to the typical conceptual framework of the sociopsychological perspective on problems in living. In this system's outlook, it is the total network of persons and interactional dynamics in the family or social system that is the target of diagnosis and treatment, not the individual alone (see Gurman & Kniskern 1981).

Moral Model

The moral model assumes that many, perhaps most, of the problems or maladjustments incurred in living are rooted in personal sin and moral deficiency. Biological, sociological, and psychological factors might be involved, but moral and spiritual factors most likely are central. Illustrative representatives of the moral model of personality dysfunction are Jay Adams (1970) and O. Hobart Mowrer (1961).

While traditional nosological (disease classification) terminology might be used in reference to psychological problems, religious concepts are often used as well to describe conditions. For example, an explanation for the cause of a neurosis or psychosis, in the ultimate analysis, is unresolved guilt because some sin has not been confessed or acknowledged, and therefore the person has not experienced cleansing, forgiveness, reconciliation, and restoration.

An Integrative Model of Etiology or Causality of Maladjustment

The conceptual framework by which Integrative Therapy describes the cause and nature of maladjustment incorporates contributions primarily of the biosocial, sociopsychological, and moral models. While the biomedical model has made contributions, its conceptual outlook per se is not fully acceptable because it overemphasizes genetic influence in the etiology of mental disorders and has a penchant for mental illness as a medical disorder. The biosocial model accounts sufficiently for the biological and physiological factors in the causation of personality dysfunction.

Integrative Therapy is also reluctant to endorse the use of pejorative terms like *psychopathology* and *abnormality* that suggest the mental-illness paradigm. The expression *problems in living* is preferred as the primary name for conditions people bring to counselors and psychotherapists for resolution. Sometimes the nature of clients' presenting problems does indicate deviance from accepted social, religious, ethical, and legal norms, but "behaviors [and personality conditions] traditionally called abnormal [or mental illness] are no different, either quantitatively or qualitatively, in their development and maintenance from other learned behaviors [and personality characteristics]" (Ullmann & Krasner 1969, 1).

The next several paragraphs identify the various etiological factors that lead to problems in living.

Physiological Factors

Many physiological changes and physical conditions influence the development of personality disorder or maladjustment. First, genetic and congenital defects sometimes contribute to disorders. Specific examples include genetic or hereditary configurations that appear to be predisposing factors, at least in some cases, for schizophrenia (Kendler 1983; Kety 1976), and prenatal conditions like infections (e.g., venereal diseases) and the effects of the mother's use of alcohol and drugs on fetal development.

Chemical or hormonal imbalances, particularly endocrine disorders, usually result in emotional, mental, and behavioral disturbances. For example, inappropriate amounts of thyroxin, insulin, estrogen, or testosterone can lead to disorders in personality and behavior. Substance abuse often impairs mental functioning, distorts perception of reality, affects motivation, and interferes with emotional and mood stability.

Postnatal infections (e.g., syphilis and encephalitis) also can produce disorders in mental functioning, emotional expressions, and behavioral patterns. Tumors and cancer (e.g., brain tumors and cancer of the pancreas) result in a variety of dysfunctions including, among others, mental confusion, depression, irritability, and loss of memory. Head injury that damages the brain is another possible causative factor in mental, emotional, and behavioral disorders.

Frustrated Satisfaction of Needs

Much of the maladjustment people experience can be traced to unmet needs. Reference was made repeatedly in the previous chapter to the negative effects of frustrated needs fulfillment and unresolved life tasks on psychological well-being. Persons who seek counseling and psychotherapy generally do not have a wholesome psychosocial identity. They are unable to actualize themselves fully and lack the skills necessary to achieve realistic, mature, effective, and self-fulfilling lives. Consequently, in order to maintain whatever sense of self they have, people with developmental deficits or deficiency needs resort to self-defeating attitudes, habits, and behavioral patterns.

Although persons who suffer from unmet needs often can function in their world, they tend to think that they are inadequate, stupid, no good, unloved, unwanted, or inferior. They are discouraged, insecure, alienated, lonely, and often without hope. This negativity interferes with interpersonal relationships, educational achievement, job performance and satisfaction, and spiritual maturation.

In some instances the deprivation can be so severe, in both the failure to fulfill needs and the inability to succeed at accomplishing developmental tasks, that people create private or make-believe worlds that have little or no correspondence with external reality. For lack of a better word, these people are the so-called psychotics who are out of touch with their true selves, other people, their environment, and life.

Inappropriate Learning

Inappropriate learning experiences constitute another major causal source of maladaptive life styles. Learning is considered to be inappropriate if it is insufficient in amount, excessive in amount, inaccurate in content, improperly timed, or experienced under unfavorable conditions. Thus, inappropriate learning is frequently an accompaniment of both unmet needs and unresolved life tasks.

A rather large proportion of problems in living consists of learned attitudes and behaviors that stem from unfortunate conditioning, undesirable patterns of reinforcement, defensive inhibitions, and poorly devised or worn-out strategies of adaptation. Behaviors that arise from inappropriate learning often become problematic due to their being either deficient or excessive in the frequency of appearance. Examples of learned problems include inappropriate or inadequate social skills, sexual deviations and dysfunctions, phobias, ineffective academic and vocational skills, and self-defeating thought patterns.

Unresolved Conflict

People experience conflict whenever they must choose between mutually exclusive desires, goals, or responses. A conflict may involve either an approach-approach, approach-avoidance, or avoidance-avoidance situation and may be either intrapersonal, interpersonal, or extrapersonal. Furthermore, conflicts may occur on the job, at home, at church, in the community, or in friendships, and they may be focused on past, present, or future.

Regardless of the situation and nature of the conflict, the individual experiencing it remains frustrated, anxious, and neurotic until it is resolved.

An example will illustrate the personality disturbance that can arise from an unresolved conflict. A married woman in her early thirties who adheres to traditional Judeo-Christian values becomes emotionally and physically attracted to another man who holds values like hers. She feels pulled in opposite directions. From a psychodynamic perspective, we could reason that she must choose either to follow the desires of her Id and approach her potential new lover or to honor the dictates of her Superego and approach loyalty to her husband and Christian values. The woman becomes neurotically secretive, defensive, and critical of others and refuses to make a choice until she has a "nervous breakdown" and is hospitalized.

Existential Crises

Sometimes problems in living can be associated with what might be called existential crises. Events like the death of a close relative or beloved friend, the loss of some prized material possession or one's job, being betrayed or abandoned by a confidant or a lover, failure to realize the fulfillment of personal plans, or being confronted with a terminal disease or disfiguring bodily injury can bring psychological disquiet to even the most self-actualizing person.

The disturbance—despondency, depression, remorse, deep sadness—may be either acute or chronic depending on the mental-emotional resilience and personality integration of the person experiencing it. During the crisis, the person may need therapy that involves nothing more than acceptance, support, nurture, and encouragement.

Immaturity

Mental, emotional, social, or spiritual immaturity frequently is an etiological factor in presenting problems. Quite often immaturity is an observable cause of dysfunction or conflict, particularly in marital, family, interpersonal, and work relationships. Individuals who lack emotional maturity, who possess ineffective interpersonal and social skills, who are deficient in spiritual discernment, and whose cognitive skills are inadequately developed will manifest maladaptive behaviors.

Some family and marital problems that stem from immaturity are symbiotic relationships between husbands and wives that involve unhealthy dependence and power needs; lack of impulse control that results in violence and abuse of spouse, children, or both; excessive jealousy and distrust; maladaptive interpersonal relationships that reflect various patterns of passivity and aggression; inability to experience intimacy with spouse and children; and alienation and withdrawal.

Sin

No concept is more spurned or viewed with more disdain by psychologists and psychotherapists than sin, with all its connotations. However, sin and its implications for problems in living cannot be ignored or dismissed by responsible psychologists and therapists.

The biblical record discloses that all pain, suffering, and cosmic disorder are the result, ultimately, of willful rebellion and disobedience. Sin originated in the rebellion of Lucifer (an archangel, also called Satan or the devil, who had been created by God to be responsive to the Creator) when he sought to usurp God's authority by manipulating human beings into following his example of opposition to God (Gen. 3:1–5). Sin is thus any departure from the revealed will of God. Adam and Eve, the original man and woman, were warned explicitly by God that their failure to honor his desire would lead to their death (Gen. 2:16–17), and Paul explains that their death affects all their posterity (Rom. 5:12). This theme is repeated throughout the Scriptures: "the wages of sin is death" (Rom. 6:23) and "sin . . . gives birth to death" (James 1:15). Death refers not only to the demise of the physical body, but also to spiritual, mental, emotional, social, and psychological deterioration.

Integrative Therapy assumes that the *ultimate* cause of all problems in living can be traced to the entry of sin into the world and the subsequent disruption of the totality of the created order (e.g., Rom. 8:18–22). The whole creation groans in pain, suffering, alienation, and frustration because of sin. The expression *theological guilt*, with all its ramifications, appropriately describes the human condition after departing from God's will.

Original sin and universal theological guilt that are the ultimate cause of all maladjustment or problems in living are only one dimension of sin in the etiological picture. Sinful actions by individuals against themselves and others are immediate factors in living disorders. For example, the sins of rape and incest result in shame, depression, fear, and sexual dysfunction among the victims and the sins of child abuse and neglect often leave victims mentally and emotionally disturbed.

Perhaps the most widely experienced consequence of personal sin is the sense of guilt. Mowrer, one of few psychologists who dared to broach the issue, was convinced that a substantial amount of mental illness results not from psychological guilt or guilt *feelings* but from *actual* guilt caused by sinful deeds (Mowrer 1961; Mowrer & Veszelovszky 1980). Menninger (1973), a highly respected psychiatrist, has also acknowledged the presence and consequences of sin in individual lives and the larger society.

While it is both appropriate and necessary to examine the role of sin in the etiology of problems in living, counselors and therapists must be cautious and exercise sound professional judgment in making their diagnoses. The extreme position advocated by Adams (1970) that all problems in living stem directly from either organic disorders or personal sin appears to be the kind of diagnostic approach one would want to avoid, seeking instead a more balanced alternative explanation.

Demonic Influence

People have believed throughout the centuries that demons or evil spirits exist and can cause physical, mental, and emotional disturbance. Demon possession was considered the primary cause of mental illness during the Middle Ages, and those who sought to exorcise demons went to foolish and punitive ends. Immersion in hot water, beatings, and starvation were among the cruel attempts to remove demons that supposedly inhabited troubled human personalities. The emergence of modern science gave rise to a more naturalistic etiology of personality disorder and a decline in attributing mental disturbance to demonic activity. The scientific view that has permeated contemporary psychotherapy seeks to explain all personality disorders in terms of biopsychological phenomena.

The Judeo-Christian Scriptures identify demons as spiritual beings (angels) that, under the leadership of Satan (the devil), disobeyed God, thus becoming evil adversaries of God and servants of Satan (Matt. 12:24; 2 Pet. 2:4; Eph. 6:11–12). Confronting demonic activity and healing the physical, emotional, mental, spiritual, and social afflictions they caused in people was a visible part of Jesus' work (e.g., Matt. 17:14–17; Luke 8:26–39). The Old Testament also gives evidence of the existence of evil spirits and their negative influence on people's personalities (e.g., 1 Sam. 18–20; Job 1:6–2:7).

In recent years there has been a resurgent interest in the possible influence of the demonic on human beings. Numerous books have been published on demonic presence and activity in the world (e.g., Montgomery 1976; Peck 1983; Unger 1971; Gross 1990). Occult activity and the worship of Satan are also growing phenomena.

Integrative Therapy assumes the reality of demons on the basis of the credible witness of the Judeo-Christian Scriptures and human experience. Also, we acknowledge the possibility of demonic involvement in human affairs and individual lives and, thus, in personality and behavioral disorders. It seems plausible that what is sometimes diagnosed merely as psychological disturbance could be a symptom of demonic oppression, influence, or even possession. Peck (1983), a self-described "hard-headed scientist," reports that 5 percent of his psychiatric patients present problems that do not fit any traditional diagnosis. He concludes that these personality disturbances can be explained only by the supernatural influence of Satan or demons (195). This might account for the ineffectiveness of some psychological interventions. A missed diagnosis results in the use of an inappropriate method or strategy.

If demonic presence and influence are, in some cases, part of the etiological make-up of a troubled life, then a most discerning diagnostician is required. Counselors and therapists should not be so foolish as to rush in where angels fear to tread. Therapists also need to avoid a current tendency among some groups of Christians to see demonic influence in virtually all personality problems (e.g., Hammond & Hammond 1973). Complicated human situations are not to be treated with simplistic and prescriptive routines.

Diagnostic and Classification Systems

An understanding of the causes of problems in living is essential to the practice of psychotherapy but provides insufficient information for both planning and implementing effective therapeutic interventions, on the one hand, and conducting well-designed psychotherapy research, on the other. "Clinicians and research investigators must have a common language with which to communicate about disorders for which they have professional responsibility. Planning a treatment program must begin with an accurate diagnostic assessment. The efficacy of various treatment modalities can be compared only if [client or] patient groups are described using diagnostic terms that are clearly defined" (DSM-III [*Diagnostic and Statistical Manual of Mental Disorders,* 3d ed.] American Psychiatric Association 1980, 1). It is fallacious to assume that all counselors and therapists adhere to a common diagnostic system, because disagreement on preferred diagnostic nomenclature parallels divergence regarding the nature and cause of problems in living (Smith & Kraft 1983). Yet, each counselor or therapist must possess a diagnostic language that is clear and understandable in order to define accurately the presenting problems of clients or patients and to communicate with other professionals about assessment, treatment, and research outcomes.

As with the divergent etiological models, the major systems for classifying and diagnosing problems in living will be identified with some elaboration. Afterward, we will develop Integrative Therapy's own position regarding diagnosing and classifying maladjusted life styles.

ICD-9-CM

The World Health Organization has developed a mammoth document called *The International Statistical Classification of Diseases, Injuries, and Causes of Death* (ICD). The ICD exists currently in the ninth edition (WHO 1977), and plans are in progress for an ICD-10, which should be available around 1992 (DSM-III-R[evised] 1987, xvii).

The ICD-9 consists of seventeen major sections that deal with diseases and morbid conditions that range from infections and parasitic diseases (Section I) to injury and poisoning (Section XVII). Other illustrative inclusions are endocrine, nutritional, and metabolic disorders (Section IV), diseases of the nervous system and sense organs (Section VI), and congenital abnormalities (Section XIV). Each of the seventeen major sections is subdivided into a specific number of conditions or categories (each tagged with a three-digit identification number) that are divided further into subcategories (with a four-digit identification number). Supplementary codes and labels focus on the classification of external causes of injury and poisoning (the E codes) and the classification of factors influencing health status and contact with health services (the V codes). The principal objective of the ICD is to allow for collection and dissemination of comparable mortality and morbidity data at the international level.

Section V of the ICD-9 classifies thirty categories of mental disorders (identified by the three-digit numbers 290–319). The ICD-9 does not lend itself easily to multiaxial classification due to inconsistency within the major sections. However, efforts are being made to use the ICD-9 multiaxially, primarily with children (Rutter et al. 1969; Tarjan & Eisenberg 1972).

Because many therapists and clinicians in the United States believed the ICD-9 lacked the level of specificity needed for their work, a special task force of American professionals prepared a revision called the *Clinical Modification of the World Health Organization's International Classification of Diseases, 9th Revision* (ICD-9-CM 1978). The clinical modification was accomplished by adding a fifth digit to the four-digit subcategories and creating additional four-digit subcategories when the required detail could not be achieved by the use of the fifth digit.

The thirty three-digit categories of mental disorders classified in the ICD-9-CM are as follows:

Psychoses (290–299)

290 Senile and presenile organic psychotic conditions
291 Alcoholic psychoses
292 Drug psychoses
293 Transient organic psychotic conditions
294 Other organic psychotic conditions

295 Schizophrenic disorders
296 Affective psychoses
297 Paranoid states
298 Other nonorganic psychoses
299 Psychoses with origin specific to childhood

Neurotic Disorders, Personality Disorders, and Other Nonpsychotic Mental Disorders (300–316)

300 Neurotic disorders
301 Personality disorders
302 Sexual deviations and disorders

303 Alcohol dependence syndrome
304 Drug dependence
305 Nondependent use of drugs

306 Physiological malfunction arising from mental factors

307 Special symptoms or syndromes, not elsewhere classified

308 Acute reaction to stress

309 Adjustment reaction

310 Specific nonpsychotic mental disorders due to organic brain damage

311 Depressive disorder, not elsewhere classified

312 Disturbance of conduct, not elsewhere classified

313 Disturbance of emotions specific to childhood and adolescence

314 Hyperkinetic syndrome of childhood

315 Specific delays in development

316 Psychic factors associated with diseases classified elsewhere

Mental Retardation (317–319)

317 Mild mental retardation

318 Other specified mental retardation

319 Unspecified mental retardation

The following example illustrates the subdivision of the major categories of mental disorders in ICD-9-CM into four-and five-digit subcategories.

309 Adjustment reaction

309.0 Brief depressive reaction

309.1 Prolonged depressive reaction

309.2 With predominant disturbance of other emotions

309.21 Separation anxiety disorder

309.22 Emancipation disorder of adolesence and early adult life

309.23 Specific academic or work inhibition

309.24 Adjustment reaction with anxious mood

309.28 Adjustment reaction with mixed emotional features

309.29 Other

309.3 With predominant disturbance of conduct

309.4 With mixed disturbance of emotions and conduct

309.8 Other specified adjustment reactions

309.81 Prolonged post-traumatic stress disorder

309.82 Adjustment reaction with physical symptoms

309.83 Adjustment reaction with withdrawal

309.89 Other

309.9 Unspecified adjustment reaction

Whatever merits the ICD-9-CM might have, its stress on the disease themes and lack of sufficient indication of appropriate therapy make it unacceptable as the central diagnostic system of Integrative Therapy.

DSM-III-R

The *Diagnostic and Statistical Manual of Mental Disorders* (DSM) of the American Psychiatric Association has become the predominant diagnostic system used by counselors and therapists in the United States. The first edition (DSM-I) was published in 1952, the second (DSM-II) in 1968, the third (DSM-III) in 1980, and a revision of the third edition (DSM-III-R) in 1987. Work on the DSM-IV is in process with publication expected in 1992 to coincide with release of ICD-10-CM.

Like the ICDs, the DSMs have been created primarily by medical practitioners. A small number of nonmedical mental-health professionals were involved as liaisons or consultants in the preparation of DSM-III and DSM-III-R. Their influence resulted in stronger emphasis on social, cultural, and environmental factors in the etiology of mental disorders; departure from the disease model of maladjustment; and removal of mental disorders from the universal rubric of medical disorders.

DSM-III-R is essentially a duplication of ICD-9-CM in that all official DSM-III-R codes and terms are included in the ICD-9-CM. The major differences between the two documents reside in the two distinct manners of arranging the various categories of disorders and in the multiaxial diagnosis characteristic of the DSM-III-R.

DSM-III-R includes more than two hundred specific disorders organized in nineteen sections (seventeen major five-digit categories and two supplementary sets of five-digit codes and labels):

    I. Disorders usually first evident in infancy, childhood, or adolescence
    II. Organic mental disorders
    III. Psychoactive substance-use disorders
    IV. Schizophrenia
    V. Delusional (paranoid) disorder
    VI. Psychotic disorders not elsewhere classified
    VII. Mood disorders
    VIII. Anxiety disorders
    IX. Somatoform disorders
    X. Dissociative disorders
    XI. Sexual disorders
    XII. Sleep disorders
    XIII. Factitious disorders
    XIV. Impulse-control disorders not elsewhere classified
    XV. Adjustment disorder
    XVI. Psychological factors affecting physical condition
    XVII. Personality disorders

XVIII. Conditions not attributable to a mental disorder that are a focus of attention or treatment (V codes)

XIX. Additional codes (other V codes, unspecified nonpsychotic mental disorder, no diagnosis or diagnosis deferred on Axis I)

One major section of the mental disorders identified in the DSM-III-R has been selected to display the breakdown into several five-digit subcategories.

Personality Disorders

301.00 Paranoid	301.82 Avoidant
301.20 Schizoid	301.60 Dependent
301.22 Schizotypal	301.40 Obsessive-compulsive
301.70 Antisocial	301.84 Passive-aggressive
301.83 Borderline	301.90 Personality disorder not
301.50 Histrionic	otherwise specified
301.81 Narcissistic	

A thorough diagnosis includes the entry of the appropriate code(s) on each of the following five axes:

Axis I. Clinical syndromes, conditions not attributable to a mental disorder that are focus of treatment (V codes), and additional codes.

Axis II. Specific developmental disorders (children) and personality disorders (adult).

Axis III. Physical disorders and conditions (e.g., diabetes, cirrhosis of the liver, viral encephalitis).

Axis IV. Severity of psychosocial stressors (a numerical rating is used to assess the overall severity of stress that is judged to have been significant in the development or exacerbation of the current disorder; the ratings range from 1, which indicates no apparent stressor present, to 6, which considers an involved stressor to be of catastrophic potential; a null—zero indicates inadequate information available or no change in condition regarding the clinical situation).

Axis V. Global assessment of functioning (GAF Scale) during the past year and at the time of evaluation. A rating scale consisting of nine intervals indicates the clinician's judgment, where 81–90 indicates good functioning in all areas and 1–10 indicates persistent danger of hurting oneself or others.

Both the ICD-9-CM and DSM-III-R present definite theoretical biases (although DSM-III-R claims to be atheoretical), are disease-based models, use nosological labels with assumed judgmentalism that can result in social injustice, feature diagnostic categories arrived at by committee vote rather than by sufficient scientific methodology and supportive research data, and depend on diagnostic nomenclature that is both unreliable and irrelevant to the task of designing a therapy program. In addition, the universal requirement by third-party payment organizations that either ICD-9-CM or DSM-III-R diagnostic codes and labels—usually the DSM—be used when seeking reimbursement for mental-health services makes for a forced-choice situation. Therefore, except for insurance purposes and supplemental diagnosis, Integrative Therapy avoids unqualified adoption of either the ICD-9-CM or DSM-III-R as its primary diagnostic approach.

Behavioral Analysis

In contrast to ICD-9-CM and DSM-III-R, which depend on nosological labels that are often vague, nonspecific, and unreliable, behavioral analysis seeks to provide a description of maladaptive behaviors in concrete, specific, and objective terms. DSM-III uses general constructs to refer to what individuals supposedly have or possess; for example, "the text of DSM-III . . . uses [expressions like] . . . 'an individual with schizophrenia'" (APA 1980, 6). Behavioral analysis, in comparison, is more operational in nature and emphasizes "what a person *does* in situations rather than [drawing inferences] about what attributes he [or she] *has* more globally" (Mischel 1968, 10).

A premise of behavioral analysis is that problems in living develop within a social environment and are functionally related to both internal and external antecedents and consequences. This functional relationship between problematic behavior and environmental events can be conceived of through the so-called ABC model (Goldfried & Sprafkin 1974; Hersen & Bellack 1976; Kanfer & Saslow 1969; Mahoney & Thoresen 1974). Behavior (B) is influenced by events that precede it, called antecedents (A), and by some events that follow it, called consequences (C). An antecedent event (A) prompts the individual to behave (B) situationally, and the consequence (C) serves either to strengthen and reinforce or to weaken and punish the behavior. For example, a relational pattern has developed in which a man's wife either says or does something displeasing to him (A), and the husband begins to abuse her verbally (B); although the man realizes that his behavior is cruelly inappropriate and damages the marital relationship, the feeling of power (C) he derives from the abusive behavior helps to sustain his maladaptive behavior. This rather simple paradigm is central to a behavioral analysis of maladaptive behavior.

A behavioral analysis begins by identifying the problem situation or target behavior. It assesses deficits and excesses, frequency, intensity, and duration of the problem condition. The targeted problem might involve behavioral, affective, cognitive, contextual, interpersonal, or somatic components. Next, the antecedents that provoke the problem situation are identified. Antecedents may be either internal or external to the client or patient and may appear in the form of either a contextual, behavioral, affective, cognitive, somatic, or relational stimulus. Finally, the consequences that influence or motivate the problem situation are examined. Like antecedents, consequences may emerge from either the internal or the external environment and their source(s) may be somatic, affective, behavioral, cognitive, contextual, or relational.

Information that discloses the targeted problem situation, together with its antecedents and consequences, may be obtained through a variety of means: direct interviews with the individual, observation of the individual in various situations, interviews with significant third parties, examination of the individual's case history, analysis of the client's social relationships, and self-report or behavioral-analysis forms completed by the client (e.g., Cautela 1977).

The Task Force on Descriptive Behavioral Classification of the American Psychological Association (Morley et al. 1977) has tried to develop a classification or schedule of personality dysfunctions. As seen in the display that follows, behavioral classification aims for operationally defined clusters of dysfunctions instead of placing individuals in global classification categories. The following presentation first provides a list of twenty possible dysfunctions without their operationally defined subentries and then selects four of the identified types of dysfunction together with their operational descriptions for illustration.

Schedule of Personality Dysfunction

1. Agitation
2. Depression
3. Psychomotor slowing
4. Activity impairment
5. Incongruous affect
6. Self-abuse
7. Withdrawal
8. Anxiety
9. Fear
10. Repetitive thoughts and impulses
11. Suspicious ideas and beliefs
12. Disorientation
13. Perceptual distortions
14. Grandiose beliefs
15. Thought disorganization
16. Unusual motor behavior
17. Role nonacceptance
18. Angry aggressiveness
19. Somataform disorders (sensory/motor dysfunctions without organic involvement; sexual dysfunction; and others

such as cardiac dysfunctions and gastrointestinal
problems)
20. Developmental dysfunctions

Operationally Defined Personality Dysfunction

Depression
  Shows little concern about physical appearance
  Experiences eating or sleep disturbances
  Blames self for past thoughts or actions
  Experiences recurrent thoughts of suicide or death;
    despondent in mood
  Experiences feelings of helplessness or hopelessness
  Cries frequently
  Experiences feelings of worthlessness
  Facial expression tired, immobile, or flat

Disorientation
  Unable to give season or month of year
  Unable to give calendar year
  Cannot report age correctly
  Cannot identify city or state where lives
  Unable to give own name
  Unable to identify one person in immediate environment

Angry Aggressiveness
  Boisterous, rowdy, loud
  Disruptive in groups
  Frequent arguments or fights
  Destructive of property
  Experiences impulses to physically harm others
  Physically harms others
  Verbally abusive toward others

Developmental Dysfunctions
  Inadequate problem-solving ability
  Specific learning disability
  Memory impairment
  Motor disability
  Sensory disability

The objective, descriptive, and easily understood language of behavioral
analysis is among its more pragmatic features. Its emphasis on operationally
defined problems also helps to indicate an appropriate mode of interven-

tion. Because of these qualities and its eschewing of the disease or mental-illness motif, Integrative Therapy considers behavioral analysis an important dimension of its diagnostic model.

Social-Interpersonal Diagnosis

Examination of psychotherapy texts, published position papers, and research data indicates that a large number of the theoretical orientations to counseling and psychotherapy adhere to the assumption that psychosocial factors are the primary influences on human behavior and personality, from both adaptive and maladaptive perspectives. It follows logically that persons embracing these orientations would hold as well the view that "the most useful aspects of psychiatric diagnostic schemata are psychosocial in nature and that most diagnoses of functional mental disorders are made, albeit implicitly, on the basis of observed interpersonal behavior" (McLemore & Benjamin 1979, 17). They prefer an interpersonal behavior taxonomy of dysfunctions that uses psychosocial terms for diagnoses, and they tend to resist traditional psychiatric nosology, which depends too much on impressionistic clinical judgment and the categorization of persons in terms of mental illness. A few of the many psychotherapists who have advocated the social-interpersonal approach to understanding maladjustment are Erik Erikson, Karen Horney, Harry Stack Sullivan, Alfred Adler, Eric Berne, Carl Rogers, and Jacob Moreno.

From the perspective of psychological assessment, a variety of personality tests is premised on factors and dynamics definitive of the social-interpersonal approach to social behavior (e.g., Actualizing Assessment Battery, California Personality Inventory, Edwards Personal Preference Schedule, and Fundamental Interpersonal Relationships Orientation). A few efforts have been made to develop diagnostic systems that follow a social-interpersonal emphasis, language, and format. Two in particular are worthy of mention: Leary's (1957) "interpersonal diagnosis" and Benjamin's (1974) "structural analysis of social behavior." I have selected Leary's model to illustrate the classification of social behaviors and the use of psychosocial terminology to describe dysfunctions. The display that follows is an adaptation of his (Leary 1957) "interpersonal circle" in which he arranged a network of social-interpersonal variables in sixteen mechanisms or reflexes that made use of two orthogonal axes, love-hate and dominance-submission. The sixteen mechanisms or reflexes are classified in eight general categories to be used for interpersonal diagnosis. Each categorical variable consists of a moderate or adaptive and an extreme or pathological level of intensity (e.g., aggressive—sadistic). Subsumed first under each categorical level of intensity are illustrations of extreme or rigid reflexes (e.g., aggressive: attack or unfriendly actions; sadistic: punitive, sarcastic, or unkind actions). Subsumed next is an indication of the type of behavior a specific interpersonal variable tends to provoke in other people (e.g., the aggressive variable tends to provoke hostility in others, while the sadistic reflex provokes passive resistance). Finally, an illustration is given of adaptive behaviors or reflexes for each variable (e.g., an adaptive behavior of the aggressive reflex is frank and forthright action; the sadistic person can behave adaptively through aggressive and firm actions). The lower-case letters *a*, *b*, and *c* identify the three subsumed variable descriptors in their respective order.

Display of Leary's Interpersonal Diagnostic System

1. Managerial (A)—Autocratic (P)
   a. Dominates   a. Seeks respect
   b. Provokes obedience   b. Provokes respect
   c. Manages   c. Guides

2. Competitive (C)—Narcissistic (B)
   a. Exploits   a. Boasts
   b. Provokes distrust   b. Provokes inferiority
   c. Acts assertively   c. Acts independently

3. Aggressive (E)—Sadistic (D)
   a. Acts unfriendly   a. Acts punitively
   b. Provokes hostility   b. Provokes passivity
   c. Forthright in action   c. Firm in actions

4. Rebellious (F)—Distrustful (G)
   a. Complains   a. Acts hurt
   b. Provokes punishment   b. Provokes rejection
   c. Unconventional action c. Realistic wariness

5. Responsible (O)—Hypernormal (N)
   a. Behaves compulsively   a. Very soft-hearted
   b. Provokes trust   b. Provokes acceptance
   c. Offers help   c. Supportive

6. Self-effacing (H)—Masochistic (I)
   a. Anxious and guilty   a. Submits too easily
   b. Provokes arrogance   b. Provokes leadership
   c. Shy and sensitive   c. Obeys and does duty

7. Docile (J)—Dependent (K)
   a. Conforms   a. Clings to others
   b. Provokes advice   b. Provokes help
   c. Respectful   c. Trusting

8. Cooperative (L)—Over-conventional (M)
   a. Agrees always   a. Effusive actions
   b. Provokes tenderness   b. Provokes love
   c. Eager participant   c. Affectionate

Leary's interpersonal diagnostic model can depict an interpersonal mode of adjustment or maladjustment and the equivalent of a standard psychiatric type of maladjustment. The FG variable can describe a realistic, skeptical personality (adjustment indicated), a passively resistant, bitter, distrustful personality (maladjustment indicated), or a schizoid personality (as defined by psychiatric nomenclature).

The primary appeal of social-interpersonal diagnosis lies in its focus on the dynamics of interpersonal behaviors and its avoidance of the judgmental overtones of psychiatric nosological terms. These emphases are desirable inclusions in the diagnostic model advocated by Integrative Therapy.

Therapy Process as Diagnosis

Framers of diagnostic systems usually assume that an accurate assessment or diagnosis of presenting problems is an absolute necessity in designing treatment programs. However, not all psychotherapists agree. Many assert that traditional diagnoses tend to interfere with therapy rather than aiding it. They consider diagnosis and therapy indistinguishable and inseparable.

No therapist has been more clear and persistent about this than Carl Rogers (1951, 219–23). Rogers assumes that therapy begins with the very first psychological contact between therapist and client and proceeds hand-in-hand with diagnosis. This means to him that therapy is not built upon diagnosis per se. Furthermore, the client- or person-centered perspective on diagnosis holds that psychological diagnosis as usually understood is nonessential to psychotherapy and may actually hinder the therapeutic process.

The basic assumptions at the foundation of the view that therapy is diagnosis can be summarized as follows: First, behavior is caused and the psychological cause of behavior lies largely in a certain perception or way of perceiving phenomena. Second, clients, with their unique sets of perceptions and experiences, are the only ones who can know and understand fully the dynamics of their perceptions and behaviors. This necessarily makes clients or patients the final diagnosticians in therapy regardless of the theoretical orientation.

Thus, "in a very meaningful and accurate sense, therapy *is* diagnosis, and the diagnosis is a process which goes on in the experience of the client, rather than in the intellect of the psychotherapist. . . . [And] one might say that psychotherapy, of whatever orientation, is complete or almost complete when the diagnosis of the dynamics is experienced by the client" (Rogers 1951, 223).

Gestalt therapists, psychodramatists, transactional analytic therapists, and Adlerian therapists are among those from other theoretical orientations who also look to the therapy process for much of the diagnostic understanding of problems in living. Mosak (1984), an Adlerian psychotherapist, sums up the matter succinctly: "Most Adlerians avoid nosological diagnosis, except for non-therapeutic purposes such as filling out insurance forms. Labels are static descriptions and ignore the *movement* of the individual. They describe what an individual *has*, but not how he moves through life" (90).

This perspective fits smoothly into Integrative Therapy's modus operandi. It seems to be the most respectful, accurate, and dynamic way to relate to clients and their unique situations in life. Problems are learned experientially, and they must be disclosed, understood, and corrected experientially via relearning avenues, including therapy.

Integrative Therapy's Diagnostic Stance

Integrative Therapy's inclination toward diagnosing maladjusted life styles can be discerned easily by observing its position about the etiology of problems in living and by scanning the commentary appended to each of the preceding discussions of diagnostic classification systems. The diagnostic and assessment procedures followed in Integrative Therapy will be presented thoroughly in chapter 7; therefore, only a synopsis is offered here.

Integrating the attitudes, emphases, processes, procedures, and terminology derived from the behavioral, social-interpersonal, and therapy-as-diagnosis approaches provides a most fitting diagnostic framework for Integrative Therapy. Viewing the therapy process itself as an experiential disclosing and unfolding of clients' problems in living is a realistic and personal approach to understanding human hurts, pains, and impasses. Since many, perhaps most, problems in living are learned in a social-interpersonal context, it seems natural to seek an understanding of the problems in a therapeutic environment that stresses social and interpersonal aspects. Furthermore, terminology that defines social behavior appears to be the most appropriate language to describe maladaptive conditions in living. Finally, the contributions of behavioral analysis both complement and supplement the preceding features in that they, too, locate the origin of problems in the social environment and use a descriptive (specific, operational, and nonmedical) rather than a categorical (general, nominal, and medical) language to describe maladjustment. The functional analysis aspect of behavioral analysis allows, additionally, for an objective clarification (when needed) of the target problem in terms of the presenting complaint together with its antecedents and reinforcing consequences.

This integrated approach to diagnosis is sufficient for all diagnostic needs in Integrative Therapy, including an understanding of spiritual problems, with one exception. Due to the existing situation regarding third-party payments for mental-health services, it is necessary to use the codes and labels of either ICD-9-CM or DSM-III-R when filling out insurance forms.

5

Theory of Personality and Behavior Change

That human beings are capable of experiencing positive behavioral and personality change in psychotherapy is an assumption accepted by all therapists of different orientations. They lack consensus, however, about the nature of the change that takes place in an individual's life style. The aim of this chapter is to identify the bases of personality change and the motives for therapeutic gain or change as perceived by Integrative Therapy.

Bases of Personality and Behavior Change

The following conditions are offered as the likely sources that account for most positive personality gains experienced by individuals in therapy. These conditions relate to the biological, mental, emotional, spiritual, and social-interpersonal domains of human behavior. This set of conditions is not an exhaustive accounting of all grounds for therapeutic gain. Much of the change people experience results from life-altering events that are concurrent with therapy but external to it.

Correction of Biological Conditions

As discussed in the preceding chapter under the heading of etiology, many biological conditions can seriously affect human personality and behavior. Elimination or even partial removal of the pathological condition is likely to result in observable, positive personality gain or change. Surgical removal of a brain tumor, correcting a chemical or hormonal imbalance, and stopping alcohol or drug abuse and dependence are examples of biological corrections that can improve personality functioning.

Learning

The acquisition of new attitudes, values, behaviors, and skills alters behavioral patterns and personality profiles. Learning may entail unlearning old, maladaptive behaviors, relearning previously acquired skills and behaviors that have become ineffective because of neglect or insufficient practice, or new learning that adds skills and behaviors previously lacking.

Learning experiences, though they may center on a particular modality of personality functioning, usually involve some change in other modalities. For example, an improvement in interpersonal relationship skills will likely be accompanied by observable changes in cognitive, affective, and behavioral aspects of personality. Similarly, positive gain or change in the biophysiological domain necessarily affects thoughts, feelings, and sensations. Authentic spiritual learning does not exclude other, particularly cognitive and interpersonal, types of learning.

Learning may result in either therapeutic reduction of behavioral and personality excesses or therapeutic increase in the functioning of a client's personality where there was previously a deficit. Examples are overcoming the self-defeating habit of dwelling obsessively on past mistakes and regaining sexual potency or joyful functioning, respectively.

Growth

Growth and learning are closely related but distinct phenomena. They are related in that most growth in the nonbiological aspects of human maturation depends at least minimally on learning. Yet they are easily distinguished conceptually. While learning is concerned mostly with gaining new knowledge or skills, growth refers more definitively to progressive development or expansion along a ground plan that involves stages in a process, as suggested by Erikson's (1980) concept of the human life cycle that follows what he referred to as the *epigenetic principle*.

Therapy and other experiences that expand people's awareness of themselves and the external world aid people in assimilating new data. Greater discovery of themselves and others also provides for more effective integration both intrapersonally and socially. For example, as a woman progresses in therapy or her life cycle, her capacity for interpersonal trust and intimacy should increase.

Counseling and psychotherapy interventions unavoidably aim to help people either to adjust to growth in particular developmental stages or to experience successful transition from one stage to the next. Jung's (1959) concept of individuation is a remarkable example of the personality change that results from growth. Individuation is growth by which a person becomes an integrated, indivisible unity or whole. All the separate parts of the personality become harmonious so that the person can approach life with balance and wholeness. The "war within" ceases and the individual is at peace with Self.

Redecision

Another source of personality gain is redecision. Decisions determine the directions or life paths for which people opt. Often these decisions are made early in life and are based on faulty perceptions and erroneous data. Such decisions result in self-defeating life styles or life scripts. Ineffective life styles or life scripts remain ineffective until people have some type of corrective experience.

Psychotherapy is one specialized format that provides an unusual opportunity for people to have corrective experiences. In therapy, people can evaluate prior decisions in terms of inappropriate data, mistaken ideas about themselves and others, and the scripts they have laid down. They can then change life lies into life truths via redecision (Goulding & Goulding 1979). Thus, when a life lie or faulty script is put to rest and an updated and accurate script is written, an individual's life has been changed.

Regeneration

The term *regeneration* (from the Greek *palingenesia*, meaning renewal, rebirth, or a being born again) is a theological word that refers to the spiritual change effected in human personality by the supernatural activity of the Holy Spirit (Titus 3:4–7). By regeneration, people are made spiritually new and gain a divine quality of life. Other scriptural terms for regeneration are *born again* (John 3:3, 7; 1 Pet. 1:23), *born of God* (1 John 3:9), and *born of the Spirit* (John 3:5–8). The new birth results in a new relationship with God, self, and other people. In sum, regeneration produces such a complete change in the total personality that the regenerate person is a "new creation; the old has gone, the new has come" (2 Cor. 5:17).

People can experience the new birth wherever and whenever they decide to trust Jesus Christ personally. The context of Christian counseling and psychotherapy is an appropriate setting for this spiritual and personal change to occur in a client's life. Secular therapists are likely to think of regeneration or new birth as neither valuable nor relevant, but Christian therapists and their believing clients recognize it as a life-transforming wonder unsurpassed by any contribution of psychotherapy.

Sanctification

This is another theological term that relates to positive change in a believer's personality and life style. Sanctification means first of all the believer's being set apart or separated to God for moral and righteous living (Rom. 12:1; Col. 3:1). It connotes as well the process of God's living and working personally and intimately in the personality of a believer to develop and bring to maturity the new life that was initiated by regeneration (1 Cor. 1:2; 6:11; 1 Thess. 5:23; Rom. 8:5–11). This ongoing process produces observable and permanent change in the Christian's personality and behavior.

Sanctification can be nurtured in counseling and psychotherapy, although that is not the immediate objective.

Motives for Entering Counseling and Psychotherapy

People who pursue counseling and psychotherapy as a career in order to provide professional mental-health services and those who enter therapy to receive professional help with their problems do so with particular motives. Following is an identification and discussion of four general, noneconomic motives for entering psychotherapy either as a professional provider or as a consumer. The first three motives were suggested by Rychlak (1981) and the fourth by McClelland (1975).

The Scholarly Motive

Professional therapists motivated by a scholarly interest are concerned just as much with understanding human behavior as they are with treating problems in living. The scholarly therapist delights in comprehending the dynamics of behavior and personality, grappling with the etiology of maladjustment, and discovering experimentally what is effective in correcting maladaptive life styles.

Clients who seek counseling and psychotherapy from a scholarly desire want to engage in a process of self-discovery. They most likely do not consider themselves to be seriously maladjusted. Rather, they are curious about how their personalities are put together and what makes them tick.

The Altruistic Motive

The altruistic motive is concerned primarily with values, meaning, relationships, growth, and social justice. Counselors and therapists who intervene in the life spaces of their fellow human beings with an altruistic interest sense at some level of awareness that they are their brother's or sister's keeper and desire to advocate someone's cause. These therapists seek to foster self-acceptance, self-realization, self-esteem, self-worth, self-determination, and self-actualization in their clients. The therapist-client relationship is viewed as a nurturing environment in which the client is prized and is given the opportunity, perhaps for the first time, to experience mutual love and respect. This therapeutic alliance generates social feelings and interest and is offered as a prototype for establishing effective social relationships outside of therapy.

Clients who are altruistically motivated want an accepting, nonthreatening, and nonjudgmental environment in which they may be themselves and learn to relate openly and honestly with a sensitive and empathic listener. They desire the involvement of another compassionate and authentic person who will stand with them in their process of self-realization. These clients are less interested in being healed of disturbances than they are in being heard and understood as they become caring persons.. They want to be prized as worthy individuals in an egalitarian relationship that is supportive and encouraging. With this kind of support, they know they can find themselves and their places in the world.

The Curative Motive

Therapists who strive for time and cost efficiency, technical accuracy, and measurable change or outcomes typically have the curative motive. Curative-minded counselors and therapists focus their interventions mostly on removing symptoms and seek to heal people as quickly as possible by manipulating both clients and their environments. Therapeutic cure is assessed on the basis of the absence or removal of the symptomatic behavior initially presented to the therapist. The technical and methodological aspects of therapy receive greater emphasis than does the interpersonal relationship between the therapist and the client.

Individuals who come to counseling and psychotherapy with a curative motive see themselves as sick, abnormal, emotionally disturbed, or mentally ill. They assume the role of a sick patient and enter therapy to get well or be cured. Often they expect to be the passive recipients of painless, magical clinical help just as they expect to get rid of a headache by swallowing aspirin. These clients tend to become resistant when they are informed that hard work might be a major part of their cure.

The Power Motive

Power-motivated psychotherapists think of themselves as strong, in control, self-directing, autonomous, and willful. They use their therapeutic expertise both to shape others and to enhance their sense of personal power. The more influential they are therapeutically, the greater is their experience of power. Theoretical orientations and methods of intervention often are chosen in terms of how well they provide for the expression and fulfillment of the therapists' power needs. The more direct and expressive orientations like Gestalt, rational-emotive, and psychodrama allow for an overt display of effective power. On the contrary, nondirective and insight orientations tend to reflect less need for visible demonstrations of personal power.

Clients who enter therapy with power needs are likely to exhibit dependence in the early stages of the process. A stated goal might be to learn to be more assertive and assume greater control over their lives. They desire a therapeutic experience that promises to maximize their ability to learn self-assertiveness and self-control. They also want to learn to derive more strength from themselves and depend progressively less on the strength or power of others.

It seems unreasonable to assume that either a therapist or a client has a consistently single or exclusive motive for pursuing counseling and psychotherapy. Rather, various combinations of these motives will operate in both the therapist and the client at different stages in personal development and in the process of therapy. One motive might be primary while any of the others exist(s) in an auxiliary role(s).

In Integrative Therapy, the ethical motive tends to be the primary interest. The scholarly and curative motives are alternately in the secondary position, depending on the specifics of a clinical situation. The power motive has significance, primarily from the desire to use the therapist's potency to instill trust in the client and to effect therapeutic movement.

Part 3

Process and Procedures of Integrative Therapy

6

Therapeutic Relationship

This chapter presents the moral, ethical, legal, and interpersonal aspects of the professional and therapeutic relationship between therapists and their clients. Particular focus will be placed on *agape* love as the ultimate ethical principle that governs both the personal and the professional conduct of therapists who adhere to a Judeo-Christian world view. Attention also will be given to special concerns such as dealing with transference and the role of physical touch.

Relating with Respect for Moral Values

Morality refers to a personal sense of ought and ought not, right and wrong, and good and bad in individual life styles. Counselors and psychotherapists frequently must make decisions in their clinical work that challenge their personal values. It is imperative that they have clarified their values and beliefs prior to entering professional relationships with clients. Unavoidably, therapists often find their values in conflict either with other value systems in the larger culture, with the values and practices of certain client-problem situations, or with some legal issue.

Sometimes there is no clear right or wrong in the decisions clients must make, or no one correct answer to their inquiry; rather, they need objective and nonjudgmental help in working through their difficult situations. Therapists need to have their moral values so intact and integrated that a personal or professional judgment can be made in value-loaded cases whether or not they have the objectivity required to provide the desired help. If the conflict in values appears to be an impediment to effective therapy, they probably will need to refer the client to another therapist.

97

Mature and effective therapists can tolerate value differences and assist individuals in resolving life issues that might involve personal beliefs different from their own. Such therapists do not dwell obsessively on the fear that they will compromise themselves when they offer professional help to persons with life styles based on different values. Therefore, competent therapists neither impose their values on clients nor attack their clients' values.

Relating According to Ethical Principles

Having a well-developed moral code as a value base for making judgments about life and work is insufficient in itself for responsible professional conduct. Such personal codes of morality are too subjective and internal to provide an objective guide for working with the lives of other people. Responsible professional practice requires a consensual set of guidelines that have an inherent concern for moral behavior but are external to therapists and serve as the standards for regulating their professional conduct. Typically these professional guidelines are referred to as ethical standards or principles.

Virtually every professional organization concerned with offering mental-health services to the public has its own guidelines or ethical standards that have been derived consensually from the members of the organization. Integrative Therapy acknowledges the Ethical Principles of Psychologists, developed by the American Psychological Association (appendix A), as the preferred code of external consensual standards for regulating the professional conduct of psychotherapists who belong to that organization. Another relevant code of ethical standards has been provided by the American Association for Counseling and Development (1988).

Relating with Knowledge of Legal Parameters

There is an ever-increasing body of statutory laws and court decisions that have a direct impact on the delivery of mental-health services. Responsible therapists seek to remain informed about these laws in order to make wise professional decisions and to offer accurate guidance to their clients.

Among the many legal issues that necessitate therapists' maintaining keen vigilance on their current status are licensing laws, freedom-of-choice legislation, workmen's compensation provisions, Medicare and Medicaid availability, public law enactments by the federal government, informed consent procedures, privileged communication provisions, limits of confidentiality, and serving as expert witnesses in judicial hearings. Since local laws and court principles vary, therapists need to know the legal parameters of practice in their specific locations and how these local conditions mesh with federal regulations.

Clearly, comprehending the moral, ethical, and legal principles surrounding professional psychotherapy is an essential element of a therapeutic relationship. However, much is required beyond the mere legal and ethical guidelines to effect a truly therapeutic environment.

Relating with Love, the Supreme Ethic

In his classic study of systems of psychotherapy, Jerome Frank (1973) observed that it is not precision of diagnosis and specific methodologies that account for successful psychotherapy. Rather, effective therapy stems from nontechnical elements common to the diverse approaches to counseling and psychotherapy. One of these elements is a particular kind of relationship between therapists and clients, regardless of theoretical orientation. The essential ingredient of the relationship is clients' confidence that their therapists are competent, genuinely accept and care about them, and sincerely desire to help. Frank's observation echoes the findings of Carl Rogers and his followers, who have stressed consistently that a facilitative relationship is the sine qua non of successful counseling and psychotherapy (e.g., Rogers 1957, 1975; Truax & Carkhuff 1967). Few counselors and therapists currently support Rogers's claim that a specific set of relationship skills constitutes the necessary *and* sufficient conditions for therapeutic gain. Neither are therapists unanimous on what specific elements represent the optimal therapeutic situation. Yet there appears to be an increasing concurrence among therapists that a caring and nurturing relationship is at least necessary (Parloff, Waskow, & Wolfe 1978).

Integrative Therapy holds firmly that an interpersonal relationship characterized by *agape* love is a necessary condition for effecting therapeutic gain. Stated more specifically, a relationship based on therapists' consistently seeking what is best for their clients is essential for effective counseling and psychotherapy. Many other counselors and therapists recognize that the truly therapeutic relationship is an expression of love. Research by Truax and Carkhuff (1967) offers evidence that each of the central ingredients of the therapeutic relationship (empathic understanding, nonpossessive warmth, prizing and valuing) is a communication of love. Patterson (1985) is even more explicit: "When one brings together the various aspects of the facilitative conditions . . . it becomes apparent that they constitute love in the highest sense or *agape* . . . " (91). Adlerian therapists voice a similar view when they acknowledge that the "necessary conditions for therapeutic effectiveness are variations of the Christian values of faith, hope, and love" (Mosak 1984, 73).

While some counselors and therapists use the term *love* to describe the therapeutic relationship, others tend to avoid it for various reasons. First, love phenomena are defined as subjective feelings that, if acted on, would interfere with therapists' clinical objectivity. Second, certain concepts about love found in Western culture are associated with the Judeo-Christian tradition, and this metaphysical influence conflicts with behavioral scientists' commitment to advancing a respectable scientific approach to human behavior. Third, therapists sometimes are reluctant to refer to love in connection with their clients because they equate love with sensuality or romantic involvement, which is unethical behavior in therapy. Fourth, perhaps the major reason for omitting love from a discussion of therapists' relationships with their clients stems largely from the vagueness, confusion, and imprecision that surrounds the word *love* in our culture.

Therapists, like all other responsible persons, are expected to love their children, friends, neighbors, and colleagues, but they are cautioned in training and in practice not to love their clients. Unfortunately, a misunderstanding of the true meaning and nature of love has resulted in many therapists, both Christian and non-Christian, refraining from acknowledging the appropriateness of loving relationships with clients.

Integrative Therapy considers mature love as the essense of relating interpersonally. The following is a profile of the loving relationship as understood and practiced in Integrative Therapy.

Understanding Love

Most people describe love as a positive feeling or attraction that one person has for another. When English-speaking people seek to describe love further, they typically use the terms *like* and *care*. The limited repertoire of English words to express the different components of love adds to the difficulty of comprehending and articulating the various nuances of love in the American culture. It is necessary to look beyond English for a vocabulary adequate for a comprehensive understanding of love. Greek has four basic but distinct words that serve excellently to profile love.

Eros

The first component in a comprehensive understanding of love is *eros,* which refers to an individual's striving for union, perfection, and self-realization. However, most of the Western world, including Sigmund Freud, has equated *eros* with sexual lust. *Eros* indeed does relate exquisitely to the personal bonding between lovers, but the concept reaches far beyond mere sexual desire. *Eros* expresses one's appreciation for the aesthetic, the true, the good, the perfect, and the beautiful. Augustine and others have stressed that, from the human perspective, *eros* leads human beings to God (Nygren 1969). The longing of human beings for union or fellowship with God in order to experience personal fulfillment in an intimate relationship with their Creator causes them to search for God. This longing and need for union with God is reflected in Augustine's cry, "O Lord . . . you made us for yourself, and our heart is restless until it finds rest in you." The longing and need of human beings for relationship extends to individuals' desiring a sense of relatedness to all creation, including interpersonal intimacy with other persons. *Eros* is the initial force that attracts persons to one another and is fundamental to the bonding process.

If *eros* is accepted with the breadth of its meaning and not reduced to sexual lust or desire, then the concept becomes a definitive component of the therapeutic relationship. When understood in its most elegant sense, *eros* could be defended plausibly as one of the grounds for therapists to view their clients as "noble and beautiful persons" (Landsman 1968). A specific value of *eros* is the provision of a basis for understanding and respecting gender differences in the relationship. It also offers an avenue for exploring and dealing with relationship issues like attraction, bonding, the need to belong, and the dynamics surrounding transference and countertransference.

Storge

The second element involved in a thorough understanding of love is *storge*, or the affection and gentle feelings one person holds toward another. *Storge* is essentially tender care for another without pretense and without bias regarding age, race, gender, and socioeconomic status (Lewis 1960). Concerned with warmth and nurturing, *storge* desires neither to hurt, nor to humiliate, nor to dominate its recipient. The characteristics of the Nurturing Parent as described in Transactional Analysis (e.g., Steiner 1974) exemplify *storge*. The Nurturing Parent relates to the loved one by affirming, protecting, caring, helping, guiding, supporting, encouraging, and positively stroking. Integrative Therapy considers *storge* an invaluable ingredient in all nurturing human relationships, particularly in parent-child and therapist-client interactions.

Philia

A third dimension of a complete profile of loving behavior is *philia*, the expression of friendship by one individual toward another. *Philia* is intelligent and selective and emerges from a relationship in which the participants are involved in some common interest that enhances the welfare of both or all parties. As C. S. Lewis (1960, 90) observed, *philia*, or friendship, is a relationship between people "at their highest level of individuality." Developmental and progressive in nature, *philia* begins at a point in time and grows to maturity as the individuals stand side by side, not face to face, to share openly the exigencies of life. The participants in these experiences reciprocate acceptance and regard in the context of mutual trust and confidentiality. Always concerned as much with authentic giving as with receiving, *philia* is a source of mutual joy to those who cooperate in this living process.

Philia seeks to be accepting, confiding, forgiving, challenging, trusting, invigorating, stimulating, corrective, instructive, and restorative. These are qualities indispensable to the therapeutic relationship and to Integrative Therapy. Although the term *philia* per se might not be used, the theme is clearly reflected in many of the major orientations to counseling and psychotherapy, particularly in those developed by Alfred Adler, Carl Rogers, William Glasser, and Eric Berne.

Agape

The supreme mode of loving behavior is *agape*, the unselfish, intelligent, and volitional seeking of the highest good for another person. *Agape* accepts the other person unconditionally, remains loyal, and consistently works to promote what is in the best interest of that person. It transcends all other kinds of love in that it has a divine origin and quality.

The supernaturalness of *agape* is indicated by its being a personal attribute of deity (1 John 4:8), which is reproduced in the Christian life through the agency of the Holy Spirit, who lives in every believer (Gal. 5:22). The classic description of *agape* (1 Cor. 13) affirms that people who practice this type of love are characteristically kind and patient. They do not envy other people and are not proud and boastful. Their behavior is free from rudeness, self-seeking, and uncontrolled anger. They keep no record of wrongs and find no pleasure in immoral and unethical activity. Rather, their joy comes from experiencing the truth and protecting the welfare of those they love. Furthermore, *agape*-lovers are full of trust, hope, and perseverance. Finally, they are dependable, not prone to failure.

Agape represents the supreme ethic in Integrative Therapy and serves as the guiding principle in the therapeutic relationship and the entire therapy process, regardless of the client and the presenting problem.

In summary, Integrative Therapy functions on the premise that authentic loving means relating to others with the belief that all people possess intrinsic beauty and nobility, in an affectionate and nurturing manner, in the context of a trusting and confidential friendship, and with an unconditional acceptance of the loved ones and a consistent commitment to promote their welfare.

Demonstrating Love

The preceding description indicates that genuinely loving behavior is not passive and subjective emotionalism. Instead, the loving therapist personally prizes and values the client as an individual with dignity and worth and communicates this through specific, observable, and purposeful actions. It is not necessary for therapists to tell clients that they are loved. Given the confusion regarding the term, in most cases therapists would be ill advised to say to their clients, "I love you." Not words but visible demonstrations of love are what count. Therapists can demonstrate therapeutic love in a variety of ways.

Accepting and loving self

The development of a therapeutic relationship begins with therapists' genuinely loving and accepting themselves. The ability to care genuinely for others stems from a mature relationship with God and self (e.g., Mark 12:30, 31). Relating harmoniously and lovingly to God and self results in therapists' possessing a sense of personal worth and dignity and the capacity to experience loving and nurturing relationships with their clients. Wholesome self-acceptance also allows therapists to be open, honest, sincere, and genuine persons. Like Nathaniel (John 1:47), authentic therapists are no phonies; they relate to God, themselves, and clients without façade, pretense, self-depreciation, or artificial role playing. Authentic therapists are congruent and recognize both their strengths and weaknesses; they have nothing to hide or defend. They can accept and express their true feelings and are willing to disclose personal experiences when that can be therapeutic for their clients.

Accepting clients unconditionally

Themselves recipients of God's *agape*, therapists demonstrate this same love to clients by accepting them unconditionally as persons with worth, dignity, and nobility regardless of their gender, race, appearance, behavior, or status. Clients are prized, respected, and valued as fellow human beings who, like their therapists, are created in the image of God. Therapists' unconditional caring is nonpossessive and does not ridicule, criticize, depreciate, or censure clients. Imperfections, failures, mistakes—and yes, sins—are accepted as typical of the human situation. Clients are accepted and loved as worthy persons although some behaviors and practices might be socially unacceptable, even deplorable. This loving acceptance does not imply, however, approval or condoning of maladaptive and irresponsible behavior.

Listening and responding with compassion

Therapists enter clients' life space and stand in clients' private worlds as trusted confidants. They listen to clients with compassionate understanding and experience deeply and accurately the pains, hurts, disappointments, failures, and aspirations clients disclose. This empathic, compassionate understanding assures clients that their therapists truly care, are able to feel with them, and can really help with life's difficulties.

Nurturing through gentleness

Therapists provide a nonthreatening, safe, and nurturing environment in which clients can be themselves for the purpose of self-disclosure, self-exploration, and experimentation with alternative modes of thinking, feeling, and behaving. In a very real sense, therapists function as gentle, nurturing parents who support and encourage clients in their efforts to develop more satisfying life styles. For many clients a kind, gentle therapist is likely to be the first person who has allowed them to express themselves without fear of rejection, punishment, or reprimand. Therapists' nonjudgmental attitudes, personal warmth, and gentleness give clients permission to be real and encourage them to actualize themselves as free and responsible individuals.

Communicating graciously and distinctly

Therapists acknowledge that the therapy process is essentially interpersonal communication. They are concerned about the effect on clients of their verbal and nonverbal communication. They use language that is gracious (Col. 4:6), distinct and easily understood (1 Cor. 14:9), free from obscenity and vulgarity (Eph. 4:29a), and appropriate to the specific need(s) of their clients (Eph. 4:29b). Not only do they choose their words carefully to fit their client's particular needs, but also they speak fluently, directly, and with kindness and respect. Therapists should always be aware that their tongues have the power of life and death (Prov. 18:21) and can either heal or hurt (James 3:1–12). Therefore, they keep a watch on their tongues in order to speak words of life, healing, comfort, and encouragement.

Appreciating gender differences

Therapists appreciate and relate to clients as sexual as well as spiritual and social beings. Clients are not just generic persons; rather, they are men and women—individuals with unique sexual identities. The quality of the psychosocial contact between therapists and clients is influenced significantly by respectful treatment of gender differences. Effective therapists recognize the common humanity and spirituality shared by males and females, but they also honor their gender differences. A personal and professional respect for the nuances of gender differences enhances the effectiveness of the therapeutic relationship. While therapists express an appreciation for gender differences and sexual identities of their clients, they refuse to seek pleasure from unethical sexual pairing and romantic eroticism with their clients.

Confronting without condemning

The slogan of a leading producer of greeting cards suggests that its card is used "when you care enough to send the best." When therapists care enough to give their best, they confront the inconsistencies, discrepancies, and mixed messages in clients' feelings, thoughts, and actions. A discrepancy might be between two verbal messages, two nonverbal messages, a verbal message and a nonverbal message, a verbal message and an action (a broken promise), or clients' having obvious talents and resources but failing to recognize and make optimal use of them.

Instead of assuming the role of easygoing nice guys, therapists dare to communicate to clients, directly but supportively, their awareness of discrepancies or incongruities so that clients may examine themselves and take corrective actions. Confrontation is an exemplary act of grace: it is offered voluntarily, thoughtfully, and solely for the good of the client. Genuine confrontation also is well-timed, constructive, and free of any attack, condemnation, harassment, and belittling.

Honoring personal values

Authentic caring for clients is demonstrated also through therapists' respecting clients' values. No effort is made ever to coerce or persuade clients to do anything that would compromise their values and harm their sense of personal dignity. Neither do therapists seek to impose their values, preferences, and beliefs on clients. They may help clients explore alternatives and examine the possible consequences of pursuing options. When appropriate, they might caution clients, even admonish or exhort them, regarding potential harm or danger associated with a particular choice or plan of action. Yet, it remains their clients' privilege and responsibility to make the decisions and experience the outcomes of their choices. Therapists' approach is similar to Joshua's; he exposed the options to his people, encouraged them to make personal choices, and affirmed his own values by opting for a preferred path without imposing it on them (Josh. 24:14–15).

Making referral

ometimes relationships between therapists and clients are nontherapeutic and, therefore, nonproductive. Among the various reasons for nontherapeutic relationships the following are typical: (1) The client's presenting problem or situation might lie beyond the training and competence of the therapist. (2) An unresolvable conflict or discrepancy might arise between the values of the therapist and those of the client. (3) Personal factors—residual pain or anger in the therapist following a major life crisis like the murder of a child—might interfere with therapeutic work with particular clients or problems. (4) Messy transference and countertransference could prevent the formation and maintenance of a therapeutic environment. Whenever conditions like these are observed, then, in the best interest of the client, referral options should be explored and arranged. The immediate therapist should cease clinical work with the client.

Relating Through Specific Procedures and Actions

The therapeutic relationship originates and develops according to a sequence of specific procedures and activities. The following discussion focuses on these dimensions of the therapy process.

Making initial contact

Therapeutic relationships begin the moment therapists and clients meet. How therapists approach clients during the initial encounter, whether by telephone or face to face, can help to either make or break the relationship. A friendly "hello," a smile, a welcoming handshake, and a cordial warmth—or lack of these—have tremendous impact on the quality of the relationship.

Clients often are running scared and need touches of social grace to allay their fright regarding therapy. They need to feel from the first greeting that their therapists are expressing verbally and nonverbally, "You're a valuable person and I care for you." They need to sense that their therapists are compassionate and Spirit-filled persons who will talk with them in kindness, relate to them with a gentle, sensitive touch, and give them hope (Matt. 12:18–20). They also need to perceive early that their therapists possess wisdom and are characterized by decency, peacefulness, altruism, humility, compassion, good naturedness, impartiality, and sincerity (James 3:13–18). When clients see these qualities expressed effectively, they begin to trust and confide in their therapists.

Therapists need to demonstrate self-confidence and professional competence, but airs of superiority, pompousness, and affected dignity have no place in the therapeutic relationship.

Regarding social amenities, therapists are like good hosts. They provide necessary directions to the therapy site, greet clients in the lounge or waiting area, and endeavor to make it easy for clients to get into the therapy room, have a seat, and become comfortable. Some light, informal talk and personal sharing can help in the early moments of the encounter. Touching on common interests and experiences (e.g., having the same name or sharing a common home town) helps clients to experience their therapists as caring fellow human beings.

Providing orientation and structure

Individuals who enter therapy for the first time or who seek the help of a therapist previously unknown to them have little or no knowledge of what to expect. A therapeutic relationship requires a mutual understanding of roles, expectations, responsibilities, commitment, and limitations of each participant. Thus, providing adequate orientation and structure is a prerequisite for a truly productive therapist-client relationship.

The orientation includes a brief explanation, in down-to-earth language, of what counseling, or psychotherapy, is. Therapists share with clients their personal approach to therapy, providing information about the relationship, how problems are identified, goals, and probable methods and strategies. Integrative Therapy emphasizes that therapy is an egalitarian and cooperative engagement in which therapists are skilled helpers who guide clients in solving personal issues, and clients are self-determining individuals who must assume a large part of the responsibility for achieving the desired outcomes. The limits of confidentiality are discussed.

Structure in the therapeutic relationship includes information regarding the length and frequency of sessions, an estimate of the total number of sessions required, the therapist's policy concerning scheduling and canceling appointments, and financial matters (the charge per session, mode and time of payments, insurance coverage, filing of claims).

Having informed clients about the nature of the therapy process, therapists carefully answer any questions and clarify any issues clients raise. Clients then either consent to continue in the therapy program or elect to seek help from another therapist.

This body of information serves to foster a sense of certainty in clients and to strengthen confidence and trust in therapists. It gives clarity and stability to the relationship, clients are spared unnecessary ambiguity, confusion, uncertainty, and anxiety, and therapists gain time efficiency and professional respectability.

Dealing with resistance

Most people enter therapy with ambivalence. They tend to oscillate between wanting professional help to resolve personal problems and opposing the need to change. Admitting the need for psychotherapy suggests weakness, dependence, inadequacy, and failure; these don't mesh with society's emphasis on self-sufficiency and independence. Clients' noncooperativeness in therapy is labeled resistance. This predictable reaction to change may be exhibited through clients' avoiding discussion of problems, arriving late for sessions, canceling appointments, acting confused to distract attention from painful situations, engaging in defensive intellectualization, finding fault with their therapists, or wanting to terminate therapy prematurely.

Therapists will do best by relating to resistant clients with patience, kindness, tolerance, and support. Wise therapists communicate appreciation for their clients' reluctance, acknowledging that it is not easy to submit to someone else for help. Submitting and entrusting one's personal life to a virtual stranger pose a threat to self-esteem, privacy, and integrity. Therapists respond best to resistance by being supportively confrontive rather than passively accepting the behavior. If clients perceive their therapists as compassionate and genuine, this will encourage movement from resistance to trust, commitment, and cooperation.

Handling transference

Clients begin to react emotionally to their therapists from the beginning of the relationship. Frequently, these emotional experiences are similar to their reactions to significant other people during childhood and adolescence. This phenomenon is recognized, especially by psychotherapists with a psychoanalytic orientation, as transference. Clients' emotional reactions toward their therapists may be either positive or negative and, when they are observed, need to be treated in ways compatible with therapists' theoretical orientations.

Integrative Therapy acknowledges the contribution of Freudian psychoanalysis to the understanding of transference, but it does not accept the Freudian idea that transference is largely the projection of emotionalized infantile images from the client's past onto the therapist. Nor is it necessarily true that the client's seeking to act out these repressed childhood emotions on the wrong object, the therapist, is a form of resistance to therapy that must be analyzed and overcome. A more plausible answer is found in the synthesis of learning theory and existential-phenomenological perspectives.

Transference, in some cases, is a special form of generalized learning (Dollard & Miller 1950). To some clients, the therapist's personality and behavior look or sound like those of a parent or other person in their past. Thus, the stimulus of the therapist elicits the same type of responses from clients as those exhibited in earlier relationships. If the therapist is seen or heard as a kind and loving person (positively reinforcing or rewarding), clients are likely to respond with attraction and affection. Should the therapist appear to be judgmental and critical (punitive), clients will tend to react with anger, fear, hostility, or rebellion.

The emotional reactions of some clients are more than generalized learning. They are emotional experiences in a here-and-now, I-Thou relationship between two equally valuable human beings. To paraphrase Medard Boss (1982, 239–40), Integrative Therapy recognizes clients' transference of love or hate toward the therapist as a genuine interpersonal reaction that clients experience in the immediate relationship with their therapists. The fact that clients sometimes behave in an infantile manner and therefore seriously misjudge the situation (because of emotional immaturity, which in turn is due to faulty training in youth) does not detract from the genuineness of their present feelings. They begin to love their therapist as soon as they become aware that they have found someone—possibly for the first in their lives—who really understands, accepts, and genuinely loves them just as they are, even though they are stunted developmentally by their problems. Clients love their therapist all the more because he or she permits them to unfold more fully their real and essential beings within a safe interpersonal relationship. In contrast, clients will hate their therapist as long as they are still open only to child-parent relationships (because of childhood experiences) that limit their perception of adults to frustrating experiences. They will hate the therapist even more—with good reason—if the therapist, because of his or her own so-called countertransference, actually behaves like one of the formerly hated significant others in the clients' formative years.

Therapists must always be aware of the influence of their behavior on clients and the therapeutic relationship. As long as clients' expressed feelings toward therapists are mature and adaptive, both may experience and enjoy them. If, however, clients' feelings appear to be unrealistic, immature, or inappropriate, the feelings should be explored in order to give clients a fuller understanding of themselves and to enhance both themselves and the therapeutic relationship. In either situation, therapists persist in prizing, valuing, and nurturing clients. Boss (1982) describes this therapist behavior as "psychotherapeutic eros," which is a unique love that must be selfless, self-restrained, and reverential in its treatment of clients.

Some clients cannot discriminate between social stimuli and thus are hindered in responding appropriately and establishing mature interpersonal relationships. Others have never learned how to give and receive affection. Still others find it hard to deal with negative emotions. These situations provide excellent opportunities for therapists to use the therapeutic alliance as an experiential laboratory in which clients can grow emotionally and socially. Mature, loving therapists serve as social models while clients learn how to understand themselves better and to relate interpersonally with mature social feelings and interest (Ansbacher & Ansbacher 1973).

Touching

Evidence abounds that physical touch during infancy and childhood is essential to healthy socialization, development of a positive identity, realistic perception of self and others, and the ability to establish long-term loving relationships (e.g., Harlow 1971; Montagu 1971; Spitz 1965). Yet, ambivalence and controversy surround the role and use of physical contact in professional helping relationships (e.g., Forer 1969; Holroyd & Brodsky 1977; Pattison 1973). Problems arise when touching either is confused with sexual eroticism or leads to sexual contact.

Jesus often touched people in his teaching, comforting, and healing ministry. The apostles encouraged the early Christians to express openly and physically their affection for one another (e.g., Rom. 16:16; 1 Pet. 5:14). Physical touch is moral, ethical, and therapeutic if it is offered with the proper motive and objective, in an appropriate manner, with awareness of cultural differences, and at the right time.

Integrative Therapy considers physical touch between therapists and clients, as well as between clients, an invaluable form of therapeutic communication. Nothing can be more encouraging, comforting, and healing than a well-timed hug, a firm grasp of the hand, or a compassionate shoulder on which to cry. This is especially true when clients are experiencing grief and bereavement. During such crises, truly effective counseling and psychotherapy often involve spontaneous, caring touch.

Touching can be risky, even dangerous. It should be avoided unless it is practiced with wisdom. If touching is the natural part of a warm and nurturing relationship, only good can come from it. But if either the therapist or the client has a selfish interest in sexual stimulation or personal gratification or in any way seeks to exploit or manipulate the other person, then touching is clearly nontherapeutic.

The most important experience in the life of a human being is to be personally appreciated as a unique sexual being, affectionately nurtured, confidentially befriended, and unconditionally accepted and supported. This enriching experience is love in its truest and fullest sense, and it is the essence of the relationship between therapist and client.

The therapeutic alliance is egalitarian and cooperative. In it, therapists use their personal and professional skills to help clients establish effective and fulfilling life styles. Therapists need to demonstrate consistently the Christian virtues of faith, hope, and love in their treatment of clients. Their loving behavior influences all dimensions of the relationship, including orienting clients to counseling and therapy, providing structure, dealing with resistance, confronting discrepancies, handling so-called transference, and physical touching.

The sum of the moral, ethical, legal, and interpersonal aspects of the therapeutic relationship in Integrative Therapy is guarded and guided by the ultimate ethic, *agape* love.

7

Problem Analysis
and Goal Statements

An accurate understanding of clients' problems in living is essential to effective psychotherapy. It is impossible to provide truly helpful psychological counseling until a thorough knowledge of presenting concerns is clearly in focus. In the simplest terms, therapists cannot aid people in their search for resolution of personality and behavior dysfunction without first comprehending the nature of the problems. This accurate knowledge regarding clients' problems provides an informed basis for both establishing realistic objectives for therapy and selecting the most suitable therapeutic strategies and methods. When problems have been identified specifically, they can be translated meaningfully into precise goal statements that lead to skillful interventions. This chapter delineates the procedures used in Integrative Therapy to diagnose problems in living and the guidelines followed in reaching consensual goals and objectives for therapy.

Diagnostic Procedures

Intake and Interview Information

People typically begin disclosing the particulars of their problems during the first contact with therapists or support staff. These bits of information represent the initial components of clients' clinical profile. The first definition of a problem by clients is often in broad, vague, and imprecise terms like "I'm having trouble with my marriage," "I had a bad dream and need some help with it," "I have a ten-year-old son who is pulling out his hair,

111

wetting the bed, and doing poorly in school, and I just don't know what to do." This early knowledge of a problem serves primarily to give therapists a basis for judging whether to try to help the inquirer directly or refer him or her to another source of help. If they schedule a first session, therapists spend some time obtaining basic information.

This information includes the individual's name, age, gender, socioeconomic status, address, telephone number, marital status, and source of referral. Therapists give close attention to clients' appearance and general conduct during the first interview in order to discern specifics regarding verbal skills, motor behavior, moods, affect, and attitudes. Clients usually are asked to identify what they consider to be their major presenting problem or concern. Information is also sought regarding their family of origin, medical and health history, previous counseling or therapy experiences, and the severity of the presenting problem, including the presence of any suicidal thoughts. Therapists again ponder these data and decide whether to contract a program of therapy or recommend other options.

Therapists continue to gather information about clients and their presenting problems through subsequent interviews. This new diagnostic knowledge is obtained primarily by direct observation of movement and conduct and specific inquiry to clarify the exact nature of clients' dysfunctions. The gathering of such interview data continues until therapists judge that the problem issues have been sufficiently explored.

The Story of My Life

Integrative Therapy endorses and applies the view of Adler (1958) that "among all psychological expressions some of the most revealing are the individual's memories . . . [which] are the reminders he carries about with him of his own limits and of the meaning of circumstances. There are no 'chance memories' [since] out of the incalculable number of impressions which meet the individual, he chooses to remember only those which he feels, however darkly, to have a bearing on his situation. Thus his memories represent his 'Story of My Life.'" (73).

It is extremely helpful to have clients, early in the therapy process, relate their unique "Story of My Life" to the therapist. I ask them to go back in their memory as far as possible and share both the good and bad things that happened to them. A client's story typically includes memories of experiences in the family of origin, early school days, vacations, times spent with grandparents, separation or divorce of parents, or fears. I also invite clients to share briefly about matters like their love experiences, courtship(s) and marriage(s), places of birth, and personal impressions of being a success or a failure.

The narration gives an indication of the traumatic experiences in clients' lives, what environmental conditions influenced their decisions about themselves and the external world, their mode(s) of coping with issues and tasks, and how they pursue their goal(s) in life. This diagnostic information suggests areas in their lives that need corrective intervention.

Pre-Therapy Questionnaire

Integrative Therapy uses a Pre-Therapy Questionnaire (PTQ) to obtain extensive information about clients and their problems in living (see appendix B). The PTQ touches, at a nearly exhaustive level, clients' general background, health record, occupational information, family of origin, personal impressions of themselves and others, religious and spiritual views, sexuality, menstrual information, marital experiences and attitudes, specific behaviors, emotions and feelings, physical sensations, dreams and fantasies, thought patterns, interpersonal relationships, experiences with drugs and other mood modifiers, and a self-description of the presenting problem(s).

The PTQ reflects an intrinsic integrative quality. First, it is holistic and seeks to provide a diagnostic profile with data about clients' behavior, affective processes and experiences, sensory reactions, altered states of consciousness, cognitive processes, social interactions, impact of particular habits or practices on mood states, and spiritual attitudes and values. Second, it incorporates ideas from a number of orientations. The major external influence is Arnold Lazarus's (1980) Multimodal Life History Questionnaire with its emphasis on the BASIC ID. It uses Adlerian and Transactional Analytic concepts to tap family-of-origin experiences and dynamics that helped shape clients' self-concept and world view. The marital section of the PTQ was influenced slightly by Stuart and Jacobson (1987). The "incomplete-sentence" portion seeks to gather personality data that harmonize with Jungian concepts.

Since the PTQ is so extensive, individuals are asked to complete it at home as their first therapeutic homework assignment. After clients respond to all the inquiries in the PTQ, they may either bring the completed questionnaire to the next scheduled session or return it to the clinic beforehand. I carefully examine the completed PTQ, highlight any items that need immediate attention (e.g., any indication of suicidal thoughts), and begin to develop an overall clinical profile that will suggest a particular program of therapy. I combine PTQ data with intake and interview data, the Story of My Life information, and other diagnostic impressions to arrive at a thorough description of clients' problematic behavior.

Experiential Diagnosis

While acknowledging the value of an accurate diagnosis or thorough understanding of clients' personal problems, Integrative Therapy functions with an attitude held by Rogers (1951, 219–23): therapy begins with the first contact and proceeds hand-in-hand with diagnosis. In the mind of the integrative therapist, therapy is not built on diagnosis per se. Since problematic behavior is caused largely by people's unique ways of perceiving reality, clients are the only ones who can know fully the dynamics of their perceptions and disturbing behavior. The final diagnostician, then, is the client or patient. Thus, in a very meaningful and accurate sense, therapy *is* diagnosis, and diagnosis occurs in the experience and awareness of the client rather than in the intellect of the clinician. One might say that psychotherapy, from this perspective, is complete or almost complete when clients experience and accept the diagnosis of the dynamics of their problematic behavior.

This experiential and person-centered attitude toward diagnosis and therapy reflects as well the pragmatic and phenomenological approach advocated by Kelly (1955), who stresses that all of an individual's experiences are personally and uniquely construed by that person and it is therefore always the client who can understand and interpret his or her problems in living, not the therapist. That led Kelly to assert that if therapists want to know what is bothering their clients, they should ask; clients might just give the answer!

Integrative Therapy attends to clients' experiences, guides them in exploring and sharing these experiences, and usually accepts their interpretations of their encounters with life. It uses a variety of experiential strategies to help clients make better contact with themselves and gain fuller awareness of the painful issues in their lives. Examples include the Couples' Pattern of Interaction (CPI), Options Clarification Test, Values Continuum, and Family Sculpting. In these and other experiential diagnostic procedures, clients engage in a series of body positioning exercises accompanied by verbal expressions to enhance and intensify their awareness of blocks, impasses, blind spots, conflicts, and faulty perceptions of issues in life. The exercises not only provide diagnostic insight into problems, but also are therapeutic interventions in themselves. This further corroborates that therapy is diagnosis and diagnosis is therapy.

Psychological Assessment

Some clinical situations require diagnostic and evaluative data beyond the scope of those obtained by the procedures already discussed. Among situations requiring additional diagnostic information are therapists' need for more objective measures of apparent psychopathology in the behavioral repertoire of particular clients or patients or definitive answers to questions about neurological functioning. Effective counseling for these types of client-problem cases depends heavily on data derived from carefully chosen, competently administered, and skillfully interpreted psychological tests. However, a routine use of psychological tests for all clients not only is unnecessary for successful therapy but also might sometimes give an inaccurate or biased view of the client, thus directly interfering with the therapeutic process.

Integrative Therapy avoids a routine use of psychological tests; rather, it seeks consistently to do psychological testing only when the specifics of a clinical case indicate the desirability or necessity of such supplemental diagnostic information. Even then the assessment is made without defining the individual with psychological nomenclature. The test data simply become an integral part of the overall diagnostic profile.

DSM-III-R

The DSM-III-R has little relevance to problem analysis that leads to specific therapeutic objectives and interventions. Consequently, Integrative Therapy uses its categorical codes and labels *only* for nontherapeutic purposes like filling out insurance forms or claims. Even when submitting insurance claims, the numerical codes alone are used unless the descriptive labels are required by the insurance company or third-party reimburser. Hardly ever is a complete multiaxial diagnosis (all five axes) prepared. Thus, the DSM-III-R is useful primarily for economic purposes and only tangentially for therapeutic objectives. (The same is true of the ICD-9-CM.)

Therapeutic Goals and Objectives

The analysis of a presenting problem shows what is wrong with an individual's personal world, but it is insufficient by itself to provide directions and objectives for therapy. Establishing specific goals naturally and necessarily follows identification of clients' problems. The following is a description of the purposes of therapy goals, the nature of objectives in therapy, and guidelines for helping clients select realistic goals for their own therapy.

Purposes of Therapy Goals

Establishing consensual goals for therapy serves a number of vital purposes (Cormier & Cormier 1985). First, these goals provide structure, order, objectivity, and direction for therapeutic movement. Without them, therapy is likely to be vague, rambling, and centered on the therapist's biases and preferences rather than pursuing clients' stated interests.

Second, clearly defined goals enable therapists to decide whether they possess the skills, interest, and expertise needed to work effectively with particular clients and their problems. If a suitable match exists between clients' goal needs and therapists' competence and values, then it is appropriate to proceed with therapy. But if there is an apparent mismatch between clients' goals and therapists' professional preparedness, then referral might be more desirable. In essence, goals help to answer the question, "Who is the best therapist for this client?"

Third, goal statements provide invaluable guidance in selecting and using particular therapeutic methods, techniques, and strategies. Without explicit goals, therapists have no rational and defensible basis for planning and making specific interventions. From this perspective, goals help to answer the question, "What treatment is most effective with this particular problem?"

Finally, goals help both therapists and clients to evaluate success in therapy. They provide a basis for monitoring progress after specific interventions and at different stages in the process. Without clearly identified goals, it is hard to ascertain how effective the therapy is at any given time.

In summary, a thorough diagnosis followed by a set of clearly defined goals permits therapists to make professional decisions regarding *"what* treatment, by *whom,* is most effective for *this* individual with *that* specific problem, and under *which* set of circumstances" (Goldfried 1980, 997).

The Nature of Therapy Goals

Two basic types of goals are involved in therapy: procedural (or process) goals and outcome goals. Process goals consist of objectives that therapists seek to fulfill in providing a therapeutic environment. Examples of process goals are building rapport, establishing a therapeutic alliance, providing orientation and structure, and facilitating client comfort and self-disclosure. These objectives characterize all therapeutic relationships and were discussed in an earlier chapter.

This chapter focuses on outcome goals, which tend to fall in either of two major categories: generic or ultimate goals, and immediate or subgoals.

Generic or ultimate goals

Individuals may have problems that generate ultimate goals that reflect generic personal needs like gaining greater awareness of the unconscious issues in their lives, eliminating faulty learning and behavior and learning more adaptive patterns of behaving, becoming more self-actualizing, developing a more realistic philosophy of life that is free of negative thinking and faulty scripts, finding more meaning in life, becoming more balanced and individuated, fulfilling one's needs in a responsible manner without interfering with the satisfaction of others' needs, achieving greater marital satisfaction, or becoming more assertive and taking responsibility for direction in one's life. Integrative Therapy will accept any one of these goals as an ultimate objective for therapy, but it seeks to give them increased specificity by creating a number of subgoals.

Immediate subgoals

Generic goals must be transformed into subgoals before they can have optimal usefulness in the therapy process. Let's assume that a couple enters therapy with the general objective of experiencing a more fulfilling marriage. This is a worthy objective, but it is too general to serve as an attainable goal. The generic objective becomes realistic and effective when translated into an appropriate number of subgoals: to learn to communicate more effectively, to experience increased joy in sex, to develop better money management skills, to learn how to play together, to become more cooperative and united in parenting, to resolve conflicts with or about in-laws, and to find a mutually acceptable place for worship. Integrative Therapy always seeks to reduce generic goals to a workable body of subgoals that are specific and concrete.

Guidelines for Establishing Therapy Goals

Integrative Therapy adheres to the following guidelines when formulating outcome goals. They have been influenced by the practice of John Krumboltz and Carl Thoresen (1966, 1969).

1. The goals must be desired and owned by the client and not the creation, possession, or imposition of the therapist.
2. The goals must be stated differently and uniquely for each client and in concrete terms that are clearly understood by the client. Ideally, the goals should be framed in the client's language.
3. The client's goals must be compatible with, though not necessarily identical to, the values of the therapist. For example, a homosexual client might have as a goal the establishment of a satisfying gay marriage. This goal would most likely be incompatible with the values of many Christian therapists. In such cases, a referral would be recommended.
4. The therapist must sense that he or she is both competent and genuinely willing to provide professional assistance to the client in the pursuit of the stated goals.
5. The goals must be stated so that it is possible to observe progress toward the identified objectives.
6. Both the therapist and the client must maintain a flexible attitude toward the established goals, realizing that therapy is progressive and goals might need to be broadened and modified as therapy unfolds. The goals, although specific and concrete, are never rigid in terms of either time or terminology.
7. The goals must be complementary to both the theoretical and the methodological tenets and interventions, respectively, of Integrative Therapy.

This chapter has delineated the principles, procedures, and guidelines relevant to performing an accurate diagnosis of presenting problems and establishing clearly defined therapy goals. Disciplined use of these procedures and guidelines provides a solid base for planning programs of psychotherapy for individuals at all points in life. When the diagnostic principles are accompanied by well-defined objectives, it is also possible to make effective interventions that are geared appropriately to the specific nuances of the client-problem profile. Finally, consistent and systematic use of these procedures and guidelines allows for an objective evaluation of the outcomes of psychotherapy.

8

Complementary Modes of Intervention (Part 1)

While the use of relationship skills remains essentially the same for all individuals, the selection of therapy methods varies with the uniqueness of each client-problem situation. Psychotherapy that is optimally effective cannot plausibly come from a single method that is used as the exclusive strategy with either all clients or the same client all the time. Different modes of intervention are just as essential to a comprehensively integrative approach to counseling and psychotherapy as are different problem analyses and individualized objectives for the therapy process. A therapist must have expertise in a variety of intervention strategies in order to ascertain what form of treatment is most preferred for a given individual with a particular set of circumstances.

This chapter and the next present a storehouse of counseling and therapy strategies that are considered to be (1) complementary to the philosophical and theoretical concepts of Integrative Therapy, (2) supplementary to one another and to the other clinical procedures involved in Integrative Therapy, and (3) compatible with the personal and professional life style of the writer. The methods and techniques are placed in seven distinct categories. The categories are arranged to reflect particular therapeutic emphases such as intrapersonal dynamics and issues, social influences and concerns, focus on behavior and environment, and specific nuances of personal experiencing. Each method identified is judged to make some unique contribution to the storehouse of intervention options. Varieties of certain interventions—such as handling dreams in therapy—are used by several orientations to counseling and psychotherapy. In such cases, the variant that best fits the world view and modus operandi of Integrative Therapy will be presented.

Psychodynamic Modalities

This section identifies counseling and therapy strategies that have been designed primarily to intervene in the subconscious or unconscious dynamics of personality and behavior. The techniques are called psychodynamic because they focus on the intrapersonal or intrapsychic domain of human experience. Frequently the terms *psychodynamic* and *psychoanalytic* are used as synonyms. However, I prefer not to restrict the use of psychodynamic psychotherapy to such a narrow and exclusive perspective. Thus, the modes of therapy described here have their origin in orientations that can be subsumed under a psychodynamic umbrella concept. All the methods discussed are premised on the assumptions that the unconscious is a distinct reality in the human psyche and that its contents have indispensable value to wholesome and integrated personality functioning. My use of the terms *subconscious* and *unconscious* refers equally to preverbal learning experiences, forgotten or hardly remembered personal data, repressed information that lies outside the individual's awareness, and mental processes not immediately or directly comprehended by the person.

Free Association

Free association was introduced to psychotherapy by Sigmund Freud and has remained a central clinical modality in the practice of Freudian psychoanalysis (Freud 1924, 1933). The technique seeks to help people express unconscious thoughts, ideas, and traumatic experiences through uncensored verbal sharing of their subjective worlds.

A nonjudgmental and permissive therapist in a caring environment encourages the client to express whatever comes to mind. The client may begin by reporting a thought, feeling, sensation, memory, experience, reflection, or dream. The therapist then encourages the client to associate freely any additional thoughts, feelings, or memories to the particulars of the initial sharing.

The process of sharing experiences and making associations is done without any concern for logic, order, system, or any form of conscious control. Clients are totally free to express themselves in a verbally random fashion without any coercion or censorship by the therapist. The free association allows contents that lie outside of awareness to come into awareness or consciousness. The therapist listens, encourages, accepts, clarifies, interprets, and gives feedback. The result is emotional cleansing, insight, and integration of personality functioning.

Clients may freely associate while either sitting or reclining. Traditionally, reclining has been preferred. The process of associating freely to personal contents is also enhanced by having clients share with their eyes closed.

Free association is particularly useful when clients report being confused, experience unexplainable uneasiness, behave anxiously or fearfully in apparently safe situations, and are bothered by repressed painful memories.

Active Imagination

Another effective mode for therapeutic release of the contents of the unconscious is active imagination, a technique derived from Jungian or analytical psychotherapy (Jung 1968). The technique assumes that by concentrating on a mental image and allowing a noninterrupted natural flow of inner experiences and visually vivid, emotionally rich events, the unconscious will produce a series of images that tell a complete story. It assumes further that the images that emerge have a unique message to relay and that a pattern of symbolic events will develop according to their own logic if the controlling influence of conscious reasoning does not interfere with the dynamic process.

As the images are produced experientially and the unconscious contents are comprehended and integrated, the maturation or individuation process is enhanced. In addition to the rational comprehension of the unconscious contributions, the story may be given symbolic expression through drama, painting, sculpting, music, writing, drawing, dancing, or other non-oral media.

The initial image, picture, or theme may arise from a dream, an impression, a memory, or any other subjective experience. Active imagination is especially useful in helping individuals work through impasses, blind spots, and emotional blocks. For example, a male client who is disturbed by dreams involving phallic symbols and reports being uncomfortable in public places like restrooms and locker rooms could be asked to focus on the phallic images and to allow his unconscious to express itself symbolically. The resulting story is likely to reveal the nature of the emotional disturbance by connecting symbolic events with day-to-day occurrences.

Primal Pain Expression

Faulty parenting and other traumatic events during childhood produce painful experiences that are recorded indelibly in children's unconscious minds. This primal or early-in-life pain becomes a major source of depression, hypersensitivity, anger, insecurity, paranoia, neurotic fear of abandonment or rejection, and other forms of emotional disturbance that appear later in adolescence and adulthood. Unconscious memory is invariably associated with the primal pain. What appear to have been forgotten are in reality memories that are too painful to be acknowledged, accepted, and integrated into the conscious. These original hurts, needs, feelings, and deprivations persist in the unconscious as intolerable pain because they have not been allowed expression. So long as these "forgotten" or repressed painful memories are denied by the conscious and left unexpressed in the unconscious, a maladaptive life style is the consequence.

The healing of painful memories is effected best through re-experiencing the primal hurts. This means not merely knowing about the pain but actually experiencing it in the present. Arthur Janov (1970, 1975) has pioneered the development of a therapeutic approach to the expression of primal pain. Other counselors and psychotherapists (e.g., Osborne 1980) have offered clinical alternatives for assisting individuals in the healing of their primal hurts and pains.

The process of releasing primal pain involves a number of experiential modes or experiences. It begins with a competent therapist's providing a therapeutic environment that is marked by nurturing warmth, compassion, and acceptance. Therapy rooms ideally are furnished either with large, comfortable couches, recliners, or mats. Subdued lighting and appropriate background music can enhance the therapeutic surroundings.

After establishing rapport with clients and orienting them to the nature of primal experiencing, therapists ask clients to close their eyes and begin to "breathe down." Breathing down consists of several repetitions of slow, deep inhaling, each followed by a complete emptying of the lungs. Therapists might ask clients for permission to make minimal physical contact such as placing a hand gently on the tummy, then instruct clients to allow the unconscious to be free to emerge and express itself. Regressing clients by having them recall and relive early-in-life experiences facilitates the release of unconscious data. Therapists encourage clients to express both verbally and nonverbally the emotions connected with painful memories. Crying loudly, sobbing, yelling, screaming, throwing tantrums, acting out baby rage by kicking or flailing the arms, and pounding a punching bag with a baseball bat or beating a doll of a particular gender and assumed age are some means of releasing the repressed, emotionally charged memories. Clients' reliving their original pain can continue for as many therapy sessions as needed to complete the releasing process.

Carefully selected literature can be used as an adjunct to inoffice therapy. Examples of useful resources are Janov's *The Primal Scream* and Osborne's *Understanding Your Past: The Key to Your Future*. Guidelines for using bibliotherapy will be provided later in this chapter.

Reparenting

The therapeutic reparenting approach used in Integrative Therapy reflects the concepts and methods derived from several orientations to counseling and psychotherapy. It could be discussed appropriately in other sections of this chapter, especially the following one, which presents sociodynamic modalities. However, it is included among the psychodynamic strategies primarily because of its concern with the repressed memories that exist in the subconscious of individuals, and the emotional content of the memories. A supplemental intervention, redecisioning, will be discussed in the next section.

Reparenting is often an essential aspect of resolving the emotional disturbances and ineffective life styles that result from primal pain experiences in dysfunctional families. Reliving the original pain, however therapeutic and healing, cannot by itself correct the whole life situation. Release of the pain must be followed by some new orientations to self, others, and life. The therapist's functioning as a permissive and nurturing parent is a necessity in the reparenting process. The therapist as nurturing parent accepts, encourages, affirms, loves, and protects the inner child of the client. The focus is on healing the memories (Seamands 1985) of the inner child (Missildine 1963; Whitfield 1987) so there can be an integration of his or her past and present experiences.

Painful memories can result from any number of traumatic experiences during childhood. Some specific examples include physical abuse, sexual molestation, neglect, feeling abandoned by one's mother when a sibling was born, and being rejected by biological parents and given to adoptive parents. In nearly all cases of primal or early-in-life pain, individuals experience an inadequate amount of loving care and attention.

Frequently, individuals carry the painful symptoms of damaged emotions but experienced the pain before they had a vocabulary adequate to explain or label their experiences. The trauma was recorded at an emotional level. Consequently, the pain and its symptoms are present but the understanding of the cause lies outside conscious awareness (Dollard & Miller 1950). When human beings are unable to know or understand what is within themselves (1 Cor. 2:11), they are out of contact with the inner self and lack control of a significant part of their personalities. A central part of therapeutic reparenting is helping individuals to contact this unknown dimension of their personal experiences.

Another important inclusion of reparenting that results in healing original hurt and pain, for clients who are receptive, is not only the personal touch of the therapist but also the gentleness and compassion of a loving God—yes, a heavenly Father who never abandons his own. It can be both comforting and encouraging to hurting persons to know that if their mothers and fathers abuse them and even forsake them, Jesus will welcome them into his care. This lovely promise by the Lord never to abandon those who trust him is repeated in both Testaments (e.g., Ps. 27:10; John 14:18; Heb. 13:5–6).

The Holy Spirit, in the role of Comforter, Helper, or Encourager (John 14:16–18), can become a healing agent in the reparenting process as he makes the deep truths of God's love (Rom. 8:15–16) real to the hurting inner child of the client. The wounded inner child can begin to experience security in the care of a loving Abba, or Daddy, who loves and accepts unconditionally. David Seamands (1982) has expressed the healing touch of the Holy Spirit dynamically: "[I]f you [an adolescent or adult with a hurt inner child] let the Holy Spirit reach down deep, cleanse your subconscious mind, and get into the depth of your heart to fill the storehouse of memory, God will give you power [and love] to actually make this one of the most creative parts of your personality" (18).

Sociodynamic Modalities

Some therapy modalities are apropos to working with problems in living that have been caused largely by sociological factors. Here we will pay particular attention to parenting and interpersonal dynamics that influence personal life styles and life scripts. Techniques that are most closely associated with either Adlerian psychotherapy or Transactional Analysis are offered here. The strategies delineated in this category of methods are useful for making interventions that result in realistic life goals, rewritten life scripts that either delete or correct erroneous early-in-life decisions, healthy concepts of self and others, effective intra- and interpersonal functioning, advancement in resolving basic life tasks, and an increase in positive experiencing.

Life Style Awareness

This intervention method incorporates Alfred Adler's concept of the "life style" and Eric Berne's "life script" phenomena. This integrative approach locates the life script at the core of the individual's life style.

A life style is a person's unique manner of expressing and molding himself or herself in the social milieu as he or she moves consistently toward a self-chosen goal (Ansbacher & Ansbacher 1956). The scripted life style can be defined further as a person's private cognitive map that points the way in the world and is formed during the first five or six years of life. This individualized cognitive map is the individual's basic orientation toward life and serves as a prototype for living. Scripted life styles are the result of young children's subjective evaluation of their experiences and the conclusions they draw about themselves, other people, the environment, and right and wrong behavior. Thus, dysfunctional life styles are based on distorted or maladaptive scripts formed by faulty perceptions, erroneous conclusions, and basic mistaken beliefs about reality. At the core of such faulty life styles are goals that are fictional in that they are founded on unreal or false "as if" beliefs about life. Consequently, these life styles often become a life lie.

Integrative therapists use the data obtained by the Pre-Therapy Questionnaire (appendix B), interviews, and other relevant sources (e.g., Eckstein, Baruth & Mahrer's *Life Style: What It Is and How to Do It* [1982] and Holloway's "Life Script Questionnaire" [1973]) to assist individuals with the discovery of the factors that shaped their scripted life styles. The make up of the family of origin is examined, including children's birth order, a comparison of clients with their brothers and sisters, and a thorough description of their parents. Particular attention is given to the attitudes and practices of the parents regarding their children in order to discover clients' experience of neglect, abuse, pampering, indulgence, injunctions (don't be . . . , don't feel . . . , don't cry), attributions (be strong, be a man, keep your legs crossed), or caring and love. Early recollections or memories also are examined to find other influential factors in the formation of faulty scripts that resulted in dysfunctional life styles.

The information reveals the specific contents of an individual's scripted approach to life. It shows the dysfunctional rules that were followed, the mistaken beliefs formed about self and others (e.g., good/OK me, bad/Not OK me, not me/a nobody, good/OK you, or bad/Not OK you), and the plan for living that was adopted early in life. Additionally, knowledge is gained regarding how effectively the client is giving and receiving mature love, pursuing meaningful work, establishing a network of friendships, having a wholesome self-concept, and growing spiritually.

This process of gaining awareness of one's scripted life style is simultaneously a diagnostic exercise and a therapeutic experience. Becoming aware of how a life style was formed not only puts people in greater control of themselves, but also prepares the way for a new orientation to life. Again, therapy is diagnosis and diagnosis is therapy.

Redecisioning and Reorienting

Becoming aware of one's scripted life style is merely the uncovering and discovering aspect of a life-changing process. Insight into the contents and dynamics of a dysfunctional approach to life must be followed by writing a new script, forming a new view of self and others, creating new goals, and adopting new coping strategies to establish a more adaptive orientation to life.

In redecisioning, which can be considered as either an extension or a modification of the reparenting process presented earlier in this chapter, therapists ask clients to recreate in present-tense language and imagery childhood experiences as they were and then proceed to redo the situations the way they want them to be (Goulding & Goulding 1979). Therapists guide clients in corrrecting mistaken beliefs, eliminating dysfunctional rules, removing self-defeating injunctions and attributions that were introjected in childhood, writing a new script based on positive beliefs and rules, establishing realistic goals, and adopting effective strategies for fulfilling life tasks in a mature and responsible way.

In essence, redecisioning and reorienting results in people's learning new ways of thinking, feeling, and behaving.

Encouragement

Since integrative therapists hold (with Adlerians) that people enter therapy in a state of discouragement, they use encouragement consistently as a primary intervention. Encouragement helps clients to develop self-confidence and self-esteem and to gain the courage they need to attempt change and pursue new goals and directions in life. Therapists assume the role of "I am my brother's or sister's keeper" and offer encouraging support. It is particularly incumbent for Christian therapists, who are indwelt by the Encourager par excellence, the Holy Spirit, to reach out to discouraged individuals in an encouraging and strengthening manner (Rom. 12:8).

Structural Analysis of Personality

Clients seldom understand how their personality is composed and functions. The most pragmatic model of the structure and functioning of human personality has been provided by Transactional Analysis (Berne 1961; Harris 1967; Steiner 1974). For individuals with little or no knowledge of the make-up of their personality, an excellent didactic intervention is a method called structural analysis.

The personality manifests itself in any of three ego or psychological states that can be labeled appropriately as Parent, Adult, and Child. Each ego state is a phenomenological reality that is produced in the here and now of everyday life by either the playback of learned data of childhood experiences or the actual enactment of current ego roles. To illustrate these phenomena, it will be necessary to do first-order and second-order analyses of personality structure. The thinking of Claude Steiner (1974) has been the primary influence for the following discussion.

Figure 3

First-Order Structure of Personality

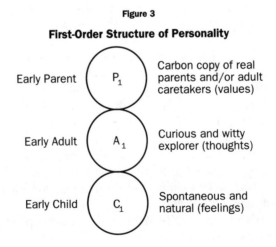

Early Parent — P_1 — Carbon copy of real parents and/or adult caretakers (values)

Early Adult — A_1 — Curious and witty explorer (thoughts)

Early Child — C_1 — Spontaneous and natural (feelings)

First-order structure of personality

The first-order structural analysis portrays the personality development of an individual at the age of four or five (see fig. 3).

The early Parent (P_1) is the introjection of the perceived values, attitudes, feelings, and behaviors of the real parents, which are incorporated into the personalities of nonverbal children before they have the cognitive ability and language to label the perceptions. These introjected Parent data may be either nurturing or critical. Early Parent data that are critical (punitive, scolding, cold, abusive, negligent) will be played back in later life as what can be called the Pig or Witch parent. The Early Parent represents the "moral, ought or taught concept" of life.

As young children observe and interact with the external world, they begin to store information about whom to trust, how to receive food, how to respond appropriately to different stimuli, and how to distinguish between themselves and others. Although this knowledge is mostly experiential and preverbal, they can use it for making rudimentary decisions. This data-processing capability is the Early Adult (A_1) and becomes what Berne called the "Little Professor." It can also be viewed as the "rational or thought concept" of life.

The Early Child (C_1) depicts the gamut of emotions, feelings, and sensations experienced by preverbal youngsters. This is the ego state that expresses the "emotional or felt concept" of life and, if not constricted or coerced, is characterized by spontaneity, naturalness, and expressiveness.

Second-order structure of personality

The ego states assume new character and complexity as individuals mature and develop advanced motor, verbal, cognitive, and social skills. Yet, most of the personality characteristics people possess at age five remain with them as adults. The structure of the adult personality is shown in figure 4.

The Later Parent (P_2) is the ego state in adults that does authentic parenting. It is characterized by mature nurturing ability and skills adequate to care responsibly for other persons.

The Later Adult (A_2) refers to the ego state that functions on the basis of grown-up reason, logic, and creative problem solving. It is the "computer" in personality that analyzes, processes, stores, and manages data that pertain to personal decision making.

The composite of early-in-life experiences, learned patterns, and the capacity for emotional experiencing form the Later Child (C_2). Should the C_2 be predominately P_1 in function, the individual will tend either to please, rebel, conform, control, or criticize. If the Later Child manifests mostly C_1, then the person is likely to be fun-loving and the life of the party. A Later Child that is dominated by the A_1 is typically observed in persons who are lively, spunky, and adventuresome.

Figure 4

Second-Order Structure of Personality

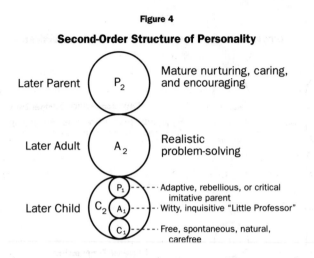

Later Parent — P_2 — Mature nurturing, caring, and encouraging

Later Adult — A_2 — Realistic problem-solving

Later Child — C_2 — P_1 — Adaptive, rebellious, or critical imitative parent
A_1 — Witty, inquisitive "Little Professor"
C_1 — Free, spontaneous, natural, carefree

Disturbed personality structure

Personality functioning becomes problematic either when any ego state is excluded from conscious awareness or when the Adult ego state is contaminated by data from the Parent or Child ego state.

If a person excludes an ego state, the consequence is a specific dysfunction. For example, someone who excludes the Child ego state from personality functioning can't play and behaves in a computer-like fashion or like an obsessive-compulsive perfectionist.

When the Adult ego state is contaminated (that is, the contents of the Parent, Child, or both seep through the boundaries of the Adult), the individual has difficulty maintaining keen awareness and distinguishing data. To illustrate, if the Adult accepts the Child statement "Adding and subtracting numbers is a boring waste of time" as fact, the consequence will be someone with a bunch of bounced checks.

Providing clients with customized knowledge of the structure of personality and the nature of any disturbance (exclusion or contamination) in the functioning of their personality produces a powerful therapeutic effect.

Transactional Analysis

Transactional Analysis offers an excellent strategy for assisting individuals to master both intrapersonal and interpersonal communication knowledge and skills. Just as the ego state is the fundamental unit in the structure of personality, the transaction is the basic unit in transactional process.

Every communication between two persons may be viewed as a transaction. A completed transaction consists of a transactional stimulus followed by a transactional response. A transactional stimulus begins when an individual "cathects" or energizes a specific ego state and sends a message to

Figure 5

Complementary, Crossed, and Ulterior Transactions

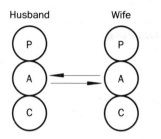

Husband   Wife

Complementary Transaction

Husband: The sermon was challenging today.
Wife: Yes, and the illustrations were moving.

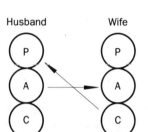

Husband   Wife

Crossed Transaction

Husband: We'll be late for the opera.
Wife: Stop blaming me.

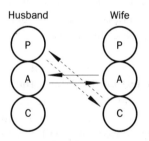

Husband   Wife

Ulterior Transaction

Husband (social): I would like to buy you some
  new pretty clothes.
Wife (social): That would be really nice.

Husband (psychological): But you're too fat.
Wife (psychological): You are always putting me
  down about my weight.

another person. The stimulus message "hooks" into and energizes an ego state of the receiver, who in return prepares a responding message for the original sender. Thus, transactions are a series of messages based on reciprocating cathecting, sending stimuli messages, hooking, and returning response messages, as shown in figure 5.

The voice on either end of the transaction may be from the Parent, the Adult, or the Child. As long as the transactional stimuli and the transactional responses follow complementary or parallel lines, communication between two persons can continue indefinitely. Complementary transactions are the basis of "good" interpersonal relationships in that they tend to minimize conflict. Whenever a stimulus message from a sending ego state hooks and evokes a response from the receiving ego state such that the vectors are nonparallel, a crossed transaction results. Uncomplementary or crossed transactions lead to conflicts, interruptions, and breakdowns in communication that produce "bad" relationships. In a third form of transaction, the ulterior transaction, the stimulus message appears to be one thing at the overt-social level but contains an ulterior message disguised at the covert-psychological level. This crooked or deceptive communication is central to interpersonal game playing.

Mature and integrated people can cathect or energize the appropriate ego state for a given situation and avoid becoming inappropriately hooked by messages from others. Persons who cannot monitor their intra- and interpersonal communications experience patterns of ineffectiveness and dysfunction. Learning to monitor, manage, and enjoy all ego states via Transactional Analysis is an invaluable therapeutic intervention for these persons.

Multiple Chairs Technique

A multiple chairs technique (Stuntz 1973) allows limitless opportunities for exploring structural analysis and Transactional Analysis. Additionally and supplementally, the dynamics of the structural and transactional analyses can be applied to both individual and multiple counseling situations that involve reparenting, redecisioning, decontamination, and communication issues. Three intervention options for using different configurations of multiple chairs are shown in figure 6.

The use of three chairs (fig. 6A) can help clients understand experien-

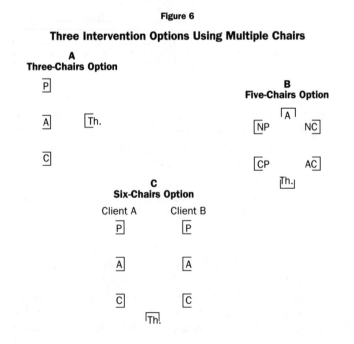

Figure 6

Three Intervention Options Using Multiple Chairs

A
Three-Chairs Option

P

A   Th.

C

B
Five-Chairs Option

A

NP   NC

CP   AC

Th.

C
Six-Chairs Option

Client A   Client B

P   P

A   A

C   C

Th.

tially the dynamics of structural analysis. Therapists can guide clients as they learn to cathect sequentially the three different ego states and learn the distinct language of each.

The five-chairs option (fig. 6B) is effective for doing second-order structural analysis, decontamination of the Adult, reparenting, and redecisioning. By sitting in and speaking from each of the five chairs that represent the Adult, Nurturing Parent, Critical Parent, Adapted Child, and Natural Child, clients, directed by therapists, can gain awareness of the different voices inside themselves. Intrapersonal conflicts (contamination, exclusion, prohibitions) can be detected and then followed by corrective interventions that result in intrapersonal integration.

When conducting therapy to resolve problems in interpersonal relationships (e.g., with married couples), the six-chairs configuration works remarkably well. Three chairs represent the Parent, Adult, and Child of each partner, respectively. The two sets of chairs are arranged so that the corresponding ego states of the partners face one another. The spouses or partners experiment with their ability to cathect and hook ego states in effective communication patterns. Work continues in the six-chairs until complementary transactions can be achieved and sustained from all ego states.

Expressive Modalities

The strategies presented in this section are largely nonverbal in nature and are particularly useful in assisting individuals with the development of greater self-awareness and self-expression, resolution of unfinished traumatic experiences, and taking more control of their lives. The interventions use dramatization, sculpting, play, and other expressive activities to deal creatively with painful, difficult, restricted, and unresolved issues in life. These strategies may be used either alone or in some combination with other interventions discussed in this chapter.

Play Therapy

The child-centered emphases of Virginia Axline (1969) and Clark Moustakas (1973) represent quite accurately the approach to play therapy used in the practice of Integrative Therapy. We start with the attitude that "play is the child's natural medium of self-expression . . . [and] play therapy is an opportunity which is given to the child to 'play out' his feelings and problems just as, in certain types of adult therapy, an individual 'talks out' his difficulties" (Axline 1969, 9). Play therapy is considered the treatment of choice for young children but can be used effectively with pre-adolescent youngsters.

Play therapy requires a colorful and cheerful room supplied with play media and materials like dolls, crayons, doll furniture, finger paints, hand puppets, spoons, bottles, boxes, scissors, paper, clay, and a sufficient number of other toys appropriate for both genders. The toys and materials are arranged in an unstructured manner so children can play out their feelings without pressure and restrictions imposed by the therapist.

Therapists build and maintain rapport with children by consistently communicating acceptance of, respect for, and belief in them. Nonjudgmental listening and reflective responding in a permissive environment are crucial in play therapy. Major focus is directed to children's affective experiences.

Structure and limits are established in terms of time (frequency and length of sessions), use of toys and materials (e.g., must be used in the designated play area and may not be taken home), and treatment of therapist and other persons (e.g., physical abuse and destruction of property will not be allowed). These limits help to provide stability, predictability, and security.

Axline (1969) summarizes succinctly the benefits of play therapy: "The play therapy experience is a growth experience [where] children are given the opportunity to get rid of their tensions, to clear the air . . . of their troublesome feelings, and by so doing . . . gain an understanding of themselves that enables them to control themselves. Through their vivid experiences in the playroom they discover themselves as persons as well as new ways to adjust to human relationships in a healthy, realistic manner" (131–32).

Activity Therapy

A step removed from play therapy per se is activity therapy, which serves well as a supplemental form of intervention with older children and adolescents. Virtually any number of activities that are appealing to youngsters can be used for either building rapport or facilitating more effective interactions between young clients and their therapists. For example, a therapist and client participating together in activities like biking, hiking, going for pizza, gardening, tennis, basketball, pool or billiards, shopping, cooking, repairing something, painting, driving, or boating can add immeasurably to the therapeutic process. It is important to secure the permission of the parent(s) or guardian(s) of any minor before becoming involved in these types of activity therapy.

A point to emphasize is that therapy or healing of troubled lives need not be confined to the therapist's office. Some of the best therapy I have ever provided for adolescents has been the "pizza therapy" conducted in a quiet corner of a restaurant while listening and responding to troubled teens over a pepperoni pizza, a plate of nachos, and a pitcher of Coke or Pepsi. This *in vivo* activity therapy parallels the life style of Jesus. He encountered people and conducted a healing ministry in their own space. Adolescents in particular are receptive to this informal but professional approach to counseling and psychotherapy.

Psychodrama

Psychodrama is an active and expressive mode of therapy pioneered by Jacob Moreno (1946) and adopted by scores of other therapists (e.g., Blatner 1973; Starr 1977). Psychodramatic interventions seek to help individuals explore and solve their problems by acting out or dramatizing them rather than merely talking about them. Psychodrama in essence is impromptu acting in which clients and their assistants play the various roles involved in their personal conflict. The process is dynamically active, transactionally powerful, emotionally intense, and highly cathartic.

The ideal setting for psychodrama is a theater-type arrangement with an actual stage, lighting, and audience. However, methods derived from psychodrama can be modified and adapted to a wide variety of settings and client situations, including interventions made in an outpatient office or clinic.

The principals in a psychodramatic enactment are the protagonist, the director, the auxiliary ego, and the audience. The protagonist is the individual (client or patient) who enacts a problem or conflict. The director is the person (counselor or therapist) who guides the protagonist in acting out the problem. The auxiliary ego refers to anyone besides the protagonist and the director who portrays a role in the psychodramatic enactment. The auxiliary ego usually plays some significant other person in the protagonist's life—a spouse, parent, sibling, employer, or lover—or some specific aspect of the protagonist's personality or behavior repertoire. An auxiliary may play any one of many roles by functioning as an antagonist, a double, a participant in role reversal, or a mirror. The audience, if present, consists of other persons present during the enactment (e.g., members of the protagonist's family, members of a psychotherapy group, trainees in a supervisory setting, or participants in a seminar or class). Rather than being passive observers, members of the audience often take an active role in protagonists' enactments of their troubled situations by giving feedback, offering encouragement, making nurturing physical contact in the form of hugs or embraces, and sharing common experiences (identifying with the protagonist).

The psychodrama involves four basic developmental phases or stages. First, a protagonist must be selected. Second, the director assists the protagonist in staging the enactment in terms of topograpy, atmosphere, and identifying auxiliary egos. Third, the working through or action stage involves exploring the core conflict(s) and behavioral practice(s) or rehearsal of the desired outcome(s). Finally, a time for feedback and sharing by the audience and completing the process follows the psychodramatic enactment.

The psychodramatic enactment may focus on past, present, or future; it may explore feelings, thoughts, behaviors, fantasies, dreams, sensations, or interpersonal relationships; it may deal with important other persons either dead or alive. Among the strategies used to assist protagonists in exploring their situations in life, in addition to those provided by the auxiliary ego and audience, are soliloquy, multiple selves, exaggeration, behavioral rehearsal, assertiveness training, and dream work. Psychodrama seeks not only to resolve unfinished business from a regressive perspective but also to be proactive in providing an opportunity to rehearse for authentic living.

Psychodramatic interventions, while most suited for groups, can also be applied to individuals, couples, and families. For example, I have discovered that my assuming the role of an alter ego with either an individual client or a spouse in marital therapy is often the most effective means of dealing with repressed, denied, or difficult issues.

Sculpting

Sculpting is a body of action-oriented methods and strategies that help people to live out spatially the meanings, images, and metaphors they hold privately about their interpersonal relationships in the systems of which they are members (Smith 1985). It taps these internal images to make them externally visible to everyone who participates in or observes the system. Thus, the private conceptualizations of interpersonal patterns or metaphorical maps become accessible to all members of a family or system. Sculpting seeks to display, experientially and nonverbally, behavior patterns that previously have been represented by words alone. For example, sculpting can be used to map spatially and actively a wife's language metaphor of "My husband and I are not close at all." The sculpting process uses real physical distance to symbolize the perceived emotional distance.

Sculpting has its historical and methodological roots in the work of Jacob Moreno, the founder of psychodrama. Other mental-health professionals with interests in human relations and family therapy have built on or adapted many of Moreno's ideas (Constantine 1981; Duhl, Kantor, & Duhl 1973; Satir 1972).

The sculpting procedure involves four different roles that parallel those in psychodrama. First, for example, a husband may volunteer to self-disclose his private view of the family or group, taking on the role of the sculptor (protagonist or client). Second, the professional who assists the sculptor in carrying out the sculpture is the monitor (director or therapist). Third, the actors (auxiliary egos or other members of the family or group) make themselves available to portray members of the sculptor's family or support group as the sculptor sees them. Finally, the audience consists of members of other families or the group who observe and give feedback to the sculptor at the appropriate time in the sculpting process.

Like psychodrama, sculpting involves a number of developmental stages. The initial phase focuses on the sculptors' establishing the specific situation or family event they desire to explore. This includes mapping out the physical space and the sculptors' associating their physical closeness and sensory experiences to this space. In the simplest terms, the first stage is concerned with setting the stage with its topography and atmosphere. The second stage involves the actual sculpting, in which the monitor or therapist has the sculptor place the actors on the stage to fill out the family or group space. The sculptor, without talking, places the actors bodily and spatially in the family or group space to give external reality to his or her private experiences of familial or group relationships. The final stage consists of processing, discussing, and giving feedback. All participants in the sculpture, including members of the audience, become active in the feedback and processing of experiences.

Sculpting can be used with individual clients, couples, entire families, family subsystems, extended families or kinship networks, multiple families, groups, and even corporations or organizations. When sculpting is used with individual clients, it is necessary for the therapist (monitor) either to assume the roles of family or group members or to substitute objects like chairs. Dyadic or boundary sculpting is particularly useful in working with couples to help them clarify issues like territoriality, physical closeness, and intimacy. Each person is asked to become aware of the availability of personal space, including the "rules" that govern the control of that space in reference to both self and the other person(s). This negotiating of space can be extended to a variety of relationships. Family and group sculpting is essentially an extension of dyadic relationship sculpting that involves a larger network of interactions in a more complicated system.

A sculpture can take the form of a line or a matrix. Linear sculpture lends itself to both unipolar representations (members of a family or group placing themselves on a continuum assessing some theme such as "frequency of initiating conversation") and bipolar situations (e.g., introverted versus extroverted or passive versus aggressive). Matrix sculpture allows for the simultaneous sculpting of the relationship between two situational variables. For example, on one line or dimension the frequency of intimate behaviors can be portrayed, while on a second line, perpendicular to the first line, the importance of intimacy can be featured.

Sculpting has unusual potential for both diagnosis and therapeutic intervention. It allows room for the individuality and creativity of therapists to be resourceful in fitting sculpting styles to their personalities and values. It also provides an opportunity for clients to deal with situations and relationships as they really are and to experiment with them the way they would like them to be.

9

Complementary Modes
of Intervention (Part 2)

Existential-Phenomenological Modalities

Most of the intervention strategies presented in this chapter are concerned with the here-and-now aspects of everyday coping. These interventions center on the immediacy of personal experiencing, and they stress gaining self-awareness, making good contact with self and others, finding meaning in life, coming to grips with one's values, forming accurate perceptions of environmental realities, and completing unfinished business. The contributions of person-centered therapy, Gestalt therapy, and logotherapy are featured along with a number of experiential techniques.

Finally, methods and strategies that emphasize the role of cognition in resolving problems round out the discussion. These cognitive-behavioral interventions place considerable focus on the here and now in personal functioning and coping.

Empathic and Reflective Responding

Discouraged, confused, troubled, and defeated people often need to be understood by the therapist before they can understand themselves accurately. The technique of empathic and reflective responding (Rogers 1951, 1957) is an indispensable intervention for facilitating the fulfillment of this need.

The therapist seeks to perceive as sensitively, fully, and accurately as possible the client's experiences from the client's own internal frame of reference, and then communicates these perceptions empathically and reflectively back to the client. In essence, the therapist becomes another self or alter ego for the client and reflects, as if through the eyes and senses of the client, the client's attitudes and feelings in a nurturing manner so the client can discern himself or herself more clearly, experience self more truly and deeply, choose more significantly, and live more authentically.

Logotherapy

A frequent complaint of many individuals is that their lives have no meaning. These persons usually lack a philosophy of life and values adequate to motivate them and give purposeful direction to their existence. Consequently, they subsist in an existential vacuum and experience mostly emptiness, apathy, boredom, loneliness, alienation, and frustration. They present clinical situations that are largely existential, philosophical, or spiritual and are more in need of logotherapy than of psychotherapy per se (Frankl 1962, 1965, 1969). Therapists can enter I-Thou relationships with such individuals and use a Socratic dialogue to assist them in a search for the undiscovered *logos* (meaning) of their personal existence. Therapists neither teach nor preach but confront clients with the lack of meaning and purpose in their lives.

Any or all of the following issues are grist for the logotherapeutic encounter: resolution of value conflicts; exploration of the meaning of life, love, work, alienation, suffering, and death; formulating a mature philosophy of life, including a personally chosen set of basic values; achieving a sense of individual uniqueness, freedom, and responsibility; and becoming committed to a meaningful task or mission in life.

In such relationships, therapists must be consistently careful not to impose their values on clients but to adhere to the clinical objective of helping them find their own meaning and values.

The techniques of *paradoxical intention* and *de-reflection,* which depend on the capacity of human beings to transcend their everyday experiences and engage in temporary self-detachment, can be adjuncts to logotherapy. By using them, therapists can assist individuals to stand outside themselves and conquer their problematic situations in life by arising humorously and defiantly above them.

Individuals sometimes react to an event by fearfully expecting its recurrence. This fearful expectation can so rule their lives as to become self-fulfilling. For example, the fear of not being able to fall asleep can trigger insomnia. Therapists can intervene in such situations with the paradoxical intention strategy, which encourages clients to deliberately intend what they fearfully anticipate. If they anticipate not being able to fall asleep, they will be encouraged to try to remain calmly awake all night. Thus, the fearful expectation is defused by the paradoxical intention or wish.

De-reflection also rests on the existential principle of self-transcendence and seeks to neutralize obsessive or compulsive self-absorption by turning clients' attention away from themselves and toward others. Should they be obsessed with the thought that nobody really likes them, therapists can ask them to ignore (de-reflect) their need to be liked and focus their energy on liking other people.

Gestalt Interventions

The Gestalt approach to counseling and psychotherapy is replete with techniques that emphasize the here and now, I-Thou, and immediacy in the therapy process (Fagan & Shepherd 1979; Perls 1973; Polster & Polster 1973; Yontef & Simkin 1989). Gestalt interventions are largely experiential and are concerned more with being and doing (process) than with thinking and talking (content). Integrative Therapy uses these experience-oriented strategies to help clients to make better contact with both themselves and their environment, to focus attention on particular problematic situations that emerge within the organism-environment field, to integrate awareness and creative action, and to restore organismic balance to personal life styles. The Gestalt options presented here are a mere sampling of the scores of possibilities and represent those most frequently used in Integrative Therapy.

Present-tense communication

Clients are encouraged to deal with all their life issues in the present tense. This helps to promote better awareness and immediacy in experiencing. It also allows individuals to make better contact with themselves, thus intensifying and personalizing their problems and experiences. Present-tense language also makes it easier for clients to integrate past experiences into their personalities in here-and-now living. Significant historical moments are relived therapeutically in the existential now.

I language

Individuals who refer to their bodies and behaviors in objective, second- and third-person, you/it language are asked to communicate their experiences in "I" statements. This enhances their perception of themselves as active, dynamic agents rather than passive, acted-on objects. I language also helps people assume greater responsibility for, involvement in, and control of their total behavior in the context of their life spaces.

The what and how of behavior

Integrative Therapists ask clients to focus on the what and how of behavior, the so-called awareness continuum, in order to guide them into making good contact with their sensorimotor selves and away from the interpretive why of behavior. Asking why tends to lead to intellectualization, defensiveness, analytical explanations, and judgmentalism. For example, should clients report that they are depressed, therapists intervene more effectively by inquiring with questions like "How long have you been depressed?" or "What is it like to be depressed?" or "How does depression interfere with your plans for living?" than by asking, "Why are you depressed?", which is less effective as a therapeutic tactic.

Dialogue

People typically enter therapy with discordant polarizations in their personality functioning. These splits or dualisms include conditions like masculine versus feminine, aggressive versus passive, or commanding versus resisting. When therapists detect these discordant poles in clients' experiences, they can have the clients engage the polarized tendencies in actual dialogue in order to integrate the fragmented parts. The discordant parts confront and encounter one another, face to face, until the two elements merge into a new, balanced integration. To illustrate, the outcome of a dialogue between aggression and passivity is assertiveness, or an encounter between masculinity and femininity leads to androgyny.

The dialogue can be carried out by using two empty chairs or the two hands. One chair or hand can represent one pole, the other the opposing quality. The dialogue may be between two differing psychological attitudes or feelings, two parts of the body, or the personality of the client and some significant other person who is involved in some type of unresolved conflict with the client. The therapist guides the dialogue until harmonization or integration is realized. The intervention is essentially a dialectic process in which a thesis (e.g., commanding) encounters an antithesis (e.g., resisting) to produce a synthesis (e.g., cooperating).

Completion of unfinished business

Individuals bring unfinished business or unresolved emotions like hurt, anger, guilt, and resentment into therapy. When these unfinished emotions surface, clients are guided in completing the work by reliving or living out these painful feelings in the here and now. Role playing, psychodrama, pillow/cushion therapy, and dialogue are some of the specific methods for working through the disturbing emotional residue.

Playing the projection

Quite often what clients dislike in others is really a projection of what they dislike about themselves. That is, a negative trait, attitude, feeling, or mode of behavior that actually belongs to the client is first attributed to another person, then perceived as directed toward the client by the other person.

Whenever clients express a projection disguised as a perception, they are encouraged to play the role of the personification involved in the projection to discover their own conflict in this area of personality or behavior. For example, a woman who says to the therapist, "Nobody really cares about me" may be asked to play the role of a noncaring person. Following the role enactment, she can be asked to examine herself to see whether this is really a disowned trait or a practice of her own.

Doing the reversal

Reversal helps people realize that manifest behavior often represents the opposite of the underlying impulse, attitude, or emotion. For example, a lonely man who states that he really likes and cares for other people but just doesn't have time to develop a social life might be asked to enact the role of a recluse who is indifferent toward others.

Here's a sentence for you

Clients frequently will reveal significant messages or behavior patterns that are not in their awareness. Therapists propose a sentence for a client to repeat verbatim and then verify its personal relevance. If the sentence is true to the client's experience, he or she can be asked to amplify the theme. Should the sentence be judged to be untrue in relation to the client, he or she can rewrite it to make it true and then amplify it. The objective is to enable clients to gain greater awareness and experience more fully and accurately their mode of being and behaving. The awareness allows for constructive changes if needed or desired. To illustrate, a young woman who is obviously male-dependent and has gone from one male to another with virtually no time gaps since she was fourteen is asked to repeat, verify the accuracy of, and amplify the sentence: "When I think of myself going six months without a man in my life to take care of me, I become frightened."

Stay with the pain

From time to time during therapy, clients will hit on a feeling, mood, or state of mind that is unpleasant and will prefer to run from the pain rather than encountering it. Instead of seeking to make things comfortable for them and allow them to avoid the painful situation, therapists encourage them to stay with the pain. This enables them to develop the ability to deal effectively with their emotional pain and to complete unfinished business that interferes with their maturation and organismic self-regulation.

Guided fantasy

An excellent opportunity for individuals to explore, clarify, and come to grips with feelings and themes in their life is provided by fantasy journeys. Clients may project themselves into numerous fantasy or make-believe situations like becoming an acorn and going through all the developmental processes from being planted to growing into a mature tree, or hiking in the mountains to visit a wise old man who has gifts and insights into life to share with his visitors, or observing their own life coming into being and unfolding the way they would like it to be ideally from conception to mature adulthood. Rather than being mere fantasy, these experiences can become genuine expressions of people's concepts of personal existence, needs, desires, hurts, disappointments, or strengths. The fantasy experience is best done while clients are deeply relaxed and their eyes are closed. The fantasy journey can be guided by either the therapist or the clients themselves after some basic instructions regarding the procedure.

Dream work

Integrative Therapy considers dreams to be existential-phenomenological self-revelations of the person. A dream is a message by the individual, to the individual, about the individual, and for the individual. In a very real sense the individual *is* the dream. Every image or symbol in a dream represents some element of unfinished or unresolved business in personality development and functioning, be it an alienated or disowned part of the self, a conflict between two opposites or polarities in the personality, a compensatory effort to fulfill unmet needs or desires, or the seeking of a resolution to some basic goal(s) in life. I concur with Perls that the dream is the "royal road to awareness and integration." Dreams, along with pain, are among our very best friends in that they tell us that something is missing, wrong, or out of balance in our lives.

Integrative Therapy takes more of an experiential than an analytical approach to dreams. Clients first narrate or report the dream in first-person and present-tense language. After reporting the dream, they are asked to identify and place an open hand on the specific location of any sensation (e.g., excitement, fright, uneasiness, tightness) in the body that is associated with the dream. I then ask them to identify any thing, event, relationship or condition in their everyday life that produces a similar sensation. This is to discover any immediate experiences that might be involved in the dream formation. Next, I ask them to identify with the various images and symbols in the dream from the most powerful or vivid to the least. Focus on images in terms of power and vividness is emphasized in order to tap clients' emotional intensity or energy investment in the dream. The greater the investment of emotional energy, the greater is the potential for therapeutic movement toward awareness and contact with self. By re-experiencing and enacting the dream in the present tense from the vantage point of each image or symbol, clients can begin to reclaim and integrate the alienated or conflicted parts of their personality.

Most interpretation of dreams is left to the clients. Therapists assist primarily by suggesting the order in which the images are encountered, helping clients deal with avoidance or resistance in confronting the disowned or conflicted parts of themselves, and suggesting when they might relate the message(s) revealed through their dreams to current living. Dialogue and other techniques can be used in dreamwork to ease integration of discordant elements of the personality revealed in dreams.

Although Gestalt emphases are the starting point of dream work in Integrative Therapy, Freudian contributions are used when dealing with certain sexual dream themes, Jungian strategies when dreams reveal specific compensatory themes, and Adlerian concepts when dreams suggest goal-oriented themes. Dream work provides one of the best opportunities for therapists to be truly integrative in their clinical interventions.

Other Experiential Interventions

The four experience-based techniques presented below are samples of the many that I have either personally created or modified to use in my clinical practice of Integrative Therapy. All of these strategies help individuals gain better awareness of themselves, clarify their values, resolve conflicts, and facilitate decision making.

Couple's Pattern of Interaction

This intervention consists of a series of experiential exercises in which marital partners or persons in committed relationships use various spatial positionings of their hands and bodies to explore how they communicate and experience intimacy in the relationship. Both partners portray how they view the couple's patterns of communication and interaction. After each spatial positioning of either hands or bodies, the partners are asked to make comparative evaluations of how accurately this specific exercise shows the nature of their relationship. For example, when using the hands to picture the level of intimacy and closeness, the right index fingers of the couple barely and feebly touch at the very tips. This suggests that intimacy hardly exists in the relationship.

When the partners have experimented with a diversity of spatial portrayals of how they experience the relationship in its present form, I ask them to show spatially how they would like the relationship to be. Then I give homework exercises and strategies to change the undesired patterns of interaction to more satisfying ones.

Options Clarification

When clients are confronted with situations in which they must choose between two or more possibilities, decisions are facilitated best by using an options clarification intervention that involves physical movement along with cognitive and affective processes.

First, all of the options are clearly identified and defined. Then chairs or corners of the therapy room are assigned to represent them. Clients go to the chair or corner that represents a particular option, make physical contact by either sitting in the chair or standing in the corner, explore the pros and cons involved with each option, and share verbally how strongly they are inclined toward each possibility. This clarification process continues until clients can narrow the options down to two so that two objects can become end points on a continuum. The therapist then asks them to position themselves bodily on the continuum to reveal how close they are to choosing one of the options. All the negatives and positives, possible losses and gains, and advantages and disadvantages of the two alternatives are explored until clients can take a position and declare, "I choose this option and like my choice because. . . ."

I have discovered that the physical movement enables individuals to make decisions much more easily and quickly than merely exploring verbally while remaining on the therapy couch. The movement facilitates their becoming more actively involved in the decision-making process.

The Door Technique

Often the decisions that individuals must make are doors to new and different lives or ways of being in the world. Opting for these new lives and different ways of being is usually marked by mixed emotions.

Several years ago, I began to use the door to my therapy room as a splendid aid in helping individuals to make difficult decisions. The technique described here grew logically out of the options clarification strategy. When a client narrows the options down to two, often the door becomes an appropriate representative for one of the possibilities. Any time individuals are faced with situations that require them either to remain where or as they are or to relocate or make major changes, the door technique works excellently.

For example, the door technique may help clarify options in a troubled marriage. A married Christian woman—who believes marriage vows are for life and divorce is wrong—enters therapy alone because her abusive husband refuses to come. She explores all the options (continue living with her husband under the present conditions, arrange a trial separation, work cooperatively to make the marriage better, or seek a divorce). Since she has previously tried separation and that didn't help, and since the husband refuses to come for counseling to work on the marriage, the woman is faced with remaining in the marriage as it is or divorcing her husband. The therapist uses a chair placed opposite the door to represent staying in the marriage as it now exists, and the door to represent divorce or the way out of the painful situation. The woman is asked to position herself bodily between the chair and the door and to face the direction in which she is most inclined at the moment. The therapist observes how close she is to the door and the direction she is facing. Should she face the door (seeking a divorce), she is encouraged to share her awareness of both what is in front of her and what is behind her—losses and gains, pain and joy, failure and success, guilt and happiness, freedom and fear. She is also asked to share what the door symbolizes to her and what she sees beyond or outside it—being alone, new adventure, financial insecurity, confidence in herself to make it on her own with God's provision, loss of family, starting a new family. The exercise is continued until the client has explored fully the two options and is ready to choose one and act on it. If she elects the door, the therapist encourages her to take progressive steps toward it and share her awareness with each step until she can take hold of the doorknob and begin her way out of her impossible situation. The therapist assures her that he or she will help her with adjusting and coping skills in either direction taken.

Backtracking

There are times when individuals come for their therapy sessions with an uneasy feeling but have no idea what is causing it. A helpful strategy in these situations is one I have dubbed backtracking, which refers to my having clients retrace their life's course from the time of entering the therapy room back to when or where the bad feeling orginated. I operate on the assumption that a memory of some negative event or experience lies recorded in the unconscious mind and is inaccesible to clients without some assistance.

I ask clients to walk around the room and begin to trace their steps backward from the moment of entering the therapy office. As they move around the room recalling the events in the immediate past, in reverse order, they share verbally all the experiences that come to mind. I make verbal interventions when necessary to facilitate accurate recall. Usually, they hit on a situation that triggered the emotional upset. When the causal event is located, I assist clients in working through the unfinished residue of that experience.

A clinical observation illustrates the backtracking intervention. A woman in her mid-forties came for therapy one afternoon. She was very anxious, but could not identify the source of her anxiety. I used the backtracking strategy with her, and she successfully traced the origin of the disturbing emotion to an occasion in her home three days previously. Her husband had become furious with her for not rinsing all the dishwashing detergent from a stainless steel coffee pot. After she had made a "ruined pot of coffee," he threw the coffee pot to the floor, denting both the pot and the floor, and screamed menacingly at her for being incompetent. Having discovered the cause of her discomfort, we focused on her becoming more assertive and not allowing her husband to intimidate her.

Cognitive-Behavioral Modalities

This section delineates strategies and techniques that can be used to assist individuals in corrective learning experiences. In some situations corrective interventions will involve unlearning old, maladaptive thoughts and behaviors and relearning adaptive ones that had been forgotten. In other cases, the focus will be on learning new adaptive ways of thinking and behaving.

The methods presented here are derived primarily from the behavioral, cognitive, rational-emotive, reality, and nouthetic approaches to therapy.

These strategies are used in Integrative Therapy without belaboring which ones are behavioral, cognitive, or rational in nature or origin. Little is gained by cutting the theoretical pie so thinly and precisely. Integrative Therapy adheres to the position that behavior, cognition, and affect exist holistically and integratedly in virtually all human actions and reactions. I do not advocate the radical behavioral emphases, like applied behavioral analysis, that focus exclusively on overt behaviors and environmental contingencies.

The techniques offered here are labeled cognitive-behavioral and integrate behavioral, cognitive, rational, and environmental nuances. The methods and strategies that exist under these rubrics are so numerous that it would be possible to fill several large volumes describing them. Consequently, only those that are used most frequently in Integrative Therapy are presented.

Positive Reinforcement

Positive reinforcement refers to a class of interventional strategies based on the operant-conditioning model, in which adaptive or desired responses are followed by positive rewards or interventions (Skinner 1953). The therapist offers positive reinforcement to strengthen particular responses and to increase the likelihood that clients will repeat them. Verbal responses, appropriate physical touch, valued objects, social recognition, client-preferred activities can be used as positive reinforcement.

Positive reinforcement appears to be indispensable to therapy (especially positively reinforcing verbal statements) and is present, whether intentional or otherwise, in some form in virtually all approaches to counseling. Thus, it can be both complementary and supplementary to all other interventions. For example, therapists' matter-of-fact behaviors like making eye contact, offering a cheerful greeting at the beginning or a goodbye at the end of a session, nodding affirmingly, touching kindly, or saying "mm-hmm," are all potential positive reinforcers that blend in with any other modes of intervening. The positive reinforcement is even more rewarding and strengthening when clients are rewarded immediately after making successful efforts in resolving their problems. A therapist's simple statements, "You are doing well," "That's a very good piece of work," or "You're making definite progress," are essential reinforcing interventions.

Bibliotherapy

Bibliotherapy, from the transliteration of the two Greek words *biblion* (book) and *therapeuo* (therapy or healing), means in the most literal sense "book therapy." The term is used more generically to describe the use of written material to help individuals change problematic behavior, thoughts, feelings, and interpersonal relationships (Atwater & Smith 1982; Smith & Burkhalter 1987).

Bibliotherapy, an auxiliary method in many contemporary approaches to psychotherapy, has its historical roots in Jewish and Christian communities. Rabbis, priests, and ministers for three millennia have directed individuals to the Scriptures and other religious literature for information, guidance, encouragement, comfort, and spiritual support and restoration. Perhaps no other literary resource has had therapeutic use and value equal to the Book of Psalms, which touches on the gamut of human emotions and experiences.

Abundant materials currently available can be bibliotherapeutic resources—books, pamphlets, periodicals, cassette tapes, video tapes, and films. Any of these can be employed as an excellent supplement to other interventions. Biography can be used as a form of social modeling (see the section Modeling for a description of this mode of intervention) to enable clients to observe how others have coped with the same problems they are facing. The Bible and inspirational literature can nurture and support clients who are discouraged, despondent, or burdened with feelings of guilt, shame, failure, anger, or regret. Self-help books can help with family life, parenting, marriage, divorce, emotional conflicts, life crises, finances, sexual problems, and scores of other issues in living. The same is true of cassette tapes, video tapes, and films. (The use of these materials could be called mediatherapy and follows the same principles that govern the use of written products.) Popular magazines and newspapers have articles designed specifically to help people deal with a variety of human needs and concerns.

Brammer and Shostrom (1977) have provided some helpful guidelines for bibliotherapy. These guidelines are similar to those followed in Integrative Therapy.

First, therapists must be familiar with the bibliotherapeutic resources they recommend. Firsthand knowledge of the source enables therapists to make appropriate suggestions in terms of topic relevance, age relatedness, experience, and language level.

Second, therapists should be able to express personal confidence in the potential of the bibliotherapy materials to help. In a very real sense, therapists' discernment, judgment, and competence are associated with the recommendation of bibliotherapy materials.

Third, the resources should be suggested or recommended rather than prescribed. Therapists' positive attitudes toward them and proposing them as optional tend both to motivate clients to use them and to enhance their overall therapeutic effectiveness.

Fourth, therapists should emphasize that bibliotherapy is an aid to therapy and not the therapy itself. Otherwise, clients might be misled into believing that merely reading, viewing, or listening will solve their problems. Clients must realize that bibliotherapy is only a supplement to their learning effective self-management.

Fifth, bibliotherapy should be introduced when therapists sense that clients are most likely to be receptive to it. Signs of clients' readiness for bibliotherapy include their understanding that the therapist considers their problems to be important and treats them with professional seriousness, accepting bibliotherapy as a significant aspect of the therapy process rather than a substitute for the therapist's involvement, judging the therapist to be competent and willing to help with other interventions as well, and experiencing little or no resistance to therapy.

Sixth, materials to be recommended should be readily accessible and reasonably priced. Both hard-to-find and expensive materials discourage, frustrate, and anger clients instead of encouraging them.

Seventh, clients' use of bibliotherapy needs to be followed by regular discussion in order to ascertain its effectiveness, to clarify misunderstandings, to examine the bibliotherapy for appropriate application to the specifics of the presenting problem(s), and to adjust the bibliotherapy for the best fit in the therapy.

Eighth, bibliotherapy should be used in small, manageable portions rather than in larger amounts. Too much material at any time might be difficult for clients to grasp and apply effectively to their situation in life, possibly making them feel overwhelmed by the excessive exposure.

Lists of suggested bibliotherapy sources, preferably with brief summaries or annotations, can be placed in locations like the waiting area for client self-referral.

When using the Bible for bibliotherapy, modern translations or paraphrases like the *New International Version* or the *Living Bible* prove to be the most understandable and useful to most people. However, should clients express a strong bias toward a particular translation or version, therapists are wise to respect their preference.

Nouthetic Training

Nouthetic training is the characteristic method in an approach to counseling and psychotherapy developed by Jay Adams (1970). The concept has its roots in the Greek word *noutheteo,* which refers specifically to putting something in the mind. More general meanings include admonition, correction, instruction, and encouragement. Historically, the practice of nouthetic training has been associated with religious bodies and Jewish and Christian communities in particular. Currently it is essentially a Christian phenomenon. Although Adams prefers the idea of nouthetic *confrontation, training* is more fitting in Integrative Therapy.

Nouthetic training, whether for encouragement or for admonition, always implies that some problem or need exists in the life of the individual that requires corrective attention. The intervention might focus on concerns ranging from the need to be encouraged to keep growing and developing toward personal maturity (Col. 1:28) to instructing or equipping a critical or abusive father for effective parenting (Eph. 6:4; Col. 3:21). Thus, the goal may be either very general or exactingly specific. In either case, the therapist's intervention is aimed at having a corrective or motivating influence on the decision-making process of the individual.

Nouthetic training consists of an active and directive verbal involvement by the therapist. While the therapist's encouraging nonverbal behavior is important, the spoken word is the central mode of therapeutic intervention. Thus, the essence of nouthetic training is a specific form of teaching.

Although therapists assume a direct role in the helping process, this in no way suggests that they have authority over or control their clients. They should never attempt to harass, attack, scold, or punish clients.

Whenever therapists sense that nouthetic training is the preferred mode of intervention, they have awareness that a number of special conditions must be present in addition to the general relationship qualities. First, it is essential that they have an accurate knowledge of both the specifics of the client's presenting situation and the relevant spiritual principles (e.g., Rom. 15:14). Second, practical wisdom is required for an effective application of spiritual and psychological principles to the client's problem (Col. 3:16). Finally, nouthetic training demands personal involvement by the therapist (e.g., Acts 20:31; 1 Thess. 2:5–8). The therapeutic value of the training rests not only on the spoken word but also on the caring and supportive attitude with which the therapist speaks.

Homework

In-session therapeutic experiences are brief and infrequent compared with the amount of time spent by clients in their daily and weekly sojourn. For optimum therapeutic gain, the in-session interventions need to be augmented by homework. Homework, from a clinical perspective, includes any tasks or activities assigned by therapists for clients to complete outside the regularly scheduled treatment sessions. These may be made for either assessment/diagnostic or therapeutic objectives. For example, the initial homework that I typically assign is completion and return of the Pre-Therapy Questionnaire (see appendix B).

Therapeutic homework assignments continue the corrective interventions clients experience face-to-face in sessions. The assigned tasks are customized and personalized to match clients' specific needs. For example, should a man be working on developing assertiveness skills, the homework assignment might consist of having him read a book like *Your Perfect Right* (Alberti & Emmons 1986) along with specified tasks to accomplish in relation to his wife, employer, supervisor, or associate. It is important to follow up all homework assignments to evaluate for success, proper fit, and understanding.

Success in therapy varies in proportion to the degree to which clients willingly cooperate by completing homework.

Natural and Logical Consequences

The use of natural and logical consequences is an excellent intervention to assist individuals in acquiring effective parenting skills. These behavior-based interventions have their origin largely in Adlerian approaches to psychotherapy (Dreikurs 1964).

Natural consequences are what happens naturally after someone misbehaves, without any specific action or interference by the parent or another person. For example, hunger is the natural consequence of forgetting to eat. Allowing children, adolescents, and even adults to experience the consequences of their acts or misdeeds provides invaluable learning experience.

When a parent or other person structures events that logically follow misdeeds, the interventions represent what we call logical consequences. For example, parents and a child may enter a contract that allows the child the freedom to come for dinner at six or play for another ninety minutes, with the mutual understanding that if the child plays, he or she will not be allowed to eat until the next regular meal. In situations like this, parents structure the subsequent events and enforce the terms of the contract. The emphasis is placed on the child's right to make choices and the responsibility to accept the consequences.

The use of natural and logical consequences helps individuals learn how to make their own decisions and to assume responsibility for them. It replaces the autocratic and punitive aspects of parenting, teaching, or supervising with a democratic approach that treats people as responsible equals. It is applicable to a wide variety of people and situations.

Behavior Rehearsal

Behavior rehearsal describes a specific therapeutic procedure that seeks to replace inadequate behaviors with more effective ones by having clients practice the desired behavior under the therapist's direction (Lazarus 1966, 1985). The primary focus of behavior rehearsal is on correcting current ineffective behavior patterns rather than completing unfinished business of the past. This procedure is particularly useful for training in social skills.

A number of activities and strategies are involved in behavior rehearsal. The behavior pattern to be modified must first be identified, and it must be ascertained whether clients' behavior constitutes a deficit or an excess. Next, the desired mode of behavior is defined and enacted or modeled by either the therapist or another person. Clients are directed in their practice or rehearsal of the behavior. Frequently role playing is used in which the therapist assumes the roles of significant persons in clients' lives, and clients enact the desired behaviors in response to the role behaviors of the therapist. As clients progress in achieving the desired manner of acting and responding, the therapist uses positive reinforcement to encourage them. Role-reversal is also used at times, with the therapist assuming clients' roles and modeling the desired verbal and nonverbal behaviors, while clients act the roles of the persons with whom they experience difficulties. When they have demonstrated effective in-session success with the behavior rehearsal, homework assignments are made for them to practice the newly acquired skills *in vivo*. Homework checks discern the need for additional rehearsal of the desired skills.

Modeling

Social modeling is a therapy procedure with roots in the pioneering work of Albert Bandura (1969) and is usually associated with imitative or observational learning. A major premise in social modeling is that "one of the fundamental means by which new modes of behavior are acquired and existing patterns are modified entails modeling and vicarious processes" (Bandura 1969, 118).

The initial step in modeling is the identification of the social behavior to be acquired or modified. This is followed by selecting a live, filmed, or imagined model. Preferably, the model will be of the same gender and approximate age of the client in order to have optimum relevance. The model also needs to be proficient, articulate, and held in reasonable esteem by the client. The model enacts the intended behavior while the client observes. Next, the client rehearses the modeled behavior (see the section Behavior Rehearsal) and is positively reinforced by the therapist, step by step, as progress is made from less to more difficult behavior patterns.

In-session modeling is always augmented by *in vivo* practice via appropriate homework. As with behavior rehearsal and other homework, routine checks evaluate success and assess the next step in the therapy.

Relaxation Training

Someone has remarked that ours is the age of anxiety. We could put it another way: ours is the tense society. Tension is an unavoidable reality for virtually everyone, but when people become overly tense in situations where extreme tension is disruptive or inappropriate, they need help acquiring special coping skills.

Relaxation training (Bernstein & Borkovec 1973; Jacobson 1938, 1964; Wolpe 1985) is an indispensable component of effective programs for controlling tension. The following is a brief delineation of the relaxation procedures used in Integrative Therapy.

Relaxation training is provided in a quiet, attractive, living-room atmosphere with indirect lighting regulated by a dimmer switch. The dimmer switch allows for maintenance of a low light that facilitates a relaxed state. The client, dressed in loose-fitting clothing (e.g., slacks and blouse or shirt with comfortable undergarments), is fully and comfortably supported by an overstuffed recliner. Skirts and dresses are discouraged in order to avoid possible embarrassment when lying down. Personal items like contact lenses, jewelry, and shoes are removed to allow for increased comfort and freedom of movement.

The procedures used in the relaxation training are discussed with clients. They are informed regarding the specific benefits that they can anticipate by reducing and controlling tension by relaxation.

The therapist, speaking in a soothing and modulated voice, instructs clients to close their eyes and begin to inhale deeply until the lungs are completely filled, then to exhale slowly until the lungs are empty. This is repeated several times. Attention is focused next on the various muscle groups. In Ingegrative Therapy I have discovered that an abbreviated relaxation procedure often works better than the more tedious and regimented forms sometimes followed. Five muscle groups are tensed and relaxed in this sequence: arms and hands; face and neck; chest, shoulders, and back; abdomen; thighs, legs, and feet. Clients are instructed to direct their attention to a particular muscle group and, on cue, tense that group. The tension is maintained for about six seconds and, again on cue, released. This is repeated two or three times for each muscle group until the sequence is complete. Should clients experience any cramping, the duration of the tensing is reduced to three or four seconds. Several in-therapy sessions often are required to train clients to become thoroughly relaxed.

Specific homework assignments are made for clients to practice relaxation procedures. If the tension is primarily job related, clients might be asked to withdraw into a quiet space once or twice daily to perform self-directed or audio-directed relaxation. Should it be connected with insomnia, then the homework will focus on a bedtime practice.

The relaxation training procedures can be intensified and expanded by the emotive imagery technique described next.

Emotive Imagery

Emotive imagery (Lazarus 1985) is a simplified variant of the systematic desensitization procedure (Wolpe 1982). It can be used by itself or in combination with relaxation therapy. These counter-conditioning strategies are based on the principle of reciprocal inhibition: experiencing either of two opposite conditions inhibits experiencing the other. For example, anxiety or tension is the opposite of relaxation; therefore, if clients can be trained to relax in the presence of the anxiety or a tension-producing situation, then the anxiety or tension can be inhibited.

The anxiety-causing situation is identified and then followed by the compilation of a graduated hierarchy of stimulus conditions that range from a nearly neutral to the actual targeted noxious situation. While in a state of deep relaxation (relaxation is optional), clients are asked to confront, step by step, their dreaded situations. As the dreaded situations, from least to most negative, are called to mind, clients are asked to imagine the feared events taking place in a positive environment like floating on a raft in a beautiful lake, listening to soothing music while watching the glow of a fireplace, lying on the beach and enjoying the wind, ocean, and sea gulls, or riding a motorcycle through an idyllic countryside. The relaxation and positive imagery combine to inhibit anxiety and tension.

In some cases it is unnecessary to compile a hierarchy of stimulus conditions. It is sufficient to train clients how to relax and use positive imagery to inhibit the intrusion of anxiety and tension on the job or in the home.

Emotive imagery can be adapted for therapy with children by having them imagine their favorite sports hero, TV or movie personality, or comic figure becoming involved in their feared experiences. For example, a little boy who fears the dentist's office can first imagine quarterback Joe Montana going to the dentist and then see himself sitting in the dental chair while Montana is in the office with him offering encouragement and cheering him for his courage. Some children might consider Jesus their hero and imagine him with them in feared situations.

Assertiveness Training

An individual's characteristic interpersonal or social behavior tends to be either aggressive, passive, passive-aggressive, or assertive. Although there can be situation-specific variations and effectiveness of interpersonal conduct, assertive social behavior (standing up for one's own rights in an honest, respectful way that does not interfere with other people's rights) is generally recognized as the most adaptive and effective style of interacting. Life styles characterized by either of the other three modes of interacting are likely to become problematic.

The initial focus in assertiveness training is to clarify the nature of clients' presenting concerns by ascertaining their characteristic modes of behaving in problematic situations. Do they act in hostile ways that violate other people's rights (aggressively), behave so that their own rights are ignored or violated (passively), or maneuver to get control by expressing themselves noncooperatively (passive-aggressively)?

Having discovered clients' typical repertoires of social behavior in the area of concern (marriage, work, friendships, parenting), an assertive option is described, modeled, and rehearsed during therapy sessions and followed by specific homework assignments. The training in assertiveness involves work on eye contact, verbal and nonverbal language, body posture, cognitions, affect, and environmental factors. The homework usually includes bibliotherapy (e.g., *Your Perfect Right* or *The Assertive Woman*) and clearly defined practice *in vivo*.

Reframing

Faulty, erroneous, or biased interpretations of one's observations can result in maladaptive response patterns and distorted world views (Greenberg & Safran 1981). Reframing or relabeling seeks to modify or correct perceptions that lead to problematic behavior. Reframing gives a situation or behavior a new label or name in terms of meaning or context. The reframed situation usually replaces a negative connotation with a positive one. For example, a father who views his son's behavior as rebellious stubbornness may be helped to see it as a normal developmental search for personal autonomy, or a woman who sees a mountainous park as the habitat of poisonous snakes and dangerous animals may be helped to revisualize it as a beautiful countryside filled with delightful flora and fauna waiting to be discovered by curious and adventuresome people.

Among the several outcomes of reframing, the most valuable is the reduction of people's defensiveness and mobilization of their resources and abilities for creative change, adventure, and new growth.

Thought Control

King Solomon observed that how people think or reason determines their basic character (Prov. 23:7 NIV margin). This maxim applies particularly to people who suffer from persistent trains of thought that are unrealistic, unproductive, self-defeating, and upsetting. Thought stopping or control (Taylor 1963; Wolpe 1982) is an effective intervention for episodic worrying, rumination, brooding, and preoccupation with negative thoughts or images. It is here described and illustrated by its use with a pregnant Christian woman who was bothered by the recurring thought that God would give her a "waterhead" baby as punishment for a poor relationship with her husband.

The first step in the thought-stopping procedure is to identify the upsetting thoughts or images. Therapists need to help clients understand that their own negative preoccupations create their discomfort. Then they can encourage them to cooperate in a corrective process that will open up a new outlook on life. In our example, the therapist needs to inform the woman that she is disturbed by allowing herself to think of or visualize a hydrocephalic baby as God's punishment for a bad marriage. Next, he explains that if she could stop thinking about and visualizing a deformed baby, she would feel much better about herself and her life. He describes the procedure to her: "I want you to sit back in the recliner, close your eyes, become relaxed, and begin to share all the thoughts and images that emerge. As soon as a thought or image of a deformed baby appears, tell me what you are thinking or seeing. I will then interrupt you and teach you how to stop these negative thoughts and images yourself whenever they begin to bother you."

The next phase in the procedure is stopping thoughts via the therapist's overt command. As the woman reclines with her eyes closed and shares her inner experiences, she eventually says, "I'm seeing an ugly hydrocephalic fetus being formed and I have these awful thoughts about God punishing me." The therapist shouts "Stop!" and has the woman ascertain whether her negative images and thoughts indeed were stopped. This procedure is repeated until the client reports the cessation of the negative experiences at the therapist's command. Subsequently, the therapist modifies the procedure and asks the woman to indicate the onset of negative thoughts and images by raising her finger. When he sees her raised finger, he interrupts with a loud "Stop!" and repeats the modified procedure until the verbal command is effective in terminating the self-defeating thoughts and images.

After learning how to control disturbing thoughts at the therapist's command, the client is instructed to interrupt negative ideation and visualization at her own command. She sits comfortably in the chair, allows thoughts and images to flow, and yells "Stop!" whenever an unwanted thought or image emerges. If the verbal command is ineffective in stopping the disturbing thought, a supplemental strategy like pinching her inner wrist often helps.

It is not always practical or desirable for people to interrupt their upsetting preoccupations with overt verbalizations. Therefore, it is necessary to train clients to move from overt to covert or subvocal interruptions. Thus they are asked to practice until they are able to control their negative thoughts and images with only the private command and, when needed, the occasional pinch of the wrist.

Merely stopping negative preoccupations or ruminations is frequently insufficient. They need be replaced by positive, self-affirming, adaptive thoughts and images. Nature hates a vacuum. The disturbing thought that "God is going to punish me with a 'waterhead' baby" needs to be replaced by "God loves my baby and me and desires the very best for both of us, and I look forward to birthing a beautiful, healthy baby."

This thought-controlling strategy is in harmony with both psychological practice and the general teaching of the Bible. For example, Christians are challenged "to take captive every thought and make it obedient to Christ" (2 Cor. 10:5) and to think about things that are noble, true, pure, lovely, admirable, excellent, and praiseworthy (Phil. 4:8). This intervention has enormous potential for skillful use in strengthening ineffective Christian life styles due to defeating thoughts and fantasies.

Cognitive Restructuring

Some negative situations require more comprehensive treatment than is provided by either the reframing or thought-stopping interventions. Cognitive restructuring is usually the treatment of choice for these more pervasive conditions.

Cognitive restructuring refers to a composite of strategies to identify and alter self-defeating thoughts or negative self-statements that cause emotional distress and ineffective performance of essential life tasks. Therapists have developed several models for cognitive restructuring. Among these, Albert Ellis's Rational-Emotive Therapy (e.g., Ellis & Grieger 1977), Aaron Beck's cognitive therapy (1976), and Donald Meichenbaum's (1977) self-instructional training are the most widely recognized. Integrative Therapy integrates the contributions of Beck and Meichenbaum into the basic format used in Ellis's Rational-Emotive Therapy (RET). Although Ellis himself is vitriolic, even hostile, toward Christianity and religious values and beliefs, he and his followers have provided a method that can be adapted by Christian therapists for effective use in an integrative fashion.

A simple A–B–C–D–E paradigm outlines the cognitive restructuring intervention. Some external event (or environment) affects someone's life. We call this an activating event (A). The individual's distorted attitudes toward, irrational beliefs about, and negative self-talk (B) about this occurrence result in undesirable emotional and behavioral consequences (C). Therapeutic correction is effected by training the person to discern and dispute (D) the irrational beliefs and negative self-talk. Logical or rational reasoning, thinking, and positive self-talk produce cognitive, emotional, and behavioral effects (E) that are adaptive.

Cognitive restructuring is demonstrated with a young man's reactions to his fianceé's breaking their engagement in order to pursue full-time study of veterinary medicine.

Activating event (A): The fianceé ends the relationship.

Beliefs, attitudes, and negative self-talk about the event (B):

". . . she had no right to end our relationship."

"How could she reject me to study cats and dogs?"

"I must be worthless."

"I'm a total failure."

"There must be something wrong with me."

"I've disappointed my family and friends."

"All women are fickle and can't be trusted."

"I'll never love another woman."

Consequences of negative thinking (C): Depression, anger, rejection, loneliness, withdrawal, resentment, exaggerated evaluation of women, and absolutistic decisions about himself and the female gender arise in his mind.

Disputing his illogical and self-defeating ideation (D): Among the options for correcting the self-defeating ideations are Socratic dialogue ("I loved her so much and she had no right to leave me" can be followed by the therapist's "Perhaps she never really loved you and needed no right to leave you, just an excuse and an opportunity.") and logical argument ("I'm a total failure" and "I must be worthless" are challenged by "Let's explore just how you have failed. Perhaps you didn't get everything you wanted with the young lady, but not getting everything one wants is hardly failure. The fact that an ambitious young woman preferred a career over marriage does not mean that you are either a failure or a worthless person. One woman's preferences do not determine your worth and success as a man.") Other corrective strategies are paradox, confrontation, humor, rhetorical questioning, suggestion, reframing, thought stopping, homework, and deliberate production of positive self-statements.

My clinical work with both Christian and non-Christian clients has indicated convincingly that Christians hold as many irrational beliefs about God, themselves, and other people as do non-Christians. Correcting crooked thinking and self-talk via cognitive restructuring is invariably the preferred treatment for these individuals. Cognitive restructuring provides an excellent opportunity to integrate environmental factors, cognitions, perceptions, emotions, and biblical principles in correcting faulty attitudes and beliefs and developing wholesome cognitive life styles.

Stress Management

Stress, not suprisingly, is a necessary force in healthy and productive life styles. Psychological problems develop when people are unable to manage stressful situations effectively and, in order to cope successfully, need to acquire special stress-management skills (Meichenbaum & Jaremko 1983; Meichenbaum 1985).

The initial phase of stress management training in Integrative Therapy focuses on educating individuals about the nature of stress and both its positive and negative roles in personality functioning. The objective is not to become stress free, because a certain amount of stress is needed to keep the human organism energized, motivated, and conditioned for a balanced life. Instead, learning how to manage stressful situations in family, work, and other relationships is the task.

The second step consists of identifying the sources of stress in people's lives and teaching them to monitor them to discover the specific physical symptoms, behavioral reactions, cognitive processes, and emotional consequences associated with each stressor. Exploration is made, too, of their dietary, sleep, and exercise practices to check for any particular habits that might exacerbate stress.

The third phase combines relaxation and emotive imagery (strategies discussed earlier in this section). Clients are taught how to use relaxation and positive imagery to counter causes of stress.

The final step in the stress-management training procedure uses a variety of other strategies like reframing, cognitive restructuring, behavior rehearsal, bibliotherapy, and physical exercise routines to teach clients how to handle stressful situations while staying calm and composed.

Guidelines for Selecting Therapy Strategies

There is no one perfect way to understand every individual's problem, nor is there any single perfect counseling strategy that fits all situations. Different techniques work differently for different people, for different problems, and for different goals (Hosford & de Visser 1974, 97). Therefore, therapists need some criteria to select methods to use with particular client-problem situations. Some suggested guidelines are:

1. Intervention strategies are more acceptable to clients after a strong therapeutic relationship has been established between them and their therapists. Clients need to know that their therapist understands their problems, sincerely cares for them as persons, and has won their trust by behaving with demonstrated empathy and respect.

2. Therapy methods are best viewed as specific modes of communication between therapist and clients. They are part of the therapist's modus operandi in relating skillfully, personally, and professionally with the people they wish to help. Counseling methods are *not* to be equated with a bag-of-tricks approach that suggests a technical expert reaching mechanically for tools to apply.

3. The chosen intervention(s) must be appropriate for the assessed problem(s). Selecting a strategy before the problem is adequately defined or using one that is mismatched with the assessment results in ineffective therapy and erosion of the client's trust and confidence in the therapist.

4. Techniques and methods must be related appropriately to the outcome goals established for the therapy. Since the goals indicate the direction clients are taking to correct their life styles, carefully chosen methods are the means of effecting the desired and indicated changes.

5. Any therapy strategy is most effective when timed with clients' readiness to commit themselves to cooperative involvement and with their gaining motivation for specific kinds of action or change.

6. Therapy strategies should be selected with the personal characteristics and preferences of the client fully in mind. For example, a provocative and expressive mode of therapy (e.g., some Gestalt methods) probably would not be best for shy and retiring clients.

7. Any limitations presented by environmental factors like time, cost, impact of significant others, and availability of resources must be considered when opting for specific interventions. Examples include recommending bibliotherapy with knowledge of the individ-

ual's ability to secure the resources and not selecting play therapy unless enough play materials are available.

8. Finally, therapists should select and use methods with which they are both competent and comfortable. Professional effectiveness in psychotherapy rests largely on therapists' expertise with poised application of modes of intervention.

10

Integrative Therapy in Practice

A truly integrative and comprehensive approach to psychotherapy enables therapists to help all ages of people from all social groups and levels with all kinds of problems. The theory and methods of the most useful forms of integrated therapy not only are potentially applicable to the gamut of psychological problems but also allow for responsible assessment of outcomes. This chapter addresses these and other pragmatic aspects of Integrative Therapy, looking at levels of intervention, specific applications, evaluation of effectiveness, termination, and follow-up.

Levels of Intervention

The problems people experience in day-to-day living tend to fall into three major social categories: intrapersonal, interpersonal, and intergroup. Behavioral and psychological problems associated with these social classifications can be defined as dispositional, situational, and structural, respectively. Integrative Therapy is concerned with all of these categories and its practices can be adapted to fit dispositional conditions (individual therapy), situational conflicts (therapy with couples, families, and groups of individuals), and social-structure issues (consultation with agencies, organizations, institutions, and corporations).

The concepts and methods incorporated in Integrative Therapy provide for a balanced practice of both developmental (primary) and crisis or remedial (secondary) interventions. Furthermore, therapists can adapt this integrative approach to either inpatient or outpatient treatment, brief or long-term therapy, re-educative or reconstructive therapy, insight or action therapy, person-centered or direct therapy. The specific needs of each clini-

161

cal situation indicate the preferred therapeutic adaptation. Thus Integrative Therapy seeks to be inclusive and open in practice rather than exclusive, closed, or rigid.

Specific Applications

Just as some methods are inappropriate for particular clients and problems, some individuals or groups of individuals are not properly fitted for certain types of therapy because of preference, readiness, motivation, response potential, clinical profile, environmental factors, and contextual conditions. Therefore, a system of counseling and psychotherapy must be amenable to a diversity of applications. As I show in the following discussion, Integrative Therapy possesses theoretical openness and methodological richness and flexibility sufficient to accommodate the range of therapy needs presented by the general public.

Therapy with Individuals

Outpatient individual psychotherapy is the setting most frequently focused on by Integrative Therapy because that is what most people need and want. Therapists must decide which therapy setting will serve clients best in light of basic intake data and essential diagnostic information obtained via interviews and the Pre-Therapy Questionnaire. The Pre-Therapy Questionnaire functions as a clinical guide with all literate clients sixteen and older. Interview, direct observation, and other carefully selected assessment strategies substitute with illiterate people, early adolescents, and children. Clients' preferences are always considered when deciding on the social unit of intervention. Although the initial intervention might be with an individual, many cases lead eventually to couples, family, or group therapy.

Children

Individual therapy with children typically consists of play therapy, activity therapy, or dyadic interviews lasting about half an hour. When conducting interviews with children, therapists seek as much as possible to enter their world and communicate interpersonally in language they can understand. They must adjust to children's thought patterns, interests, and levels of comfort with new learning experiences. Projective exercises such as drawing a person (self, father, mother, brother, sister), using play media to portray family scenes, sharing favorite fairy tales, and talking about the happy and sad rooms in the family house add invaluable insight into children's developmental experiences. Frequently therapists sit or sprawl on the floor with a child rather than sitting face to face, as they do with adults. This physical accommodation enhances the therapist-child relationship and eases effective sharing and communication.

Consultation sessions are scheduled with parents, teachers, and other significant persons involved in child clients' daily routines. These consultations allow for both a more realistic appraisal of problems and an *in vivo* check on how effective the therapeutic interventions are.

Adolescents

In addition to interview data and information garnered from the Pre-Therapy Questionnaire, problem check lists (e.g., The Mooney Problem Check Lists and SRA Youth Inventory) are helpful in uncovering issues with which adolescents are struggling. These check lists provide a noncoercive or voluntary response pattern and identify problems without labeling individuals. These qualities are especially important to adolescents, who often are sensitive to labeling and external forces about their personal choices.

As with children, parents and other adults who have significant involvement in adolescent clients' lives are usually consulted to see what they understand about the presenting concerns and what effects they have observed from the therapy. These contacts are made with adolescents' knowledge and consent.

Most of the modes of intervention identified in the previous chapter can be adapted and used effectively with adolescents. Particularly applicable are activity therapy, cognitive-behavior strategies, interventions using natural or logical consequences, and Transactional Analysis. Successful therapy with adolescents depends as much, perhaps, on therapists' patience, nonjudgmental attitude, toleration of ambiguity, and nondefensiveness when challenged or tested as on expert diagnosis and skillful interventions. Therapists have made enormous strides in helping young people when they have learned to become adolescents' trusted older counselors and friends, possess youthful spirits, relate respectfully to young people with wit and humor, show sincere interest in them as worthy persons, and believe in their potential.

Therapy sessions with adolescents are typically about forty-five to fifty minutes long. Therapists must tolerate their tendency to sit or sometimes recline in awkward and amusing manners. Adolescents often use jargon that jars adults' ears. Wise therapists accept and flow with their unconventional posturing and speech. They relate with adolescents best by becoming comfortable with them but not trying to be like them. Adolescents open up to adults whom they consider cool but distrust those who try to act like kids.

Adults

Adults who are single, who are married but whose spouses refuse to enter therapy, or who desire to resolve personal issues, and who state a clear preference for one-to-one therapy for various reasons usually are treated individually. Interview data, observation, and information provided by the Pre-Therapy Questionnaire are supplemented, when needed, by other assessment and diagnostic devices (e.g., psychological tests, problem check lists, interest inventories, value clarification routines, baseline counts).

Virtually all the methods and strategies identified in chapter 9 can be used with adults. Most adults who seek psychotherapeutic treatment present problems connected in some degree to family-of-origin experiences. In most cases, therefore, I use some combination of expressive, redecisioning or restructuring, and re-educative methods. Expressive strategies (e.g., Gestalt, primal, psychodrama) are effective with repressed feelings and painful memories. Having released these painful stored-up emotions from the past, clients can engage in redecisioning to build effective life styles. Methods that reflect the rational-emotive, Adlerian, cognitive-behavioral, and transactional analytic orientations are particularly apropos for redecisioning interventions. Finally, re-educative interventions draw primarily on behavioral and cognitive-behavioral methods and strategies.

Some adults enter therapy with concerns that have little to do with early-in-life experiences. Parenting issues, financial problems, work and career matters, dealing with aging parents, coping with personal loss, and physical health are among their immediate concerns. Support therapy, skill-building interventions, exploration and clarification of values and interests, establishing priorities, and forming realistic plans of attack represent typical clinical work with these kinds of problems.

A unique feature of Integrative Therapy, I believe, is that it encourages clients to view dreams and pain as two of their best friends, since both serve to inform them that something is out of balance, incomplete, or lacking in the life style. It follows naturally that I use dream analysis or dream work in all my therapeutic interventions. I also caution clients to be as drug-free as possible, including both prescribed and nonprescribed chemical substances. Why? Because headaches tell us something is wrong and needs attention. Instead of taking aspirin, we should find out what's wrong (e.g., improper diet, poor vision, withdrawal from caffeine or another chemical, stressful sleeping or sitting position). Giving in to the temptation to medicate the symptom away means not dealing honestly with its cause.

Individual sessions with adults are scheduled initially on a weekly basis for fifty to sixty minutes. With progress, sessions are likely to be reduced to every other week.

Clinical Work with Groups

Many people prefer group counseling or psychotherapy. The group setting provides unique features that are lacking in individual therapy (Yalom 1985). Group members can experience a sense of universality by observing that other people struggle with the same problems they have. This identification with others reduces their feeling of being alone in their pain. The group experience also helps to instill hope as members see fellow members make visible improvement. Group interaction can include corrective recapitulation of family-of-origin experiences with members playing the roles they held in their primary family system.

The group setting offers an excellent opportunity to develop more adaptive social skills. An integral aspect of socialization is group members' gaining therapeutically from imitative learning by participating vicariously in each other's experiences. Interpersonal learning in groups also makes it possible for members to experience genuine support while correcting distorted perceptions of both themselves and others. And group members can do authentic reality testing and deal with unfinished emotional situations, resulting in corrective emotional experiences. Finally, group therapy becomes essentially a social microcosm in which members exhibit the problematic behaviors typical of their interpersonal styles in the real world, thus allowing a more realistic approach to understanding and correcting ineffective life styles.

The concepts, principles, and methods incorporated in Integrative Therapy lend themselves readily to various forms of group work. Among the many possible modes or types of group intervention to which it is adaptable, the three most frequently used are personal growth groups, structured groups, and group psychotherapy that follows a psychodynamically oriented process.

Personal growth groups

Personal growth groups are formed for individuals who do not present serious personality disturbance but want to work on issues like developing better self-awareness, fostering a more positive identity, learning how to trust themselves and others, gaining more self-respect and self-confidence, acquiring more effective social and communication skills, and becoming more sensitive to the feelings, interests, and needs of others. Growth groups are not intended for psychotherapy per se but do produce definite therapeutic gains for their participants.

Growth groups are useful with children, adolescents, adults, and the elderly. They are typically closed (only a limited number of members are selected, usually six to ten) and meet for a specific number of sessions (typically twelve to sixteen, but sometimes more). Group sessions with children tend to last forty to fifty minutes, while sessions with adolescents and adults usually run one to two hours, respectively. The average length of an adult group session is about one and one-half hours. Play and activity therapy are helpful group work with children and adolescents.

Structured groups

While personal growth groups tend to be unstructured regarding themes and interventions, structured groups tend to focus on specific problems. All the members of a particular structured group work on a common central theme or issue. Structured groups can be used effectively with all age groups. Normally, structured groups are closed, meet for one to two hours weekly, and endure from six weeks to several months depending on the nature of the problems for which members seek more effective coping skills.

Possible themes for structured groups with children are dealing with their parents' divorce, learning to express feelings, getting along with friends or classmates, handling violent or angry outbursts, and coping with fear (e.g., darkness, nightmares, being alone).

Among the scores of themes apropos for structured groups with adolescents are peer relationships, body image, dating, peer pressure, alcohol and drugs, study habits, family problems, loneliness, vocational exploration, values clarification, relating to authority figures, finding a job, and leaving home.

Adult themes for structured groups include assertiveness training, divorce, re-entering the dating world, mid-life crises, career changes, caring for aging parents, financial issues, developing effective parenting skills, stress management, adult children of alcoholics, empty nest syndrome, "boomerang kids," love and intimacy, death and dying, dream work, and preparing for retirement.

Group psychotherapy

Group psychotherapy can be used with older children, adolescents, and adults. The group therapy approach integral to Integrative Therapy is democratic and focuses on both the sociodynamics and the psychodynamics of the group process. Here-and-now experiencing and responsible I language are emphasized. Although present-tense experiencing is emphasized, unfinished business from the past can be shared in the immediacy of the present.

Most of the unique features of group work identified earlier characterize group psychotherapy. For example, a corrective recapitulation of family-of-origin traumas, dysfunctional rules, and ineffective coping styles or roles is an anticipated development in the group process. These issues are manifested in some form of transference, interpersonal conflict, or role enactment in the group. Since Integrative Therapy considers the formation and functioning of the nuclear family as the ideal prototype of group process, it is natural to expect the developmental phases, dynamics, and procedures observed in group therapy to reflect the same kind of sociopsychological phenomena that occur in families.

Unlike the interpersonal issues found most commonly in personal growth groups and structured groups, the issues treated in group psychotherapy tend to be more deeply rooted in the intrapersonal dynamics of the group members. Usually, the more deeply rooted the problems are in the psyche, the more painful are the memories. These deep, painful problems require more time for therapeutic resolution. Therefore, psychotherapy groups usually endure considerably longer than do growth groups and structured groups.

Psychotherapy groups may be either closed (a limited number of members are selected with no later additions) or open (new members may join as old members meet their goals and move on). A psychotherapy group typically meets weekly basis for two-hour sessions. It may last from six months to more than a year, while an open group could endure easily for several years.

A male and a female therapist working together can usually achieve better results in group therapy than either one therapist working alone or two of the same sex working together. This is so whether the group is mixed or not. Such cotherapy provides opportunities for group members to enact their family-of-origin roles in a group that corresponds to the family. Nonetheless, parental stimulus effects in group therapy reminiscent of the bio-family can be achieved effectively without leadership by both a man and a woman.

It is important that cotherapists, whether male or female, have compatible basic values and intervention styles. There will be enough personal differences between compatible leaders to accomplish family-of-origin recapitulations. The squabbling of malfitted parental models distracts from group life rather than enhancing it. In contrast, honest differences and clean "fights" between cotherapists can be therapeutic for group members.

A democratic process that stresses personal responsibility and distribution of power uses a variety of experiential and expressive methods to enhance the helpfulness of communication among therapists and members. Interventions may be either individual, dyadic, or group focused.

Integrative group therapists always try to practice the "three p's" of psychotherapy: potency, permission, and protection (James 1977). Their potency is evidenced by their competence, credibility, dependability, trustworthiness, authenticity, composure, and down-to-earth professionalism in relating to group members' concerns and needs. Effective group therapists give verbal and nonverbal permission to group members to experience their feelings, thoughts, and behaviors regarding themselves and others openly and freely without fear of reprimand. Finally, they protect the members by discouraging inappropriate self-disclosure (e.g., too much too soon) or attacks by other members. Doing these things helps to build a safe and comfortable therapeutic environment.

Relationship or Couples Therapy

Relationship or couples therapy is counseling with two individuals who desire to improve the quality of the long-term relationship to which they are committed. The two people might want to enhance their marriage or be seeking premarital counseling. They might disagree about the exact nature of their relationship (e.g., is it friendship or romance from either perspective or both?) and want to clarify their true feelings, thoughts, and plans. They might be roommates who need to reduce conflict or interpersonal tension and create a more cooperative living arrangement, or they might be involved in a gay or lesbian relationship that is frustrating, vague, and problematic, including bisexual attachments. Some might be involved in third-person affairs and need help resolving the triangulated situation.

My practice of Integrative Therapy is open to all types of relationship work except assisting (a) gays and lesbians in establishing same-sexed "marriages," (b) individuals who are engaged in any form of fraud, deception, or duplicity that can hurt or cheat others, and (c) people who are abusing others physically, sexually, emotionally, or mentally and refuse to change. In such cases, I will provide individual therapy but not relationship therapy until I observe success at the individual level. Sometimes it is possible to conduct concurrent individual and relationship therapy with persons whose problems are not so serious and who are not destructive to others.

Among the many concerns addressed in relationship therapy, the following are some of the most frequently treated: communication, decision making, sexuality, emotional availability, intimacy, compatibility of interests and values, relationships with friends and relatives, financial matters, sex roles, desire for children, parenting, recreation and leisure, dual careers, trust and commitment, forgiveness and reconciliation, jealousy and possessiveness, and forgetting the past.

Many of the therapeutic modalities featured in chapters 8 and 9 are applicable to relationships, but those drawn from the Transactional Analysis, experiential, and cognitive behavioral approaches work best in most cases. Carefully selected homework activities are invaluable parts of relationship therapy. I also use bibliotherapy with virtually all clients who have ineffective, dysfunctional, unhappy, or troubled relationships.

Family Therapy

Integrative Therapy seeks a balanced treatment of the family as a system while respecting individuals as unique members of the family. An existential appreciation for the uniqueness and realness of the individual leads us to see that the dynamic interactions and role assumptions of individual personalities combine to create the social network we call a family. Thus, from my point of view, the best family therapy uses integrated treatment of the individual in the context of the family.

As we try to understand and treat a family with conflicts, we invariably observe and examine both the behavioral profiles of the individual members and how they relate to each other. Observation made from an object-relations perspective provides valuable information about bonding patterns, attachment and separation experiences, object losses, capacity for love and intimacy, and distancing within both the immediate nuclear or blended family and previous families, including the parents and spouses in their families of origin. It is also important to discover any subgroup in the family, for instance, dyadic and triadic arrangements in both present and former families. Discerning these increases understanding of the sociopsychological forces operating in the family. We also need to discover or uncover the rules, both functional and dysfunctional, that have persisted across generations and now regulate family life.

In Integrative Therapy, we emphasize repeatedly that no one family member will be singled out and treated as the "identified patient." Rather, if anyone has a problem or is hurting, then the entire family has a problem and is hurting. In many cases certain members of a family are more disturbed than others, but our focus on the whole family removes the onus and stigma of being "sick" or "crazy" from any particular person.

Integrative Therapy views family therapy as a special form of group therapy. It is not surprising to observe many of the same dynamics, procedures, and interventions in both group and family therapy. If the nuclear family can be seen as the ideal prototype of the therapy group (as Integrative Therapy sees it), it follows that family therapy is the most natural form of group therapy. The roles assumed at home by the family members are brought into the therapy room and are quickly identified by the therapist(s).

A major function of the integrative therapist in family therapy is to facilitate a therapeutic environment in which each member of the family is free to feel, think, and behave as a unique and valuable person. The same "three p's" (potency, permission, and protection) emphasized in group psychotherapy are practiced in family therapy as well. We try to create an open and participatory democracy in which all members of the family have genuine freedom to make real choices, behave responsibly toward themselves and others, give valuable input to family decisions, and communicate openly and honestly. They are accepted and respected without imposed conditions of worth, are appreciated for any contribution(s) they make to the success and welfare of the family, receive positive recognition for appropriate behavior, have a voice in defining right and wrong conduct, and accept the consequences of personal misconduct. They are not punished for honest mistakes, and they assume a share in the distribution of power in the family system appropriate to their status (parent or child) and age (adult, adolescent, young child). This needs to be accomplished with full respect for the distinct roles and responsibilities of parents and children.

Virtually any of the methods profiled in the previous chapter can be used in family therapy to assist particular members or the family as a whole. I often use family sculpting for both diagnosis and treatment. I customize homework for each family and design it to include as many aspects of the family's total milieu as possible. These homework assignments appear to be among the most helpful interventions, according to most client families.

Treating Addictive Behaviors

Most addicts require two stages of treatment for successful recovery (Larsen 1985). Stage I consists of detoxification, becoming sober, and breaking the addiction. As a general rule, successful Stage I treatment requires the individual's commitment to a controlled, structured environment for intensive inpatient therapy. This holds true for most addictions: drugs, alcohol, food, sex, relationships, gambling. This stage usually necessitates locating the addicted person so that he or she has no access to the addictive substance or situation.

The second stage of recovery involves the personal change or growth the individual makes after breaking the addiction. For some persons, Stage II recovery is experienced in a self-help group (e.g., Alcoholics Anonymous, Narcotics Anonymous, Overeaters Anonymous). Many others profit from ongoing professional therapeutic interventions.

The principles and methods of Integrative Therapy lend themselves to both inpatient and outpatient treatment but are particularly relevant to Stage II interventions. The Twelve Steps popularized by Alcoholics Anonymous can become a part of the integrated approach. I have revised and adapted the Twelve Steps (see appendix D) to make them more compatible with the tenets of Integrative Therapy; for example, my adaptation reflects more accurately the belief in a personal God than does AA's theme of the "higher power."

Stage I treatment rids the individual of the bad consequences of the addiction, but it does little with the cause(s). Stage II psychotherapy examines and treats issues like dysfunctional rules that existed in the family of origin and their impact on the client, early life decisions, poor self-concept, low self-esteem, and environmental conditions that influence choices and life style. Treatment focuses on forming new attitudes toward self and others, making new decisions, developing more adaptive coping and living skills, and forming a more realistic orientation to life. A definite focus is placed on the need for love and grace (May 1988) in a mature relationship with God and other men and women of faith who share in the quest for authentic and successful living.

Group therapy is the preferred mode of treatment for individuals who are recovering from addictive behaviors. The advantages of the group option were identified earlier in this chapter.

Training and Supervision

Pre-practicum training

Integrative Therapy, as developed here, represents a plausible approach to both the mastery of the theoretical aspects of open systems or nonexclusive psychotherapy (didactic training) and the acquisition of the generic helping skills required in counseling and therapy (experiential training). It provides a model for developing a personal orientation to therapy that includes a view of the human being, a theory of personality, a theory of personality dysfunction, a paradigm for diagnosing problems, a set of guidelines for ethical conduct, therapeutic relationship skills, steps to follow in setting goals for therapy, principles for selecting intervention methods and techniques, and a body of complementary modes of therapy.

Although this book tends more toward didactic training, the instructor or trainer can easily create experiential learning activities to supplement and parallel its theoretical, conceptual, and methodological emphases. It is more effective for individual trainers to develop experiential learning exercises that closely match their specific preferences than for me to provide a handbook or how-to manual. Instructors' crafting their own counseling laboratory activities adds to the authenticity, originality, intensity, realism, and personal presence and involvement in the training process.

The themes and methods featured in this book can serve easily and effectively as the text for either a complete course on integrative, open systems, or broad spectrum therapy, or as a special unit in a course that examines various schools, systems, and approaches to psychotherapy.

Supervised clinical practice

Supervised clinical practice is an invaluable part of training professional counselors, psychotherapists, and psychologists. First, the supervised practica and internships of counselors and therapists shape their professional style, sharpen their skills, and refine their expertise as therapists. Second, clinical supervision is a major, perhaps the primary, influence on a therapist's adopting a particular orientation to counseling and psychotherapy (e.g., Cummings & Lucchese 1978). As is true of pre-practicum training in the theory and practice of open systems therapy, Integrative Therapy is equally applicable to the supervised practicum. This therapeutic model can serve as the preferred supervisory emphasis in training programs that advocate the integrative orientation, or it can be one of the elective options in programs that are eclectic or nonexclusive. Supervision may be offered for all modes of therapy—individual, group, couples/relationship, family, child, adolescent, adult.

As a trainer of counseling psychologists in an accredited program (American Psychological Association) in a large state university, I stress the theoretical and practical emphases detailed here in the various clinical practica I supervise, particularly with students who choose to do elective training with me.

Consultation

Frequently other professionals involved in agencies, institutions, or organizations that deliver human services need assistance to improve their quality and effectiveness. Intervening in the activities of such community or public systems is usually called consultation. Consultants provide indirect services to the public or clientele served by professionals in the agencies that seek their help. Consultation is becoming an increasingly important input to human-service systems.

Integrative Therapy has been used successfully to provide consultation for public school systems, community mental-health centers, vocational training centers, private psychiatric hospitals, churches, professional groups, educational institutions, and social-service agencies. Among the many targeted issues of the consultation services have been classroom management, building social skills, conflict resolution, interviewing skills, interpersonal relationships, marital enrichment, and parenting skills.

Consultation may occur virtually anywhere using virtually any interventions. Examples include inservice workships for teachers, counselors, nurses, ministers, parents, police, and managers; employee assistance programs (EAPs); continuing education professional groups; skills acquisition and enhancement for professional members of mental-health delivery systems; designing training programs in educational and professional institutions; and developing or modifying treatment programs in public or community agencies.

Community Focus

An assumption integral to Integrative Therapy is that a comprehensive practice of psychotherapy cannot be restricted solely to in-office treatment. Rather, clients must be diagnosed and treated whenever appropriate or possible: in the family, within their total social environment, with input from other professional helpers, and with the support and nurture of significant other caring persons. The overall concern is to facilitate the development, adjustment, growth, and healing of the whole person in a system that includes all available resources (sociological, psychological, vocational, educational, spiritual, medical). An interdisciplinary model is used as much as possible. This might include consultation with family physicians and teachers; pastors, priests, or rabbis; parents or children; employers and supervisors; referring persons or anyone with knowledge or skills relevant to the client and problem. All this is conducted according to professional ethics and with the client's informed consent.

The outlook voiced here is harmonious with the Judeo-Christian tradition that stresses a community of believers functioning as an interdependent body in which each member makes special contributions to the welfare of others. This theme is emphasized repeatedly in the Bible, especially in the writings of the apostle Paul (e.g., Rom. 12; 1 Cor. 12–14; Gal. 6:1–10; Eph. 4:1–6:9; Phil. 2:1–4; Col. 3:1–4:1; 1 Thess. 5:12–15; Philem.). The principles of *agape* love, *koinonia* (fellowship, sharing things in common), mutual commitment to building one another up spiritually and otherwise, and assuming personal responsibility for being the keeper, healer, restorer, encourager, counselor, comforter, and burden-bearer of one's brother or sister are apropos to the practice of Integrative Therapy.

How do I use community in my practice? Quite frequently, people who enter therapy suffer from loneliness, lack of friends and support system, family-of-origin abuse or deprivation, disappointment, and discouragement. In addition to my in-office therapy sessions, I routinely ask these clients to visit local churches, clubs, and civic groups of their choice and to become actively involved. Sometimes I will give the names and telephone numbers of carefully selected resource persons whom they can contact for help with introductions. Many former or current clients are happily involved in churches in my community because of a homework assignment in therapy. Several individuals who entered therapy as agnostics, skeptics, cynics, or doubters about God, church, and spiritual realities have become joyful believers while searching for community in response to my assignment.

Evaluating the Effectiveness of Therapy

The procedures followed in Integrative Therapy for diagnosing problems, establishing therapeutic goals, and planning and making interventions allow for a straightforward evaluation of the therapy. While no paper-and-pencil evaluative devices have been developed and used with clients to date to provide a quantitative data base with statistical analyses of outcomes, ongoing assessment is being made. Neither have any longitudinal or long-term follow-up evaluations been conducted on either complex clinical cases or large numbers of randomly selected clients. Nonetheless, regular follow-up checks do serve as a useful means to assess outcomes of therapy. More formal means of evaluation that can be used to obtain numerical data for generating statistical results are envisioned. Currently, evaluations are based on information gathered by the methods discussed below.

At the end of each therapy session, I inquire about what was gained, learned, or experienced during that hour. I frequently ask some down-to-earth questions like, "What have you gotten from this session that is useful to you?" or "What are you taking home in your 'shopping bag' today that will make life more productive for you?" or "What issue with which you are struggling has been clarified, resolved, or reduced today and how?" I do not want clients to leave my office until they can identify some specific gain or success. This does not imply that they always depart in an upbeat mood; that is desirable but hardly realistic. Sometimes clients learn in therapy how to deal honestly with anger and might leave sessions in touch with that aspect of their personality or behavior. This would be evaluated as successful therapy if constructive expression of anger had been stated as a therapeutic objective.

Periodically, I check my clients' level of comfort in the therapy. I am especially concerned to monitor the quality of the therapeutic relationship and their satisfaction with it. I inquire specifically about their sense of being respected, understood, cared for, and treated with sensitivity and kindness.

During each session I try to obtain information about the amount of progress clients are experiencing toward the fulfillment of therapeutic goals related to specific problematic behaviors, emotions, sensations, dreams or images, thoughts, interpersonal or relationship factors, mood changes, self-concept, or sexuality. I also check routinely on the completion of homework. I process this information and enter it into the clients' files. It provides a ready basis for making a comparative judgment about the status of each client's progress to date.

Satisfactory fulfillment of the goals of therapy is the primary criterion for measuring therapeutic effectiveness. Successful achievement of goals is based on the consensual confirmation of three essential sources of empirical validation: the client's self-reporting of satisfaction with the positive gains in personality and behavior change as specified by the established goals; the therapist's observing the same improvements directly or as reported by the client; and corroboration from external witnesses, including the results of *in vivo* practice and observations by significant others (spouse, employer, teacher, child, supervisor). The combined data from these three sources provide a fairly reliable basis for assessing effective outcomes of counseling and psychotherapy.

Termination of Therapy

Therapy begins with the awareness that it will be a temporary involvement of the therapist in the client's concerns with living. Temporary, of course, is relative to both clients and problems. While some therapy requires only a single session, some lasts for weeks, months, or even years. Whatever the duration, when the therapist and client agree that the client no longer needs professional help, therapy ends. The following discussion focuses on particular realities associated with ending counseling.

Termination: A Constant Issue

Termination needs to be a central issue in therapy from the beginning. Since clients are respected as free and responsible individuals with the right to be self-determining and self-directing, they are encouraged early to assume responsibility for deciding whether to continue in therapy. This is part of the informed-consent procedure (see appendix C). Although therapists always endeavor to provide the conditions and skills that are necessary and sufficient for effective psychotherapy, it remains clients' prerogative to judge whether they are gaining enough to warrant continuing.

Even though it is clients' right to terminate whenever they wish, we expect them to evaluate their progress objectively before choosing to stop. Clients who recognize substantial progress toward fulfilling their therapeutic objectives usually want to continue.

Thus, we work on the assumption that the entire process can be enhanced by seeing termination as a viable option beginning with the initial interview, and clients work with full awareness that the final decision to continue or end therapy is theirs.

Confronting Premature Termination

Accepting clients' right to terminate and encouraging them to assume ultimate responsibility for the decision does not mean that therapists never challenge their desire to terminate prematurely. Experienced therapists know that clients reach points when they prefer to depart rather than come to grips with themselves and their problems. They recognize these potential turning points and confront clients' resistance to corrective, possibly painful, changes in their lives. I typically ask my clients to assess the possible losses and gains from staying in therapy or stopping. Becoming aware that their desires to terminate tend to be unreasonable and superficial and that the likely gains from continuing outweigh those they might expect from stopping helps motivate them to continue. The therapist's nonjudgmental support, encouragement, and acceptance of their resistance helps to resolve their desire for premature termination.

Sooner or later every therapist, no matter how competent and compassionate, encounters that first client who communicates, either by words or by missing an appointment and refusing efforts to reschedule, that the therapist or therapy is no longer desired. Whenever possible, therapists will want to discuss openly with these clients their reasons for termination, express respect for their decision, and share their own true feelings about the situation—including possible disappointment at not having the opportunity to assist clients through to the attainment of their goals. Instead of viewing this premature termination as an affront or challenge to their professional competence, therapists would do well to (1) discern what might be learned from this experience in terms of relationships, skills, and procedures; (2) accept as reality that it is impossible to be effective with all clients; (3) make efforts to arrange for an appropriate referral if desired; and (4) proceed to work with the next scheduled client with increased wisdom and renewed commitment to help as many people as possible to the best of their personal and professional ability.

Occasionally therapy is terminated before the client's goals have been fulfilled because of events in the life of the therapist, like relocating to a place far from the client's home, closing an office or agency, or a major crisis (e.g., incapacitating injury or illness or a devastating relationship change). If these events are anticipated, the client can be prepared by being informed as early as possible. When the occurrences arise unexpectedly, special efforts must be made to assist the client in making new adjustments. Should the therapist and client have formed a strong relationship, the client is likely to feel betrayed or abandoned by a trusted friend. Anger, hurt, fear, and resentment often emerge as the client reflects on how he or she revealed personal information in confidence and now the trusted person is walking out. The therapist must provide time to work through both the client's emotions and his or her own feelings in open, honest sharing. If the client desires another therapist, the departing therapist must do everything possible to assist with referral and transition.

Fulfilled Goals

Ideally, therapy ends only after the specified goals have been met successfully. One criterion discussed earlier in the chapter requires an observation of the extent to which clients achieve the stated goals for therapy. After the appropriate therapeutic methods have been applied in order to produce the desired change or changes in personality or behavior, it's time to stop.

As stated earlier, both clients and therapists must be able to observe change in terms of achieving the expected outcomes of therapy. The change must be observed not only in the therapy room but also in life. For example, should an individual's goal be to gain the ability to write exams without excessive anxiety, termination would be inappropriate until the client's real test performance reached the level specified by the goal.

When clients stand assured that they have satisfied their therapy objectives and are able to corroborate self-reports with evidence from real life and the confirming witness of the therapist and (whenever possible) other observers, termination of therapy is both timely and appropriate.

Saying Good-bye

Terminating a genuinely therapeutic relationship frequently generates mixed emotions in both the client and the therapist. Both are happy that progress has been made and the client no longer needs the therapist's help. Both also experience a tinge of sadness because they have become friends, fellow human beings who have encountered one another in real life and now must discontinue the relationship. Both have gained by sharing in the pain and joy of life—the client by receiving healing help, and the therapist by giving unselfishly for the welfare of another and so being blessed by the other's new hope.

In therapy, clients open their souls and reveal their inner secrets in trust and confidence to therapists. Therapists respond with compassion, gentleness, and courage to clients' pain and struggles. When all the goals have been reached, both feel that it would be nice to meet again next week, but both know that it is better not to. So, they shake hands, maybe share a gentle embrace or hug, smile affectionately, and say good-bye.

As clients walk away, they sense deep in their hearts that they have found someone who not only cares but also has touched them in a healing, strengthening, encouraging way. They know that the therapist's door is always open and they can return for more help if the need arises.

As I lean back in my chair and look out the window, I, too, feel deep within that I have helped to make life a bit more meaningful for another person. And I feel that that person has made life more full for me. I never heal without being healed, give without receiving, touch without being touched. And I never encourage without being encouraged.

Follow-up

A final evaluation of the effectiveness of counseling and psychotherapy can be made by therapists' contacting clients for follow-up assessment of sustained outcomes. Clients should be informed during the exit interview that a follow-up evaluation will be conducted in a few months. Preferably, the follow-up will be made at no cost to the clients; this enhances their awareness that therapists are genuinely interested in their welfare.

A follow-up assessment should not be made until at least three or four months have passed. The longer the time between termination and follow-up, the greater is the assurance that clients are maintaining, without therapists' assistance, the behavioral, cognitive, or emotional changes gained in therapy.

Cormier and Cormier (1985) have identified several practical approaches to follow-up: (1) Schedule in-office interviews to evaluate the extent of success in coping with former concerns. (2) Mail postage-paid questionnaires on which clients can indicate how well they are maintaining the changes achieved in therapy. (3) Write to clients requesting written responses to specific questions about the current status of the problems brought to therapy. (4) Conduct telephone interviews to obtain oral reports on sustained success. (5) Ask clients to self-monitor or self-rate their own observed success at maintaining the achieved goals. Clients could do this for two or more weeks about four to six months after termination of therapy. A copy of the self-rating or charting of observed success can be returned to the therapist for evaluation.

Should the follow-up assessment indicate that success has been sustained, therapists can compliment clients for their success and wish them continued mastery of life issues. They can remind clients that the door is always open should they ever need help with the same or other problems. However, should the follow-up reveal that clients are not coping satisfactorily with their problems, therapists can either invite them to return for further therapy or encourage them to seek additional help from someone else. The latter option is better when either clients prefer not to return to their original therapists or therapists judge that clients will be served better by working with someone else. The original therapist will assist with referral as needed.

The seasoned and wise therapist knows well that some of the best psychotherapy is not done in a professional office. Rather, splendid healing and renewing of human souls and spirits occur in beautiful bonding experiences between a man and woman in love or between mothers and fathers and their children; walks in meadows filled with birds, butterflies, and flowers; eating watermelon with friends; singing praises to the Lord in the splendor of a natural or human sanctuary; canoeing down a wilderness river with a trusted confidant; reflecting on the love and grace of God while reveling in creation at the top of a mountain or on an ocean's shore; touching the face of a lonely little boy or girl; being licked affectionately by a puppy; watching raindrops on green leaves and window panes; finishing a job of which you are proud; any of these and ten thousand more.

Growth and healing are never finished for any person. Therefore, the in-touch therapist encourages clients to seek out all possible opportunities for new growth, healing, renewal, and restoration, to seek balance and integration, to be responsibly vulnerable and take risks, and to be at peace with themselves, God, and other people.

Wise therapists know and demonstrate that life is beautiful and good because the Lord is good and is eager to give abundantly to us out of his goodness (John 10:10).

Epilogue

I have tried to provide a respectable orientation to counseling and psychotherapy that stands on a firm foundation. In summary, five basic assumptions form the foundation of Integrative Therapy. First, a personal, sovereign Supreme Being exists and is the source of all truth, whether observed in nature or revealed in the Holy Scriptures. Second, human beings were created and exist in the image of God and can discover and know the truth through disciplines as diverse as theology, anthropology, biology, mathematics, philosophy, astronomy, physics, and psychology. Third, the most plausible search for truth is provided by an empiricism that is open to all sources of data, including the supernatural. Fourth, no single approach to counseling and psychotherapy possesses either sufficient theoretical contructs to comprehend the personality and behavior of human beings or adequate therapeutic methods to assist a cross-sectional clientele presenting the gamut of problems encountered in living. Rather, the whole of psychotherapeutic truth lies in the systematic integration of the complementary methods, principles, and concepts derived from the Scriptures, systems of counseling and psychotherapy, and all relevant disciplines. Finally, a bona fide integrative approach to counseling and psychotherapy that is responsive to the myriad of human concerns will reflect the Zeitgeist of the hour.

While stating these presuppositions firmly, the book is offered to its readers as an open-minded model for the integrative process in crafting and implementing a personalized orientation to psychotherapy. I desire that those who use the book refuse tenaciously to accept it as *the* approach to counseling and psychotherapy. I have simply tried to demonstrate one way to frame a perspective on therapy.

I hope that the book will prove useful as a training resource, a practice handbook, an integration guide, and a growth stimulator. Whatever purpose it serves, I suggest that it be appreciated as either a supplement or a complement to your own creative involvement in counseling and psychotherapy. I sincerely encourage you not to allow it to become a substitute for your own creativity. If I point the way and provide a plausible model for integrative therapy, then my primary objective will have been accomplished.

I have tried to produce a product that is attractive to both the curiously interested nonreligious individual and the open-minded Christian. No effort was made to straddle the fence or speak out of both sides of my mouth. Rather, my intent was to use language, attitude, and writing style that are honest, realistic, nonguarded, and adaptive to the pragmatic and pluralistic world in which both believers and nonbelievers live and interact. I hope nonreligious readers will allow the supernatural or metaphysical overtones in the book to flow freely into the consciousness and bounce around for a while before discarding them arbitrarily. I invite religious or Christian readers to remember that truth is one and to avoid rejecting concepts and methods merely because they are not derived from the Scriptures per se. Truly effective counseling or psychotherapy depends on the truths derived from both the natural and the supernatural realms. May all readers become and remain open to both of these truth sources and allow the truth parts to fall into their proper place in the integrative process.

Appendix A

Ethical Principles of Psychologists

Preamble

Psychologists respect the dignity and worth of the individual and strive for the preservation and protection of fundamental human rights. They are committed to increasing knowledge of human behavior and of people's understanding of themselves and others and to the utilization of such knowledge for the promotion of human welfare. While pursuing these objectives, they make every effort to protect the welfare of those who seek their services and of the research participants that may be the object of study. They use their skills only for purposes consistent with these values and do not knowingly permit their misuse by others. While demanding for themselves freedom of inquiry and communication, psychologists accept the responsibility this freedom requires: competence, objectivity in the application of skills, and concern for the best interests of clients, colleagues, students, research participants, and society. In the pursuit of these ideals, psychologists subscribe to principles in the following areas: 1. Responsibility, 2. Competence, 3. Moral and Legal Standards, 4. Public Statements, 5. Confidentiality, 6. Welfare of the Consumer, 7. Professional Relationships, 8. Assessment Techniques, 9. Research with Human Participants, and 10. Care and Use of Animals.

Acceptance of membership in the American Psychological Association commits the member to adherence to these principles.

Psychologists cooperate with duly constituted committees of the American Psychological Association, in particular, the Committee on Scientific and Professional Ethics and Conduct, by responding to inquiries promptly and completely. Members also respond promptly and completely to inquiries from duly constituted state association ethics committees and professional standards review committees.

Principle 1: Responsibility

In providing services, psychologists maintain the highest standards of their profession. They accept responsibility for the consequences of their acts and make every effort to ensure that their services are used appropriately.

a. As scientists, psychologists accept responsibility for the selection of their research topics and the methods used in investigation, analysis, and reporting. They plan their research in ways to minimize the possibility that their findings will be misleading. They provide thorough discussion of the limitations of their data, especially where their work touches on social policy or might be construed to the detriment of persons in specific age, sex, ethnic, socioeconomic, or other social groups. In publishing reports of their work, they never suppress disconfirming data, and they acknowledge the existence of alternative hypotheses and explanations of their findings. Psychologists take credit only for work they have actually done.

b. Psychologists clarify in advance with all appropriate persons and agencies the expectations for sharing and utilizing research data. They avoid relationships that may limit their objectivity or create a conflict of interest. Interference with the milieu in which data are collected is kept to a minimum.

c. Psychologists have the responsibility to attempt to prevent distortion, misuse, or suppression of psychological findings by the institution or agency of which they are employees.

d. As members of governmental or other organizational bodies, psychologists remain accountable as individuals to the highest standards of their profession.

e. As teachers, psychologists recognize their primary obligation to help others acquire knowledge and skill. They maintain high standards of scholarship by presenting psychological information objectively, fully, and accurately.

f. As practitioners, psychologists know that they bear a heavy social responsibility because their recommendations and professional actions may alter the lives of others. They are alert to personal, social, organizational, financial, or political situations and pressures that might lead to misuse of their influence.

Principle 2: Competence

The maintenance of high standards of competence is a responsibility shared by all psychologists in the interest of the public and the profession as a whole. Psychologists recognize the boundaries of their competence and the limitations of their techniques. They only provide services and only use techniques for which they are qualified by training and experience. In those areas in which recognized standards do not yet exist, psychologists take whatever precautions are necessary to protect the welfare of their clients. They maintain knowledge of current scientific and professional information related to the services they render.

a. Psychologists accurately represent their competence, education, training, and experience. They claim as evidence of educational qualifications only those degrees obtained from institutions acceptable under the Bylaws and Rules of Council of the American Psychological Association.

b. As teachers, psychologists perform their duties on the basis of careful preparation so that their instruction is accurate, current, and scholarly.

c. Psychologists recognize the need for continuing education and are open to new procedures and changes in expectations and values over time.

d. Psychologists recognize differences among people, such as those that may be associated with age, sex, socioeconomic, and ethnic backgrounds. When necessary, they obtain training, experience, or counsel to assure competent service or research relating to such persons.

e. Psychologists responsible for decisions involving individuals or policies based on test results have an understanding of psychological or educational measurement, validation problems, and test research.

f. Psychologists recognize that personal problems and conflicts may interfere with professional effectiveness. Accordingly, they refrain from undertaking any activity in which their personal problems are likely to lead to inadequate performance or harm to a client, colleague, student, or research participant. If engaged in such activity when they become aware of their personal problems, they seek competent professional assistance to determine whether they should suspend, terminate, or limit the scope of their professional and/or scientific activities.

Principle 3: Moral and Legal Standards

Psychologists' moral and ethical standards of behavior are a personal matter to the same degree as they are for any other citizen, except as these may compromise the fulfillment of their professional responsibilities or reduce the public trust in psychology and psychologists. Regarding their own behavior, psychologists are sensitive to prevailing community standards and to the possible impact that conformity to or deviation from these standards may have upon the quality of their performance as psychologists. Psychologists are also aware of the possible impact of their public behavior upon the ability of colleagues to perform their professional duties.

a. As teachers, psychologists are aware of the fact that their personal values may affect the selection and presentation of instructional materials. When dealing with topics that may give offense, they recognize and respect the diverse attitudes that students may have toward such materials.

b. As employees or employers, psychologists do not engage in or condone practices that are inhumane or that result in illegal or unjustifiable actions. Such practices include, but are not limited to, those based on considerations of race, handicap, age, gender, sexual preference, religion, or national origin in hiring, promotion, or training.

c. In their professional roles, psychologists avoid any action that will violate or diminish the legal and civil rights of clients or of others who may be affected by their actions.

d. As practitioners and researchers, psychologists act in accord with Association standards and guidelines related to practice and to the conduct of research with human beings and animals. In the ordinary course of events, psychologists adhere to relevant governmental laws and institutional regulations. When federal, state, provincial, organizational, or institutional laws, regulations, or practices are in conflict with Association standards and guidelines, psychologists make known their commitment to Association standards and guidelines and, wherever possible, work toward a resolution of the conflict. Both practitioners and researchers are concerned with the development of such legal and quasi-legal regulations as best serve the public interest, and they work toward changing existing regulations that are not beneficial to the public interest.

Principle 4: Public Statements

Public statements, announcements of services, advertising, and promotional activities of psychologists serve the purpose of helping the public make informed judgments and choices. Psychologists represent accurately and objectively their professional qualifications, affiliations, and functions, as well as those of the institutions or organizations with which they or the statements may be associated. In public statements providing psychological information or professional opinions or providing information about the availability of psychological products, publications, and services, psychologists base their statements on scientifically acceptable psychological findings and techniques with full recognition of the limits and uncertainties of such evidence.

a. When announcing or advertising professional services, psychologists may list the following information to describe the provider and services provided: name, highest relevant academic degree earned from a regionally accredited institution, date, type, and level of certification or licensure, diplomate status, APA membership status, address, telephone number, office hours, a brief listing of the type of psychological services offered, an appropriate presentation of fee information, foreign languages spoken, and policy with regard to third-party payments. Additional relevant or important consumer information may be included if not prohibited by other sections of these Ethical Principles.

b. In announcing or advertising the availability of psychological products, publications, or services, psychologists do not present their affiliation with any organization in a manner that falsely implies sponsorship or certification by that organization. In particular and for example, psychologists do not state APA membership or fellow status in a way to suggest that such status implies specialized professional competence or qualifications. Public statements include, but are not limited to, communication by means of periodical, book, list, directory, television, radio, or motion picture. They do not contain (i) a false, fraudulent, misleading, deceptive, or unfair statement; (ii) a misinterpretation of fact or a statement likely to mislead or deceive because in context it makes only a partial disclosure of relevant facts; (iii) a statement intended or likely to create false or unjustified expectations of favorable results.

c. Psychologists do not compensate or give anything of value to a representative of the press, radio, television, or other communication medium in anticipation of or in return for professional publicity in a news item. A paid advertisement must be identified as such, unless it is apparent from the context that it is a paid advertisement. If communicated to the public by use of radio or television, an advertisement is prerecorded and approved for broadcast by the psychologist, and a recording of the actual transmission is retained by the psychologist.

d. Announcements or advertisements of "personal growth groups," clinics, and agencies give a clear statement of purpose and a clear description of the experiences to be provided. The education, training, and experience of the staff members are appropriately specified.

e. Psychologists associated with the development or promotion of psychological devices, books, or other products offered for commercial sale make reasonable efforts to ensure that announcements and advertisements are presented in a professional, scientifically acceptable, and factually informative manner.

f. Psychologists do not participate for personal gain in commercial announcements or advertisements recommending to the public the purchase or use of proprietary or single-source products or services when that participation is based solely upon their identification as psychologists.

g. Psychologists present the science of psychology and offer their services, products, and publications fairly and accurately, avoiding misrepresentation through sensationalism, exaggeration, or superficiality. Psychologists are guided by the primary obligation to aid the public in developing informed judgments, opinions, and choices.

h. As teachers, psychologists ensure that statements in catalogs and course outlines are accurate and not misleading, particularly in terms of subject matter to be covered, bases for evaluating progress, and the nature of course experiences. Announcements, brochures, or advertisements describing workshops, seminars, or other educational programs accurately describe the audience for which the program is intended as well as eligibility requirements, educational objectives, and nature of the materials to be covered. These announcements also accurately represent the education, training, and experience of the psychologists presenting the programs and any fees involved.

i. Public announcements or advertisements soliciting research participants in which clinical services or other professional services are offered as an inducement make clear the nature of the services as well as the costs and other obligations to be accepted by participants in the research.

j. A psychologist accepts the obligation to correct others who represent the psychologist's professional qualifications, or associations with products or services, in a manner incompatible with these guidelines.

k. Individual diagnostic and therapeutic services are provided only in the context of a professional psychological relationship. When personal advice is given by means of public lectures or demonstrations, newspaper or magazine articles, radio or television programs, mail, or similar media, the psychologist utilizes the most current relevant data and exercises the highest level of professional judgment.

l. Products that are described or presented by means of public lectures or demonstrations, newspaper or magazine articles, radio or television programs, or similar media meet the same recognized standards as exist for products used in the context of a professional relationship.

Principle 5: Confidentiality

Psychologists have a primary obligation to respect the confidentiality of information obtained from persons in the course of their work as psychologists. They reveal such information to others only with the consent of the person or the person's legal representative, except in those unusual circumstances in which not to do so would result in clear danger to the person or to others. Where appropriate, psychologists inform their clients of the legal limits of confidentiality.

a. Information obtained in clinical or consulting relationships, or evaluative data concerning children, students, employees, and others, is discussed only for professional purposes and only with persons clearly concerned with the case. Written and oral reports present only data germane to the purposes of the evaluation, and every effort is made to avoid undue invasion of privacy.

b. Psychologists who present personal information obtained during the course of professional work in writings, lectures, or other public forums either obtain adequate prior consent to do so or adequately disguise all identifying information.

c. Psychologists make provisions for maintaining confidentiality in the storage and disposal of records.

d. When working with minors or other persons who are unable to give voluntary, informed consent, psychologists take special care to protect these persons' best interests.

Principle 6: Welfare of the Consumer

Psychologists respect the integrity and protect the welfare of the people and groups with whom they work. When conflicts of interest arise between clients and psychologists' employing institutions, psychologists clarify the nature and direction of their loyalties and responsibilities and keep all parties informed of their commitments. Psychologists fully inform consumers as to the purpose and nature of an evaluative, treatment, educational, or training procedure, and they freely acknowledge that clients, students, or participants in research have freedom of choice with regard to participation.

a. Psychologists are continually cognizant of their own needs and of their potentially influential position vis-à-vis persons such as clients, students, and subordinates. They avoid exploiting the trust and dependency of such persons. Psychologists make every effort to avoid dual relationships that could impair their professional judgment or increase the risk of exploitation. Examples of such dual relationships include, but are not limited to, research with and treatment of employees, students, supervisees, close friends, or relatives. Sexual intimacies with clients are unethical.

b. When a psychologist agrees to provide services to a client at the request of a third party, the psychologist assumes the responsibility of clarifying the nature of the relationships to all parties concerned.

c. Where the demands of an organization require psychologists to violate these Ethical Principles, psychologists clarify the nature of the conflict between the demands and these principles. They inform all parties of psychologists' ethical responsibilities and take appropriate action.

d. Psychologists make advance financial arrangements that safeguard the best interests of and are clearly understood by their clients. They contribute a portion of their services to work for which they receive little or no financial return.

e. Psychologists terminate a clinical or consulting relationship when it is reasonably clear that the consumer is not benefiting from it. They offer to help the consumer locate alternative sources of assistance.

Principle 7: Professional Relationships

Psychologists act with due regard for the needs, special competencies, and obligations of their colleagues in psychology and other professions. They respect the prerogatives and obligations of the institutions or organizations with which these other colleagues are associated.

a. Psychologists understand the areas of competence of related professions. They make full use of all the professional, technical, and administrative resources that serve the best interests of consumers. The absence of formal relationships with other professional workers does not relieve psychologists of the responsibility of securing for their clients the best possible professional service, nor does it relieve them of the obligation to exercise foresight, diligence, and tact in obtaining the complementary or alternative assistance needed by clients.

b. Psychologists know and take into account the traditions and practices of other professional groups with whom they work and cooperate fully with such groups. If a psychologist is contacted by a person who is already receiving similar services from another professional, the psychologist carefully considers that professional relationship and proceeds with caution and sensitivity to the therapeutic issues as well as the client's welfare. The psychologist discusses these issues with the client so as to minimize the risk of confusion and conflict.

c. Psychologists who employ or supervise other professionals or professionals in training accept the obligation to facilitate the further professional development of these individuals. They provide appropriate working conditions, timely evaluations, constructive consultation, and experience opportunities.

d. Psychologists do not exploit their professional relationships with clients, supervisees, students, employees, or research participants sexually or otherwise. Psychologists do not condone or engage in sexual harassment. Sexual harassment is defined as deliberate or repeated comments, gestures, or physical contacts of a sexual nature that are unwanted by the recipient.

e. In conducting research in institutions or organizations, psychologists secure appropriate authorization to conduct such research. They are aware of their obligations to future research workers and ensure that host institutions receive adequate information about the research and proper acknowledgement of their contributions.

f. Publication credit is assigned to those who have contributed to a publication in proportion to their professional contributions. Major contributions of a professional character made by several persons to a common project are recognized by joint authorship, with the individual who made the principal contribution listed first. Minor contributions of a professional character and extensive clerical or similar nonprofessional assistance may be acknowledged in footnotes or in an introductory statement. Acknowledgement through specific citations is made for unpublished as well as published material that has directly influenced the research or writing. Psychologists who compile and edit material of others for publication publish the material in the name of the originating group, if appropriate, with their own name appearing as chairperson or editor. All contributors are to be acknowledged and named.

g. When psychologists know of an ethical violation by another psychologist, and it seems appropriate, they informally attempt to resolve the issue by bringing the behavior to the attention of the psychologist. If the misconduct is of a minor nature and/or appears to be due to lack of sensitivity, knowledge, or experience, such an informal solution is usually appropriate. Such informal corrective efforts are made with sensitivity to any rights to confidentiality involved. If the violation does not seem amenable to an informal solution, or is of a more serious nature, psychologists bring it to the attention of the appropriate local, state, and/or national committee on professional ethics and conduct.

Principle 8: Assessment Techniques

In the development, publication, and utilization of psychological assessment techniques, psychologists make every effort to promote the welfare and best interests of the client. They guard against the misuse of assessment results. They respect the client's right to know the results, the interpretations made, and the bases for their conclusions and recommendations. Psychologists make every effort to maintain the security of tests and other assessment techniques within limits of legal mandates. They strive to ensure the appropriate use of assessment techniques by others.

a. In using assessment techniques, psychologists respect the right of clients to have full explanations of the nature and purpose of the techniques in language the clients can understand, unless an explicit exception to this right has been agreed upon in advance. When the explanations are to be provided by others, psychologists establish procedures for ensuring the adequacy of these explanations.

b. Psychologists responsible for the development and standardization of psychological tests and other assessment techniques utilize established scientific procedures and observe the relevant APA standards.

c. In reporting assessment results, psychologists indicate any reservations that exist regarding validity or reliability because of the circumstances of the assessment or the inappropriateness of the norms for the person tested. Psychologists strive to ensure that the results of assessments and their interpretations are not misused by others.

d. Psychologists recognize that assessment results may become obsolete. They make every effort to avoid and prevent the misuse of obsolete measures.

e. Psychologists offering scoring and interpretation services are able to produce appropriate evidence for the validity of the programs and procedures used in arriving at interpretations. The public offering of an automated interpretation service is considered a professional-to-professional consultation. Psychologists make every effort to avoid misuse of assessment reports.

f. Psychologists do not encourage or promote the use of psychological assessment techniques by inappropriately trained or otherwise unqualified persons through teaching, sponsorship, or supervision.

Principle 9: Research with Human Participants

The decision to undertake research rests upon a considered judgment by the individual psychologist about how best to contribute to psychological science and human welfare. Having made the decision to conduct research, the psychologist considers alternative directions in which research energies and resources might be invested. On the basis of this consideration, the psychologist carries out the investigation with respect and concern for the dignity and welfare of the people who participate and with cognizance of federal and state regulations and professional standards governing the conduct of research with human participants.

a. In planning a study, the investigator has the responsibility to make a careful evaluation of its ethical acceptability. To the extent that the weighing of scientific and human values suggests a compromise of any principle, the investigator incurs a correspondingly serious obligation to seek ethical advice and to observe stringent safeguards to protect the rights of human participants.

b. Considering whether a participant in a planned study will be a "subject at risk" or a "subject at minimal risk," according to recognized standards, is of primary ethical concern to the investigator.

c. The investigator always retains the responsibility for ensuring ethical practice in research. The investigator is also responsible for the ethical treatment of research participants by collaborators, assistants, students, and employees, all of whom, however, incur similar obligations.

d. Except in minimal-risk research, the investigator establishes a clear and fair agreement with research participants, prior to their participation, that clarifies the obligations and responsibilities of each. The investigator has the obligation to honor all promises and commitments included in that agreement. The investigator informs the participants of all aspects of the research that might reasonably be expected to influence willingness to participate and explains all other aspects of the research about which the participants inquire. Failure to make full disclosure prior to obtaining informed consent requires additional safeguards to protect the welfare and dignity of the research participants. Research with children or with participants who have impairments that would limit understanding and/or communication requires special safeguarding procedures.

e. Methodological requirements of a study may make the use of concealment or deception necessary. Before conducting such a study, the investigator has a special responsibility to (i) determine whether the use of such techniques is justified by the study's prospective scientific, educational, or applied value; (ii) determine whether alternative procedures are available that do not use concealment or deception; and (iii) ensure that the participants are provided with sufficient explanation as soon as possible.

f. The investigator respects the individual's freedom to decline to participate in or to withdraw from the research at any time. The obligation to protect this freedom requires careful thought and consideration when the investigator is in a position of authority or influence over the participant. Such positions of authority include, but are not limited to, situations in which research participation is required as part of employment or in which the participant is a student, client, or employee of the investigator.

g. The investigator protects the participant from physical and mental discomfort, harm, and danger that may arise from research procedures. If risks of such consequences exist, the investigator informs the participant of that fact. Research procedures likely to cause serious or lasting harm to a participant are not used unless the failure to use these procedures might expose the participant to risk of greater harm, or unless the research has great potential benefit and fully informed and voluntary consent is obtained from each participant. The participant should be informed of procedures for contacting the investigator within a reasonable time period following participation should stress, potential harm, or related questions or concerns arise.

h. After the data are collected, the investigator provides the participant with information about the nature of the study and attempts to remove any misconceptions that may have arisen. Where scientific or humane values justify delaying or withholding this information, the investigator incurs a special responsibility to monitor the research and to ensure that there are no damaging consequences for the participant.

i. Where research procedures result in undesirable consequences for the individual participant, the investigator has the responsibility to detect and remove or correct these consequences, including long-term effects.

j. Information obtained about a research participant during the course of an investigation is confidential unless otherwise agreed upon in advance. When the possibility exists that others may obtain access to such information, this possibility, together with the plans for protecting confidentiality, is explained to the participant as part of the procedure for obtaining informed consent.

Principle 10: Care and Use of Animals

An investigator of animal behavior strives to advance understanding of basic behavioral principles and/or to contribute to the improvement of human health and welfare. In seeking these ends, the investigator ensures the welfare of animals and treats them humanely. Laws and regulations notwithstanding, an animal's immediate protection depends upon the scientist's own conscience.

a. The acquisition, care, use, and disposal of all animals are in compliance with current federal, state or provincial, and local laws and regulations.

b. A psychologist trained in research methods and experienced in the care of laboratory animals closely supervises all procedures involving animals and is responsible for ensuring appropriate consideration of their comfort, health, and humane treatment.

c. Psychologists ensure that all individuals using animals under their supervision have received explicit instruction in experimental methods and in the care, maintenance, and handling of the species being used. Responsibilities and activities of individuals participating in a research project are consistent with their respective competencies.

d. Psychologists make every effort to minimize discomfort, illness, and pain of animals. A procedure subjecting animals to pain, stress, or privation is used only when an alternative procedure is unavailable and the goal is justified by its prospective scientific, educational, or applied value. Surgical procedures are performed under appropriate anesthesia; techniques to avoid infection and minimize pain are followed during and after surgery.

e. When it is appropriate that the animal's life be terminated, it is done rapidly and painlessly.

This version of the *Ethical Principles of Psychologists* was adopted by the American Psychological Association's board of directors on June 2, 1989. On that date, the board of directors rescinded several sections of the Ethical Principles that had been adopted by the APA Council of Representatives on January 24, 1981. Inquiries concerning the substance or interpretation of the *Ethical Principles of Psychologists* should be addressed to the Administrative Director, Office of Ethics, American Psychological Association, 1200 Seventeenth Street, N.W., Washington, D.C. 20036.

These ethical principles apply to psychologists, to students of psychology, and to others who do work of a psychological nature under the supervision of a psychologist. They are intended for the guidance of nonmembers of the Association who are engaged in psychological research or practice.

These ethical principles have previously been published as follows:

American Psychological Association. 1953. *Ethical Standards of Psychologists,* Washington, D.C.

American Psychological Association. 1958. Standards of ethical behavior for psychologists. *American Psychologist* 13: 268–71.

American Psychological Association. 1959. Ethical standards of psychologists. *American Psychologist* 14: 279–82.

American Psychological Association. 1963. Ethical standards of psychologists. *American Psychologist* 18: 56–60.

American Psychological Association. 1968. Ethical standards of psychologists. *American Psychologist* 23: 357–61.

American Psychological Association. 1977, March. Ethical standards of psychologists. *The APA Monitor,* 22–23.

American Psychological Association. 1979. *Ethical Standards of Psychologists,* Washington, D.C.: APA.

American Psychological Association. 1981. Ethical principles of psychologists. *American Psychologist* 36: 633–38.

Request copies of the *Ethical Principles of Psychologists* from the APA Order Department, P.O. Box 2710, Hyattsville, Md. 20784; or phone (703) 247-7705.

Appendix B

Pre-Therapy Questionnaire

Purpose

This questionnaire is used to gather information about your personal background and current problems in living. You will add much to your counseling/therapy program by answering these questions as fully and accurately as possible. If there are items or sections of the questionnaire that do not apply to you, simply mark N/A. Should there be questions that you do not want to answer, write "Prefer not to answer."

This information about you will remain *strictly confidential. No third party will be permitted to see it without your written permission.*

Date _____

General Information

1. Name:_____Age:_____Sex: _____
2. Address: _____
   Street   City   State   Zip
3. Telephone Numbers: (Day)_____(Evening) _____
4. Date of Birth:_____Place of Birth: _____
5. Height:_____Weight:_____Handicap: _____
6. Education:_____Special Training: _____
7. Marital/Relationship Status (Circle One): Single, Engaged, Living Together, Committed, Married, Separated, Divorced, Widowed, Remarried
8. Do you own your home?___Yes___No. Type of housing: _____
9. Person(s) with whom you are now living: _____
10. Have you ever been arrested?___Yes___No. If yes, give date and reasons: _____
11. Referred by: _____
12. Are you covered by health insurance?___Yes___No. If yes,
    Name of Insurance Company _____
    Address_____
    Telephone number _____
13. Person to contact in an emergency: Name _____
    Relationship_____ Telephone _____
    Address_____

Health Information

1. Your physician's: Name_____Telephone_____
   Address _____
2. Date and results of your last physical examination: _____
   _____
3. Prescribed medicines (What kind, amount, how long, and who wrote
   prescription): _____
   _____
4. List any illnesses or diseases you had during childhood and adolescence: _____
   _____
5. Identify any serious accidents or surgery (Give your age at the time of
   occurrence): _____
   _____
6. Describe any addiction problems you have ever had: _____
   _____
7. Describe any problem such as alcoholism, substance abuse, diabetes,
   allergies, etc. in your family:_____
   _____
8. Were you ever hospitalized for psychological problems?___No___Yes.
   If yes, give date(s), place(s), and problem(s):_____
   _____
   _____
9. Have you ever attempted suicide?___No___Yes. If yes, share when and
   how: _____
10. Has any close relative attempted or committed suicide?___No___Yes.
    If yes, share who and when: _____
    _____
11. How do you rate your general health?___Excellent ___Good ___Fair
    ___Poor___Very Poor. Comments:_____
    _____

Occupational Information

1. Your occupation: _____
2. Your present job:_____Beginning date: _____
3. Current employer: Name_____Telephone _____
   Address _____
4. How satisfied are you with your present job?_____
   _____
5. How well does your income meet your financial needs?_____
   _____
6. Types of jobs held in the past and how long for each? _____
   _____
   _____

7. What are your career or vocational goals at this time?_____
_____

8. How have your career goals and ambitions changed during the last five years? _____
_____

9. What are your plans, thoughts, feelings regarding the idea of retirement? _____
_____

Family of Origin Information

1. Your parents:

	Father	Mother
Living or deceased?		
If dead, your age at death?		
Cause of death?		
Your reaction to death?		
If alive, present age?		
Health?		
Education?		
Occupation?		
Place of birth?		
Present location?		

2. Give a description of your father's personality and how he treated you and other members of the family: _____
_____

3. Give a description of your mother's personality and how she treated you and other members of the family: _____
_____

4. If you were reared by someone other than your natural parents, please identify who they were and describe how they treated you and other members of the family: _____
_____

5. List all the children in your natural family, from the oldest to the youngest, in order (include yourself):

Name	Birthdate	Education	Career

6. Give the names and ages of any stepbrothers and stepsisters:_____
   _____
   _____
   _____

7. Identify a child in your family, including yourself and any stepbrothers and/or stepsisters, with each of the following (If you are an only child, substitute your parents):

Most intelligent _____	Least intelligent _____
Hardest worker _____	Laziest_____
Most conforming_____	Most rebellious _____
Most successful_____	Least successful _____
Most awkward _____	Most athletic_____
Most violent _____	Most gentle _____
Most immoral_____	Most religious _____
Most considerate _____	Most critical _____
Most friends _____	Least friends _____
Most generous _____	Most selfish_____
First to marry _____	Last to marry _____
Family black sheep_____	Family pet_____
Most punished _____	Most pampered _____
Most neglected_____	Most indulged _____
Most attractive _____	Least attractive _____
Strongest_____	Weakest_____
Most submissive_____	Most defiant_____
Happiest _____	Saddest _____
Most life father_____	Most like mother _____
Most like you _____	Least like you _____
Daddy's boy _____	Mama's boy _____
Daddy's girl _____	Mama's girl_____
Most healthy_____	Most sickly _____
Most loved _____	Least loved _____

8. Give an impression of your childhood home environment (What kind of relationships existed between the parents, between parents and children, and between children?): _____
   _____
   _____
   _____

9. What "do" and "don't" messages did you hear most often from your parents (e.g., "Don't cry," "Be a big man," "Don't be a sissy")? _____
   _____
   _____
   _____

10. What was your favorite fairy tale when you were a child? _____
_____

11. Give two or three recollections of things that happened to you during your first ten years (Identify specific events, the persons involved, the places, and your feelings at the time.): _____
_____
_____
_____
_____

12. Draw a circle around the following conditions that applied to you during your childhood:

Bedwetting	Loved	Praised
Sleepwalking	Ridiculed	Pampered
Happy childhood	Insecure	Neglected
Sexually molested	Nailbiting	Rejected
Unhappy childhood	Fears	Lonely
Abused	Ignored	Angry
Stuttering	Unwanted	

Other(s):_____

13. Share any other experiences and memories that you wish concerning your childhood: _____
_____

Personal Impressions

1. Complete the following incomplete sentences by writing the first thought, impression, or feeling you have for each:

I like _____
I want _____
My family _____
I must _____
Church is _____
I hope _____
I can't _____
If I ever_____
I love_____
I feel _____
When I'm alone_____
Children are _____
I often_____
When I think of death_____
My father _____
God_____
I hate_____

People _____

Someday I _____

I wish _____

My mother _____

I was happiest when _____

I miss _____

Love _____

I need _____

I think of myself_____

My dreams _____

Home _____

My worst fault _____

I believe _____

Men_____

The devil_____

I failed_____

My past_____

Sisters _____

I fear _____

My greatest success _____

Women _____

My sins _____

Marriage _____

I think_____

Brothers _____

I regret _____

Sex_____

Life _____

My spouse _____

The future _____

2. Pretend that you can become any animal you wish. Identify which animal you would like to be and share your reason for this choice: _____

_____

_____

3. Describe where you would like to go, whom you would prefer to go with you, and what you would most want to do if given a three-week vacation with all expenses paid: _____

_____

_____

_____

4. List your four major strengths or abilities:

_____   _____

_____   _____

5. If you could go back to a specific age and start your life over, at what age would you choose to begin anew and what would you do differently the second time around? _____

_____

_____

_____

Religious and Spiritual Information

1. Do you consider yourself a religious person?___Yes___No
2. Religious preference:_____Church membership:_____
3. What does "spiritual" mean to you? _____
4. Describe any spiritual experiences you have had:_____

_____

5. Circle any of the following that apply to you and your beliefs:

Atheist	Skeptic	Agnostic
Pantheist	Christian	Angry with God
Evangelical	Paying for my sins	Fearful of God
A lost soul	Saved	Loved by God
Religion is fake	I hate religion	Condemned
Can't please God	Afraid of death	I like church
Born again	God is unfair	God is love
Unable to believe	Filled with guilt	Forgiven
Searching for God	Want to believe	I hate God
Punished by God	Fundamentalist	Hopeless
Am losing my faith	Bothered by demons	Spirit filled
Hurt by church	I need God	Confused
Rejected by God	Bothered by sin(s)	Charismatic
Out of God's will	Need forgiveness	Can't pray
Faith is a crutch	Turned off to church	God is myth

Other(s):_____

6. Compatibility of your beliefs with those of other significant persons (e.g., parents, spouse, children): _____

_____

7. Your thoughts and feelings about the religious training you received as a child or adolescent: _____

_____

8. Describe how your religious training and values have either helped or hurt you in coping with life's problems:_____

_____

9. Identify any religious/spiritual questions or problems that are of concern to you: _____

_____

_____

Information about Sexuality

1. Describe your parents' attitude toward sex: _____
   _____

2. When and how did you get your first knowledge about sex? _____
   _____

3. When did you first become aware of your own sexual feelings or
   impulses?_____
   _____

4. Describe any unpleasant memories about sexual experiences: _____
   _____

5. Give information about forced or traumatic sexual incidents such as
   rape and molestation: _____
   _____

6. Provide information about any unwanted pregnancies and the consequences: _____
   _____

7. Circle the term that best describes your sexual identity: Heterosexual,
   Homosexual, Gay, Lesbian, Bisexual, Asexual, Other: _____
   _____

8. Provide information about any sexual relationships that are or have
   been of concern to you: _____
   _____

9. Describe any sexual inhibitions or problems that you might have at
   this time:_____
   _____

10. Is your present sex life satisfactory?___Yes___No. If no, please explain:
    _____

11. Other information about your sexuality that you might want to pro-
    vide: _____
    _____

Menstrual Information

1. How old were you when you had your first period? _____
2. Were you informed?___Yes___No. If no, describe your reaction to the
   first period:_____
   _____

3. Are you regular?___Yes___No. If no, describe the nature of your
   irregularity and how it affects you: _____
   _____

4. Duration:_____Date of last period: _____
5. Describe any pain: _____

6. Are you bothered by premenstrual syndrome?___Yes___No. If yes, please describe: _____

_____

7. Describe any mood changes you experience: _____

_____

8. At what age did your mother enter menopause? _____

9. Describe any surgery, diseases, or medications that affect your menstrual cycle:_____

_____

10. What is your attitude toward your own menopause? _____

_____

11. Other information you wish to offer: _____

_____

_____

Marital Information

1. Name of spouse:_____Age:___Phone: _____
2. Address of spouse:_____
3. Occupation of spouse: _____
4. Religious preference of spouse: _____
5. How long did you know your spouse before marriage? _____
6. Date of marriage:_____Your age then:___Spouse's age:_____
7. Any separations from your present spouse:_____No_____Yes. If yes, tell when and for what reason(s): _____

_____

8. Has either spouse ever filed for divorce?___No___Yes. If yes, who filed and when?_____

9. Information about children from present marriage:

Name	Sex	Age	Education	Marital Status
_____	__	___	_____	_____
_____	__	___	_____	_____
_____	__	___	_____	_____
_____	__	___	_____	_____

10. How many previous marriages?_____How many divorces? _____
Comments about previous marriages:_____

_____

11. Give name, sex, age, education, and marital status of any children from previous marriage(s): _____

_____

_____

12. Any in-law problems?___Yes___No. If yes, explain: _____

_____

_____

13. List the things you like about your spouse:

_____   _____
_____   _____
_____   _____

14. List things you wish your spouse would do
              More often: Less often:

_____   _____
_____   _____
_____   _____

15. Identify interests you share with your spouse:

_____   _____
_____   _____
_____   _____

16. Indicate your satisfaction with how decisions are made in your marriage by circling a number for each item below:

	Very Dissatisfied		Satisfied		Very Satisfied
Where couple lives	1	2	3	4	5
What job husband takes	1	2	3	4	5
What job wife takes	1	2	3	4	5
Whether wife works	1	2	3	4	5
Whether husband works	1	2	3	4	5
Number of children	1	2	3	4	5
Who disciplines child	1	2	3	4	5
How to discipline child	1	2	3	4	5
Being with friends	1	2	3	4	5
Visits with relatives	1	2	3	4	5
Managing/spending money	1	2	3	4	5
Attending church	1	2	3	4	5
Planning vacations	1	2	3	4	5
When to have meals	1	2	3	4	5
How to use free time	1	2	3	4	5
Who does which chore	1	2	3	4	5
Other_____	1	2	3	4	5

17. How satisfied are you with the communication in your marriage? Indicate your level of satisfaction by circling the appropriate number for each of the following items:

	Very Dissatisfied		Satisfied		Very Satisfied
Showing affection	1	2	3	4	5
Mutual trust	1	2	3	4	5
Being understood	1	2	3	4	5
Open sharing of feelings	1	2	3	4	5
Freedom to be myself	1	2	3	4	5

Expressing appreciation	1	2	3	4	5
Feeling safe to disagree	1	2	3	4	5
Letting desires be known	1	2	3	4	5
Nonjudgmental listening	1	2	3	4	5
Offering encouragement	1	2	3	4	5
Being supportive	1	2	3	4	5
Giving compliments	1	2	3	4	5
Having a sense of humor	1	2	3	4	5
Smiling	1	2	3	4	5
Enjoying one another	1	2	3	4	5
Other_____	1	2	3	4	5

18. Indicate your level of sexual satisfaction with your spouse by circling a number for each item below:

	Very Dissatisfied		Satisfied		Very Satisfied
When to have sex	1	2	3	4	5
Where to have sex	1	2	3	4	5
How to have sex	1	2	3	4	5
Frequency of sex	1	2	3	4	5
Amount of foreplay	1	2	3	4	5
Gentleness	1	2	3	4	5
Amount of afterplay	1	2	3	4	5
Talking openly about sex	1	2	3	4	5
Openness to try new ways	1	2	3	4	5
Doing romantic things	1	2	3	4	5
Other_____	1	2	3	4	5

19. Indicate the amount of happiness you experience in your marriage and how happy you think your spouse is by checking a percentage for each of you below.

My happiness is about:
___95% or better
___75%
___50%
___25%
___5% or less

My spouse's happiness is about:
___95% or better
___75%
___50%
___25%
___5% or less

20. How committed are you to the marriage, and how optimistic are you that the marriage will improve? _____

_____

21. If you could get one important message to your spouse, what would you most want him or her to hear and receive? _____

_____

_____

_____

Information about Specific Behaviors

1. Circle any of the following behaviors that apply to you:

Aggressive behavior	Late for appointments	Gambling
Overeating	Passive behavior	Insomnia
Using drugs	Eating problems	Cheating
Attempting suicide	Unable to keep a job	Vomiting
Taking too many risks	Moving too often	Smoking
Unable to have fun	Financial problems	Stealing
Can't control temper	Procrastination	Lying
Sleep disturbance	Working too hard	Crying
Unable to concentrate	Drinking problem	Too lazy
Phobic reactions	Too impulsive	Cursing

   Other(s) _____

2. Identify habits, practices or behaviors that you would like to change: _
   _____

Information about Emotions and Feelings

1. Circle any of the following emotions or feelings that apply to you:

Angry	Depressed	Optimistic	Remorseful
Miserable	Anxious	Relaxed	Guilty
Shameful	Excited	Crushed	Bored
Lonely	Panicky	Abandoned	Sad
Scared	Hateful	Hurt	Calm
Insecure	Hostile	Unhappy	Hopeless
Helpless	Agitated	Restless	Fearful
Dejected	Desperate	Regretful	Elated
Envious	Enthusiastic	Contented	Tense
Alienated	Conflicted	Hopeful	Upset
Happy	Overwhelmed	Nervous	Empty
Joyful	Discouraged	Energetic	
Annoyed	Frustrated	Jealous	

   Other(s) _____

2. Identify the feelings you would like to experience
   More often: _____
   _____

   Less often: _____
   _____

3. What are your four greatest fears?

   _____   _____

   _____   _____

Information about Physical Sensations

1. Circle any of the following conditions that apply to you:

Headaches	Hearing problems	Stiffness
Stomach trouble	Skin problems	Chest pains
Dry mouth	Bad odors	Dizziness
"Butterflies"	Floating sensation	Fatigue
No appetite	Burning or itchy skin	Tics
Visual problems	Sexual problems	Tension
Back pain	Palpitations	Rashes
Blackouts	Don't like being	Numbness
Excessive sweating	touched	Tingling
Fainting spells	Unable to relax	Muscle spasms
Watery eyes	Bowel disturbance	Twitches
Tremors	Rapid heart beat	Hot flashes
Nausea	Flushes	Sore joints

Other(s) _____

2. List the sensations that are especially
Pleasant for you: _____

_____

Unpleasant for you:_____

_____

Information about Images, Dreams, and Fantasies

1. Circle any of the following images or mental pictures you sometimes see regarding yourself or other people:

Being hurt	Hurting others	Being alone
Doing pleasant sex	Being abused as child	Not coping
Being helpless	Being seduced	Being loved
Seducing someone	Doing unpleasant sex	Failing
Loving someone	Losing control of self	Succeeding
Being followed	Being trapped	Running away
Being laughed at	Being promiscuous	Being raped
Raping someone	Being talked about	Being killed
Killing someone	Being in charge	Being old
Being abandoned	Being poor	Being rich

Other(s) _____

2. Share what you most often see or do in your daydreams:_____

_____

3. What are the themes, symbols, persons, places, events, etc. you experience most often in your night dreams? _____

_____

Information about Thoughts

1. Circle any of the following words or phrases that you use to describe yourself and your experiences:

Worthless	A nobody	Useless	Unlovable
Intelligent	Unattractive	Incompetent	Crazy
Undesirable	Confident	A failure	Stupid
Confused	Hard worker	Attractive	Naive
Life's unfair	Conflicted	Inadequate	Honest
Suicidal	Considerate	Worthwhile	Loyal
Unstable	A mistake	Responsible	An asset
Irresponsible	Optimistic	Desirable	Humorous
A success	Trustworthy	Ambitious	Devious
Sensitive	Impatient	Inconsiderate	Gentle
Life is empty	A deviant	Pessimistic	A lover

Other(s) _____

2. Identify any irrational, negative, or "horrible" thoughts that bother you: _____
_____
_____

Information about Interpersonal Relationships

1. Circle any of the following words or expressions that describe you socially and interpersonally:

A loner	Leader	Altruistic
Extroverted	Life of the party	Unwanted
Easygoing	Unselfish	A lover
Demanding	Attention seeker	Democratic
Unfriendly	An encourager	Outgoing
Autocratic	A social star	Critical
Unhappy	A "things" person	Friendly
Egocentric	Intimate	Awkward
A nurturer	Play it safe	Rejected
A people person	Shy	Humorous
Like parties	Reclusive	Poised
Isolated	Accepting	A giver
Distrustful	Permissive	Timid
Risk taker	Popular	Uptight
Gregarious	Avoided	Happy
Socially active	Introverted	Aloof
Judgmental	A taker	Trusting
Laid back	Bashful	A hater
Sought out	A follower	

Other(s) _____

2. Identify the persons who make up your support system (those who offer encouragement, comfort, companionship): _____
_____
_____

3. How many close friends do you have?____. Make a few statements about these people: _____
_____
_____

Should you not have any close friends, share what this is like:_____
_____
_____

4. For the following social situations, place a "G" before the ones that provide "good" relationships for you and a "B" before those where you have "bad" relationships:

___Family of origin   ___Immediate family   ___Marriage
___Job   ___School   ___Church
___Spouse's family   ___Club   ___Children
___Fiance(e)'s family   ___Professional groups   ___Friends

Other(s) _____
Comments:_____
_____

5. Describe any relationships that give you
Joy: _____
_____
_____

Grief:_____
_____
_____

6. Provide additional information you would like about any relationships that are of concern to you: _____
_____
_____
_____

Information about Drugs and Other Mood Modifiers

1. Indicate which of the following practices or habits is true for you by placing an "X" under the appropriate category:

	Never	Rarely	Often	Very Often
Marijuana use				
Use birth-control pills				
Physical exercise				
Use tranquilizers				
Take aspirin				

	Never	Rarely	Often	Very Often
Eat balanced meals				
Use painkillers				
Use alcohol				
Use cocaine				
Meditate				
Listen to music				
Drink coffee				
Have allergies				
Smoke cigarettes				
Smoke pipe				
Chew tobacco				
Use snuff				
Eat "junk food"				
Use narcotics				
Take diet pills				
Aerobic dancing				
Take sedatives				
Take stimulants				
Take vacations				
Go to movies				
Do relaxation exercise				
Go to concerts				
Attend sporting events				
Watch TV				
Caffeinated beverages				
Use hallucinogens				
Other_____				
Other_____				
Other_____				

2. Provide information about the effect of the above habits or practices on your moods and emotions (Also, make any comment you wish about other concerns you have about similar issues in your life.):_____

_____
_____
_____
_____

Other Relevant Information

1. State in your own words what you consider to be the nature of your main problem(s): _____

_____
_____
_____

2. Describe when and how your problem(s) began: _____

_____

_____

_____

_____

3. I estimate the severity of my problem(s) to be: (Check one of the following):

___Just an irritant   ___Very severe

___Mildly upsetting   ___Extremely severe

___Moderately severe   ___Totally incapacitating

4. Have you sought other professional help with this problem? ___Yes___No. If yes, give name(s) and professional title(s) of the therapist(s) and date(s) of treatment(s) and results:_____

_____

_____

5. Provide any information not covered in this questionnaire that might help your therapist to understand you and your problem(s) more thoroughly: _____

_____

_____

_____

_____

The influences of Alfred Adler, Arnold Lazarus, and Richard Stuart are acknowledged.

Appendix C

Informed Consent

Description of services: Counseling psychology is a specialized science that seeks to understand and improve human behavior. I, a counseling psychologist (sometimes called a counselor, therapist, or psychotherapist), am a trained and licensed professional who uses my special skills to help persons with their efforts to lead effective and satisfying lives. I am prepared to work with individuals, couples, groups, and entire families. I provide guidance for my clients as they present their problems or concerns and set goals for the counseling process. I then assist them in reaching their goals. I use a variety of counseling methods and strategies in my office and assign appropriate homework activities to aid my clients in learning how to help themselves and run their own lives successfully.

Confidentiality: What you say and do in the sessions with me will be kept in strict confidence. Information concerning you will not be shared with other persons without your permission. Nor will diagnostic terms or codes be used to describe you and your behavior to third parties such as insurance companies without your consent. You need to know, however, that if ever there is reason for me to believe that you are likely to do harm to either yourself or another person, then it is my professional responsibility to notify the appropriate persons or authorities.

Length, frequency, and number of sessions: Individuals usually meet once a week for sessions that run about fifty minutes with adults and thirty minutes with children. Sessions with couples are also scheduled weekly and last about sixty minutes. Groups and families normally meet weekly as well but for ninety minutes. Group counseling sessions for children are weekly fifty-minute sessions. In some cases, it is possible to schedule appointments every two or three weeks. The number of sessions varies with individuals and the nature of their particular problems, but a minimum of ten to twelve sessions should be expected.

Client freedom and responsibility: I respect your values and will not ask you to do anything that would cause you to feel badly about yourself. Nor will I attempt to force you to do anything against your will or good judgment. Although you are encouraged to remain in counseling until you have successfully reached your goal(s), termination or quitting counseling is your right from the very beginning. I don't have any "magic" or power to change your life or solve your problems without your doing some hard work; therefore, it is important that you cooperate with me in carrying out the plans you make for your therapy program. *You* have the ultimate responsibility for the growth and change you make in counseling and therapy.

Fees: All the services I provide will be billed at the rate of $_____ per session. Clients with insurance coverage, after meeting their annual deductible amount, may choose either to pay the full scheduled fee and be reimbursed later by their insurance company or pay their percentage part and assign payment of the insurance portion directly to me. Clients who are not covered by mental-health insurance will pay the full scheduled fee. Special adjustments can be made for persons who do not have insurance coverage or those who have other difficult financial situations.

Payment of fees: It is expected that you pay either the full scheduled fee or your percentage part when the services are received. You will be given a receipt for each payment for your personal records. If you have insurance and wish to be reimbursed for the total cost of psychological counseling, I will prepare itemized statements to assist you with the reimbursement procedure. If you choose to pay only your percentage part and assign payment of the insurance portion directly to me, you are expected to provide me with an official insurance form that is dated and signed by you and/or the authorized party, indicating that payment has been assigned to me.

Canceled appointments: Fees are charged for all scheduled appointments. You will be billed for the full scheduled fee for any appointment that is canceled or broken without twenty-four hours' advance notification. Exceptions will be made in emergency situations such as illness or a death in the family.

Other services: My practice of counseling psychology is one of several options for receiving professional mental-health services in this community. I want you to be fully aware of this now and be assured that I will assist you in seeking another source of help if/when either you or I consider a referral to be in your best interest. Also, it is desirable that you know about the other services before you consent to begin a therapy program with me.

Questions: You are encouraged to discuss openly and freely with me any question or concern you might have about your counseling program at any time you wish.

Consent: I have read, discussed with you the psychologist, and understand what I can expect from a counseling or therapy program offered by you. I give my consent to enter a psychological counseling program with this understanding. I agree to pay $_____ for each scheduled appointment. I understand that my signing this form does *not* commit me to a binding contract but merely indicates my consent to begin therapy with you.

_____   _____
Signature   Date

Appendix D

Twelve Steps to Wholeness

1. I admit that I am powerless without the enabling grace of God to be the kind of person I desire to be and that my life is unmanageable in my own hands.
2. I believe that the love and grace of God can restore and enable me to become the person I want so much to be.
3. I decide here and now to turn my will and whole life over to the care and guidance of God, and I surrender to God to be healed and made whole by any means God wills for my life.
4. I resolve to make a searching and fearless personal inventory of my life in order to discover and face the "shadow" part of my life—to deal with the things I have denied, repressed, and feared.
5. I will admit and confess to God, to myself, and to another human being whom I trust the exact nature of all the wrongs, faults, and dysfunctions I see in me and my life.
6. I am completely ready and willing to have God give me new life and remove all these faults and dysfunctions that controlled my former life.
7. I humbly and honestly ask God to renew me, to give me Christ-like character, and to remove all the shortcomings and dysfunctions from my life.
8. I will make a list of all the persons whom I have harmed or injured and will make amends to them.
9. I will make direct amends to the people whom I have hurt or harmed wherever possible, except when to do so would injure them or others.
10. I will make a continuous personal inventory of my life and, when I am in the wrong, promptly admit it and make an honest effort to correct the wrong.
11. I will seek through prayer, meditation, and reading to improve my conscious awareness of and contact with God and to ask God for

knowledge of the divine will for me and the power to carry out this will.

12. Having gained a spiritual awakening as the result of this personal journey, I commit myself to carrying this message to and sharing it with others, and to practice these principles in all the affairs of my life.

The Twelve Steps of Alcoholics Anonymous

1. We admitted we were powerless over alcohol—that our lives had become unmanageable.
2. Came to believe that a Power greater than ourselves could restore us to sanity.
3. Made a decision to turn our will and our lives over to the care of God *as we understood Him.*
4. Made a searching and fearless moral inventory of ourselves.
5. Admitted to God, to ourselves, and to another human being the exact nature of our wrongs.
6. Were entirely ready to have God remove all these defects of character.
7. Humbly asked Him to remove all our shortcomings.
8. Made a list of all persons we had harmed, and became willing to make amends to them all.
9. Made direct amends to such people wherever possible, except when to do so would injure them or others.
10. Continued to take personal inventory and when we were wrong promptly admitted it.
11. Sought through prayer and meditation to improve our conscious contact with God *as we understood Him,* praying only for knowledge of His will for us and the power to carry that out.
12. Having had a spiritual awakening as the result of these steps, we tried to carry this message to alcoholics, and to practice these principles in all our affairs.

References

Ackerman, N. 1958. *The psychodynamics of family life*. New York: Basic.

Adams, J. E. 1970. *Competent to counsel*. Grand Rapids: Baker.

Adler, A. 1958. *What life should mean to you*. New York: Perigee.

Adler, D. A. 1981. The medical model and psychiatric tasks. *Hospital and Community Psychiatry* 32:387–92.

Alberti, R. E., and M. L. Emmons. 1986. *Your perfect right*. San Luis Obispo, Calif.: Impact.

Allport, G. W. 1937. *Personality: A psychological interpretation*. New York: Holt.

Allport, G. W. 1955. *Becoming*. New Haven: Yale University Press.

Allport, G. W. 1962. Psychological models for guidance. *Harvard Educational Review* 32:373–81.

Allport, G. W. 1964. The fruits of eclecticism: Bitter and sweet. *Acta Psychologica* 23:27–44.

Allport, G. W. 1968. *The person in psychology*. Boston: Beacon.

American Association for Counseling and Development. 1988. Ethical Standards. 3d rev. ed. *Journal of Counseling and Development* 67: 4–8.

American Psychiatric Association. 1980. *Diagnostic and Statistical Manual of Mental Disorders*. 3d ed. Washington, D.C.: APA.

American Psychiatric Association. 1987. *Diagnostic and Statistical Manual of Mental Disorders*. 3d ed. rev. Washington, D.C.: APA.

Ansbacher, H. L., and R. R. Ansbacher, eds. 1956. *The individual psychology of Alfred Adler*. New York: Harper and Row.

Ansbacher, H. L., and R. R. Ansbacher, eds. 1973. *Alfred Adler: Superiority and social interest*. New York: Viking.

Arlow, J. A. 1984. Psychoanalysis. In *Current psychotherapies*, 3d. ed., ed. R. J. Corsini. Itasca, Ill.: Peacock.

Atwater, J. M., and D. Smith. 1982. Christian therapists' use of bibliotherapeutic resources. *Journal of Psychology and Theology* 10:230–35.

Augustine. No date. *The confessions of St. Augustine.* Trans. E. B. Pusey. New York: Nelson.

Axline, V. M. 1969. *Play therapy.* Rev. ed. New York: Ballantine.

Bandura, A. 1969. *Principles of behavior modification.* New York: Holt, Rinehart, and Winston.

Bandura, A. 1977. *Social learning theory.* Englewood Cliffs, N.J.: Prentice-Hall.

Baruth, L. G., and D. G. Eckstein. 1981. *Life style: Theory, practice, and research.* 2d ed. Dubuque, Iowa: Kendall/Hunt.

Beck, A. T. 1976. *Cognitive therapy and the emotional disorders.* New York: International Universities Press.

Bell, J. E. 1961. *Family group therapy.* Washington, D.C.: Department of Health, Education, and Welfare.

Benjamin, L. S. 1974. Structural analysis of social behavior. *Psychological Review* 81:392–425.

Berkouwer, G. C. 1962. *Man: The image of God.* Grand Rapids: Eerdmans.

Berne, E. 1961. *Transactional analysis in psychotherapy.* New York: Grove.

Bernstein, D. A., and T. D. Borkovec. 1973. *Progressive relaxation training.* Champaign, Ill.: Research.

Beutler, E. L. 1983. *Eclectic psychotherapy: A systematic approach.* New York: Pergamon.

Blatner, H. A. 1973. Acting-in: *Practical applications of psychodramatic methods.* New York: Springer.

Blocher, D. H. 1966, 1974. *Developmental counseling.* 1st and 2d eds., respectively. New York: Ronald.

Bordin, E. S. 1968. *Psychological counseling.* 2d ed. New York: Appleton-Century-Crofts.

Boring, E. G. 1929. The psychology of controversy. *The Psychological Review* 36:97–121.

Boring, E. G. 1950. *A history of experimental psychology.* 2d ed. New York: Appleton-Century-Crofts.

Boss, M. 1982. *Psychoanalysis and Daseinanalysis.* New York: Da Capo.

Bowen, M. 1978. *Family therapy in clinical practice.* New York: Aronson.

Brammer, L. M. 1969. Eclecticism revisited. *Personnel and Guidance Journal* 48:192–97.

Brammer, L. M., and E. L. Shostrom. 1960. *Therapeutic psychology.* Englewood Cliffs, N.J.: Prentice-Hall.

Brammer, L. M., and E. L. Shostrom. 1977. *Therapeutic psychology.* 3d ed. Englewood Cliffs, N.J.: Prentice-Hall.

Breuer, J., and S. Freud. 1895. *Studies in hysteria.* 2d ed. of vol. 2 of *The complete psychological works of Freud.* London: Hogarth.

Bube, R. 1971. *The human quest.* Waco: Word.

Carkhuff, R.R., and B. G. Berenson. 1967. *Beyond counseling and psychotherapy.* New York: Holt, Rinehart and Winston.

Carter, J. D., and B. Narramore. 1979. *The integration of psychology and theology.* Grand Rapids: Zondervan.

Cautela, J. R. 1977. *Behavior analysis forms for clinical intervention.* Champaign, Ill.: Research.

Clements, B. T., and D. Smith. 1973. *The counselor and religious questioning and conflicts.* Boston: Houghton Mifflin.

Collins, G. R. 1969. *Search for reality: Psychology and the Christian.* Santa Ana, Calif.: Vision House.

Collins, G. R. 1976. *How to be a people helper.* Santa Ana, Calif.: Vision House.

Collins, G. R. 1977. *The rebuilding of psychology: An integration of psychology and Christianity.* Wheaton: Tyndale.

Collins, G. R. 1980. *Christian counseling.* Waco: Word.

Constantine, L. C. 1981. Family sculpture and relationship mapping technique. In *Family therapy,* 2d ed., ed. G. D. Erickson and T. P. Hogan. Monterey, Calif.: Brooks/Cole.

Cormier, W. H., and L. S. Cormier. 1985. *Interviewing strategies for helpers.* 2d ed. Monterey, Calif.: Brooks/Cole.

Corsini, R. J. 1981. *Handbook of innovative psychotherapies.* New York: Wiley.

Corsini, R. J. 1984. *Current psychotherapies.* 3d ed. Itasca, Ill.: Peacock.

Corsini, R. J. and D. Weddington, eds. 1989. *Current psychotherapies.* 4th ed. Itasca, Ill.: Peacock.

Crabb, L. 1975. *Basic principles of biblical counseling.* Grand Rapids: Zondervan.

Crabb, L. 1977. *Effective biblical counseling.* Grand Rapids: Zondervan.

Cummings, N. A., and G. Lucchese. 1978. Adoption of a psychological orientation: The role of the inadvertent. *Psychotherapy: Theory, Research and Practice* 15:323–28.

Di Loreto, A. O. 1971. *Comparative psychotherapy.* Chicago: Aldine-Atherton.

Dilts, R., J. Grinder, L. Bandler, and J. De Lozier. 1980. *Neuro-linguistic programming: The study of the structure of the subjective experience.* Vol. 1. Cupertino, Calif.: Meta.

Dobson, J. C. 1970. *Dare to discipline.* Wheaton: Tyndale.

Dollard, J., and N. E. Miller. 1950. *Personality and psychotherapy.* New York: McGraw-Hill.

Drakeford, J. 1967. *Integrity therapy.* Nashville: Broadman.

Dreikurs, R. 1964. *Children: The challenge.* New York: Hawthorn.

Duhl, F. J., D. Kantor, and B. S. Duhl. 1973. Learning, space, and action in family therapy: A primer of sculpture. In *Techniques of family therapy,* ed. D. A. Bloch. New York: Grune and Stratton.

Dustin, R., and R. George. 1973. *Action counseling for behavior change.* New York: Intext.

Eckstein, D. G., L. G. Baruth, and D. Mahrer. 1982. *Life style: What it is and how to do it.* 2d ed. Dubuque, Iowa: Kendall/Hunt.

Ellenberger, H. 1970. *The discovery of the unconscious.* New York: Basic.

Ellis, A. 1975. The case against religion: A psychotherapist's view. In *Counseling and psychotherapy: Classics on theories and issues,* ed. B. N. Ard. Rev. ed. Palo Alto, Calif.: Science and Behavior.

Ellis, A. 1977. Characteristics of psychotic and borderline psychotic individuals. In *Handbook of rational-emotive therapy,* ed. A. Ellis and R. Grieger. New York: Springer.

Ellis, A., and R. Grieger. 1977. *Handbook of rational-emotive therapy.* New York: Springer.

English, H. B., and A. C. English. 1958. *A comprehensive dictionary of psychological and psychoanalytic terms.* New York: Longmans and Green.

Erickson, E. H. 1980. *Identity and the life cycle.* New York: Norton.

Eysenck, H. J. 1952. The effects of psychotherapy: An evaluation. *Journal of Consulting Psychology* 16:319–24.

Eysenck, H. J. ed. 1960. *Behavior therapy and the neuroses.* Oxford: Pergamon.

Fagan, J., and I. L. Shepherd, eds. 1979. *Gestalt therapy now.* New York: Harper and Row.

Fisher, K. 1986. DSM-III-R: Amendment process frustrates non-MDs. *APA Monitor* 17(2):17–18, 24.

Ford, D. H., and H. B. Urban. 1963. *Systems of psychotherapy.* New York: Wiley.

Forer, B. R. 1969. The taboo against touching in psychotherapy. *Psychotherapy: Theory Research and Practice* 6:229–31.

Frank, J. E. 1973. *Persuasion and healing.* Rev. ed. Baltimore: Johns Hopkins University Press.

Frankl, V. E. 1962. *Man's search for meaning.* Boston: Beacon.

Frankl, V. E. 1965. *The doctor and the soul.* 2d ed. New York: Knopf.

Frankl, V. E. 1969. *The will to meaning.* New York: New American Library.

Fromm, E. 1963. *The art of loving.* New York: Bantam.

Freud, S. 1913/1946. *Totem and taboo.* New York: Random House.

Freud, S. 1924. *A general introduction to psychoanalysis*. New York: Simon and Schuster.

Freud, S. 1928/1955. *The future of an illusion*. New York: Liveright.

Freud, S. 1933. *New introductory lectures on psychoanalysis*. New York: Norton.

Garfield, S. L. 1980. *Psychotherapy: An eclectic approach*. New York: Wiley.

Garfield, S. L., and R. Kurtz. 1974. A survey of clinical psychologists: Characteristics, activities, and orientations. *The Clinical Psychologist* 28:7–10.

Garfield, S. L., and R. Kurtz. 1976. Clinical psychologists in the 1970s. *American Psychologist* 31:1–9.

Garfield, S. L., and R. Kurtz. 1977. A study of eclectic views. *Journal of Consulting and Clinical Psychology* 45:78–83.

Glasser, W. 1965. *Reality therapy*. New York: Harper and Row.

Goldfried, M. R. 1980. Toward the delineation of therapeutic change principles. *American Psychologist* 35:991–99.

Goldfried, M. R., and J. Sprafkin, J. 1974. *Behavioral personality assessment*. Morristown, N.J.: General Learning.

Goulding, M. M., and R. L. Goulding. 1979. *Changing lives through redecision therapy*. New York: Brunner/Mazel.

Greenberg, L. S., and J. D. Safran. 1981. Encoding and cognitive therapy: Changing what clients attend to. *Psychotherapy: Theory, Research and Practice* 18:163–69.

Grinder, J., and R. Bandler. 1976. *The structure of magic II*. Palo Alto, Calif.: Science and Behavior.

Gross, E. 1990. *Miracles, Demons, and Spiritual Warfare: An Urgent Call for Discernment*. Grand Rapids: Baker.

Grounds, V. 1984. *Radical commitment: Getting serious about Christian growth*. Portland: Multnomah.

Gurman, A. S., and D. P. Kniskern, eds. 1981. *Handbook of family therapy*. New York: Brunner/Mazel.

Hammond, F., and I. M. Hammond. 1973. *Pigs in the parlor: A practical guide to deliverance*. Kirkwood: Impact.

Harlow, H. F. 1958. Nature of love. *American Psychologist* 13:673–85.

Harlow, H. F. 1971. *Learning to love*. San Francisco: Albion.

Harris, T. A. 1967. *I'm OK—You're OK*. New York: Harper and Row.

Hart, J. T. 1983. *Modern eclectic therapy: A functional orientation to counseling and psychotherapy*. New York: Plenum.

Havinghurst, R. J. 1972. *Developmental tasks and education* 3d ed. New York: McKay.

Hersen, M., and A. S. Bellack. 1976. *Behavioral assessment: A practical handbook.* New York: Pergamon.

Holloway, W. H. 1973. Life script questionnaire. Akron, Ohio: Midwest Institute for Human Understanding.

Holmes, A. 1977. *All truth is God's truth.* Grand Rapids: Eerdmans.

Holroyd, J. C., and A. M. Brodsky. 1977. Psychologists' attitudes and practices regarding erotic and non-erotic physical contact with patients. *American Psychologist* 32:843–49.

Horney, K. 1945. *Our inner conflicts.* New York: Norton.

Hosford, R. E., and L. de Visser. 1974. *Behavioral approaches to counseling.* Washington, D.C.: American Association for Counseling and Development.

Hulme, W. 1956. *Counseling and theology.* Philadelphia: Fortress.

ICD-9-CM. 1978. *The international classification of diseases, 9th revision, clinical modification.* Ann Arbor: Commission on Professional Hospital Activities.

Ivey, A. E. 1980. Counseling 2000: Time to take charge. *The Counseling Psychologist* 8(4):12–16.

Ivey, A. E., and L. Simek-Downing. 1980. *Counseling and psychotherapy.* Englewood Cliffs, N.J.: Prentice-Hall.

Jackson, D., ed. 1960. *The etiology of schizophrenia.* New York: Basic.

Jackson, D., ed. 1968. *Therapy, communication and change.* Palo Alto, Calif.: Science and Behavior.

Jacobson, E. 1938. *Progressive relaxation.* Chicago: University of Chicago Press.

Jacobson, E. 1964. *Anxiety and tension control.* Philadelphia: Lippincott.

James, M. 1977. *Techniques in transactional analysis.* Reading, Mass.: Addison-Wesley.

James, W. 1907. *Pragmatism.* New York: Longmans and Green.

Janet, P. M. F. 1924. *Principles of psychotherapy.* New York: Macmillan.

Janet, P. M. F. 1925. *Psychological healing.* New York: Macmillan.

Janov, A. 1970. *The primal scream.* New York: Putnam.

Janov, A. 1975. *The primal man.* New York: Crowell.

Jung, C. G. 1933. *Modern man in search of a soul.* New York: Harcourt Brace.

Jung, C. G. 1959. Conscious, unconscious, and individuation. In *The archetypes and the collective unconscious,* by C. G. Jung. New York: Pantheon.

Jung, C. G. 1968. *Analytical psychology: Its theory and practice.* New York: Vintage.

Kanfer, F. H., and G. Saslow. 1969. Behavioral diagnosis. In *Behavior therapy: Appraisal and status,* ed. C. M. Franks. New York: McGraw-Hill.

Kelly, E. L. 1961. Clinical psychology—1960. Report of survey of findings. *Newsletter: Division of Clinical Psychology of the American Psychological Association* 14:1–11.

Kelly, E. L., L. R. Goldberg, D. W. Fiske, and J. M. Kokowski. 1978. Twenty-five years later: A follow-up study of the graduate students in clinical psychology assessed in the V.A. selection research project. *American Psychologist* 33:746–55.

Kelly, G. A. 1955. *The psychology of personal constructs.* New York: Norton.

Kendler, K. S. 1983. Overview: A current perspective on twin studies in schizophrenia. *American Journal of Psychiatry* 140:1413–25.

Kety, S. S. 1976. Genetic aspects of schizophrenia. *Psychiatric Annals* 6:11–32.

Kohlberg, L. 1981. *The philosophy of moral development.* San Francisco: Harper and Row.

Koteskey, R. L. 1980. *Psychology from a Christian perspective.* Nashville: Abingdon.

Koteskey, R. L. 1983. *General psychology for Christian counselors.* Nashville: Abingdon.

Krumboltz, J. D. 1966. Behavioral goals for counseling. *Journal of Counseling Psychology* 13:153–59.

Krumboltz, J. D., and C. E. Thoresen, eds. 1969. *Behavioral counseling.* New York: Holt, Rinehart and Winston.

Kurtz, P., and E. H. Wilson, eds. 1973. Humanist Manifesto II. *The Humanist* 33(5):4–9.

Landsman, T. 1968. Positive experience and the beautiful person. Presidential address, Southeastern Psychological Association.

Larsen, E. 1985. *Stage II recovery: Life beyond addiction.* New York: Harper and Row.

Lazarus, A. A. 1966. Behavior rehearsal vs. non-directive therapy vs. advice in effecting behavior change. *Behavior Research and Therapy* 4:209–12.

Lazarus, A. A. 1967. In support of technical eclecticism. *Psychological Reports* 21:415–16.

Lazarus, A. A. 1976. *Multimodal behavior therapy.* New York: Springer.

Lazarus, A. A. 1980. *The multimodal life history questionnaire.* Kingston, N.J.: Multimodal Therapy Institute.

Lazarus, A. A. 1981. *The practice of multimodal therapy.* New York: McGraw-Hill.

Lazarus, A. A. 1985. Emotive imagery. In *Dictionary of behavior therapy techniques,* ed. A. S. Bellack and M. Hersen. Elmsford, N.Y.: Pergamon.

Lazarus, A. A. 1985. Behavior rehearsal. In *Dictionary of behavior therapy techniques,* ed. A. S. Bellack and M. Hersen. Elmsford, N.Y.: Pergamon.

Leary, T. 1957. *Interpersonal diagnosis of personality: A functional theory and methodology for personality evaluation.* New York: Ronald.

Lewin, K. 1935. *A dynamic theory of personality.* New York: McGraw-Hill.

Lewis, C. S. 1952. *Mere Christianity.* New York: Macmillan.

Lewis, C. S. 1960. *The four loves.* New York: Harcourt, Brace, Jovanovich.

Lief, A., ed. 1948. *The common sense psychiatry of Adolf Meyer.* New York: McGraw-Hill.

Lowe, C. M. 1976. *Value orientations in counseling and psychotherapy.* 2d ed. Cranston, R.I.: Carroll.

Mahoney, M. J., and C. E. Thoresen, eds. 1974. *Self-control: Power to the person.* Monterey, Calif.: Brooks/Cole.

Maskin, A. 1960. Adaptations of psychoanalytic technique to specific disorders. In *Science and psychoanalysis,* vol. 3, ed. J. H. Masserman. New York: Grune and Stratton.

Maslow, A. H. 1967. A theory of meta motivation: The biological rooting of the value life. *Journal of Humanistic Psychology* 7:93–127.

Maslow, A. H. 1970. *Motivation and personality.* 2d ed. New York: Harper and Row.

Maslow, A. H. 1971. Personality problems and personality growth. *College Student Journal* 5:1–13.

May, G. G. 1988. *Addiction and grace.* New York: Harper and Row.

McClelland, D. C. 1975. *Power: The inner experience.* New York: Irvington.

McLemore, C. W., and L. S. Benjamin. 1979. Whatever happened to interpersonal diagnosis? A psychosocial alternative to DSM-III. *American Psychologist* 34:17–34.

Meehl, P., ed. 1958. *What, then, is man?* St. Louis: Concordia.

Meichenbaum, D. H. 1977. *Cognitive behavior modification.* New York: Plenum.

Meichenbaum, D. H. 1985. *Stress innoculation training.* New York: Pergamon.

Meichenbaum, D. H., and M. E. Jaremko, eds. 1983. *Stress reduction and prevention.* New York: Plenum.

Menninger, K. 1973. *Whatever became of sin?* New York: Hawthorne.

Mischel, W. 1968. *Personality and assessment.* New York: Wiley.

Missildine, W. H. 1963. *Your inner child of the past.* New York: Simon and Schuster.

Montagu, A. A. 1970. A scientist looks at love. *Phi Delta Kappan* 51:463–67.

References 225

Montagu, A. A. 1971. *Touching: The human significance of the skin.* New York: Columbia University Press.

Montgomery, J. W. 1976. *Demon possession.* Minneapolis: Bethany Fellowship.

Moreno, J. L. 1946. *Psychodrama.* Beacon, N.Y.: Beacon.

Morley, B., chairman. 1977. *Final report, phase I.* Task Force on Descriptive Behavioral Classification, Board of Professional Affairs, American Psychological Association. Washington, D.C.: APA.

Mosak, H. H. 1984. Adlerian psychotherapy. In *Current psychotherapies,* ed. R. J. Corsini. 3d ed. Itasca, Ill.: Peacock.

Moustakas, C. 1973. *Children in play.* rev. ed. New York: Aaronson.

Mowrer, O. H. 1961. *The crisis in psychiatry and religion.* Princeton, N.J.: Van Nostrand.

Mowrer, O. H., and A. V. Veszelovszky. 1980. There indeed may be a "right way": Response to James D. Smrtic. *Psychotherapy: Theory, Research and Practice* 17:440–47.

Narramore, C. 1960. *The psychology of counseling.* Grand Rapids: Zondervan.

Norcross, J. C., ed. 1986. *Handbook of eclectic psychotherapy.* New York: Brunner/Mazel.

Nygren, A. 1969. *Agape and eros.* New York: Harper and Row.

Osborne, C. G. 1980. *Understanding your past: The key to your future.* Burlingame, Calif.: Yokefellow.

Osipow, S. H., and W. B. Walsh. 1970. *Strategies in counseling for behavioral change.* New York: Appleton-Century-Crofts.

Palmer, J. E. 1980. *A primer of eclectic psychotherapy.* Monterey, Calif.: Brooks/Cole.

Parloff, M. B., I. E. Waskow, and B. F. Wolfe. 1978. Research on therapist variables in relation to process and outcome. In *Handbook of psychotherapy and behavior change,* 2d ed., ed. S. L. Garfield and A. E. Bergin. New York: Wiley.

Patterson, C. H. 1959. *Counseling and psychotherapy.* New York: Harper and Row.

Patterson, C. H. 1974. *Relationship counseling and psychotherapy.* New York: Harper and Row.

Patterson, C. H. 1980. *Theories of counseling and psychotherapy.* 3d ed. New York: Harper and Row.

Patterson, C. H. 1985. *The therapeutic relationship: Foundations for an eclectic psychotherapy.* Monterey, Calif.: Brooks/Cole.

Patterson, C. H. 1986. *Theories of counseling and psychotherapy.* 4th ed. New York: Harper and Row.

Pattison, J. E. 1973. Effects of touch on self-exploration and the therapeutic relationship. *Journal of Consulting and Clinical Psychology* 40:170–75.

Peck, M. S. 1983. *The people of the lie.* New York: Simon and Schuster.

Perls, F. 1973. *The Gestalt approach and eye witness to therapy.* Palo Alto, Calif.: Science and Behavior.

Polster, E., and M. Polster. 1973. *Gestalt therapy integrated.* New York: Brunner/Mazel.

Prochaska, J. O., and J. O. Norcross. 1983. Contemporary psychotherapists: A national survey of characteristics, practices, orientations and attitudes. *Psychotherapy: Theory, Research and Practice* 20:161–73.

Rogers, C. R. 1942. *Counseling and psychotherapy.* Boston: Houghton Mifflin.

Rogers, C. R. 1951. *Client-centered therapy.* Boston: Houghton Mifflin.

Rogers, C. R. 1957. Empathic: An unappreciated way of being. *The Counseling Psychologist* 5(2):2–14.

Rogers, C. R. 1959. A theory of therapy, personality, and interpersonal relationships as developed in the client-centered framework. In *Psychology: A study of a science,* vol. 3, *Formulations of the person and the social context,* ed. S. Koch. New York: McGraw-Hill.

Rogers, C. R. 1961. *On becoming a person.* Boston: Houghton Mifflin.

Rogers, C. R. 1979. Person-centered therapy. In *Current psychotherapies,* 2d ed. ed. R. J. Corsini. Itasca, Ill.: Peacock.

Rutter, M., et al. 1969. A tri-axial classification of mental disorders in childhood. *Journal of Child Psychology and Psychiatry* 10:41–61.

Rychlak, J. F. 1981. *Introduction to personality and psychotherapy.* 2d ed. Boston: Houghton Mifflin.

Satir, V. 1972. *People making.* Palo Alto, Calif.: Science and Behavior.

Seamands, D. A. 1982. *Putting away childish things.* Wheaton: Victor.

Seamands, D. A. 1985. *Healing of memories.* Wheaton: Victor.

Shostrom, E. L. 1976. *Actualizing therapy.* San Diego: EDITS.

Sim, M. 1983. Psychiatric diagnosis: What we have and what we need. *Psychiatric Annals* 13:757–59.

Sire, J. W. 1988. *The universe next door.* 2d ed. Downers Grove: InterVarsity.

Skinner, B. F. 1938. *The behavior of organisms: An experimental analysis.* New York: Appleton.

Skinner, B. F. 1953. *Science and human behavior.* New York: Macmillan.

Skinner, B. F. 1969. The machine that is man. *Psychology Today* (April): 20–25, 60–63.

Skinner, B. F. 1971. *Beyond freedom and dignity.* New York: Knopf.

Skinner, B. F. 1974. *About behaviorism.* New York: Knopf.

Smith, D. 1974. Integrating humanism and behaviorism: Toward performance. *Personnel and Guidance Journal* 52:513–19.

Smith, D. 1975. *Integrative counseling and psychotherapy.* Boston: Houghton Mifflin.

Smith, D. 1978. Humanist manifesto II: Five years later. *The Humanist* 38(6):55–57.

Smith, D. 1979. Response to the philosophical bias of humanist manifesto II. *Journal of Psychology and Theology* 7:118–24.

Smith, D. 1980. The impact of world views on professional lifestyling. *Personnel and Guidance Journal* 58:584–87.

Smith, D. 1982. Trends in counseling and psychotherapy. *American Psychologist* 37:802–9.

Smith, D., and W. A. Kraft. 1983. DSM-III: Do psychologists really want an alternative? *American Psychologist* 38:777–85.

Smith, D. 1985. Family sculpting. In *Baker encyclopedia of psychology,* ed. D. G. Benner. Grand Rapids: Baker.

Smith, D., and J. K. Burkhalter. 1987. The use of bibliotherapy in clinical practice. *Journal of Mental Health Counseling* 9:184–90.

Spitz, R. A. 1949. Role of ecological factors in emotional development of infants. *Child Development* 76:145–46.

Spitz, R. A. 1965. *The first year of life.* New York: International Universities Press.

Starr, A. 1977. *Psychodrama: Rehearsal for living.* Chicago: Nelson Hall.

Stein, M. J., ed. 1961. *Contemporary psychotherapies.* New York: Free Press.

Steiner, C. M. 1974. *Scripts people live.* New York: Grove.

Stuart, R. B., and B. Jacobson. 1987. *Couple's pre-counseling inventory.* Champaign, Ill.: Research.

Stuntz, E. C. 1973. Multiple chairs technique. *Transactional Analysis Journal* 3(2):29–32.

Swan, G. E., and M. L. McDonald. 1978. Behavior therapy in practice: A national survey of behavior therapists. *Behavior Therapy* 9:799–807.

Szasz, T. S. 1960. The myth of mental illness. *American Psychologist* 15:113–18.

Szsaz, T. S. 1974. *The myth of mental illness.* Rev. ed. New York: Harper and Row.

Tarjan, G., and L. Eisenberg. 1972. Some thoughts on the classification of mental retardation in the United States of America. *American Journal of Psychiatry* (May supplement).

Taylor, J. G. 1963. A behavioral interpretation of obsessive-compulsive neuroses. *Behavior Research and Therapy* 1:237–44.

Thorndike, E. L. 1913. *The psychology of learning.* New York: Teachers College.

Thorne, F. C. 1955. *Principles of psychological examining.* Brandon, Vt.: Clinical Psychology.

Thorne, F. C. 1961. *Personality: A clinical eclectic viewpoint.* Brandon, Vt.: Clinical Psychology.

Thorne, F. C. 1967. *Integrative psychology.* Brandon, Vt.: Clinical Psychology.

Thorne, F. C. 1968. *Psychological case handling.* 2 vols. Brandon, Vt.: Clinical Psychology.

Thorne, F. C. 1973. An eclectic evaluation of psychotherapeutic methods. In *Direct psychotherapy,* vol. 2, ed. R. M. Jurgevich. Coral Gables, Fla.: University of Miami Press.

Tournier, P. 1957. *The meaning of persons.* New York: Harper and Row.

Tournier, P. 1962. *Guilt and grace.* New York: Harper and Row.

Truax, C. B., and R. R. Carkhuff. 1967. *Toward effective counseling and psychotherapy.* Chicago: Aldine.

Tweedie, D. 1961. *Logotherapy and the Christian faith.* Grand Rapids: Baker.

Ullmann, L. P., and L. Krasner. 1969. *A psychological approach to abnormal behavior.* Englewood Cliffs, N.J.: Prentice-Hall.

Unger, M. F. 1971. *Demons in the world today.* Wheaton: Tyndale.

Urban, W. J. 1978. *Integrative therapy: Foundations for holistic and self healing.* Los Angeles: Guild of Tutors.

Urban, W. J. 1981. *Integrative therapy.* In *Handbook of innovative psychotherapies,* ed. R. J. Corsini. New York: Wiley.

Vance, F. L., and T. C. Volsky. 1962. Counseling and psychotherapy: Split personality or Siamese twins. *American Psychologist* 17:565–70.

Van Kaam, A. 1966. *Existential foundations of psychology.* Pittsburgh: Duquesne University Press.

Van Kaam, A. 1968. *Religion and personality.* New York: Doubleday.

Vitz, P. C. 1985. Psychology as religion. In *Baker encyclopedia of psychology,* ed. D. G. Benner. Grand Rapids: Baker.

Wallen, R. 1971. Gestalt therapy and gestalt psychology. In *Gestalt therapy now,* ed. J. Fagan and J. L. Shepherd. New York: Harper and Row.

Watson, J. B. 1919. *Psychology from the standpoint of a behaviorist.* Philadelphia: Lippincott.

Watson, J. B., and R. Rayner. 1920. Conditioned emotional reaction. *Journal of Experimental Psychology* 3:1–14.

Watson, J. B. 1925. *Behaviorism.* New York: Norton.

Whitfield, C. L. 1987. *Healing the child within*. Deerfield Beach, Fla.: Health Communications.

Wolberg, L. R. 1954. *The technique of psychotherapy*. New York: Grune and Stratton.

Wolpe, J. 1958. *Psychotherapy by reciprocal inhibition*. Stanford, Calif.: Stanford University Press.

Wolpe, J. 1982. *The practice of behavior therapy*. 3d ed. New York: Pergamon.

Wolpe, J. 1985. Deep muscle relaxation. In *Dictionary of behavior therapy techniques*, ed. A. S. Bellack and M. Hersen. New York: Pergamon.

Woodworth, R. S. 1931, 1948, 1964. *Contemporary schools of psychology*. 1st, 2d, 3d eds., respectively. New York: Ronald.

Woody, R. H. 1971. *Psychobehavioral counseling and therapy*. New York: Appleton-Century-Crofts.

World Health Organization. 1977. *Manual of the international statistics classification of diseases, injuries and causes of death*. Geneva: WHO.

Yalom, I. D. 1985. *The theory and practice of group psychotherapy*. 3d ed. New York: Basic.

Yontef, G. M., and J. S. Simkin. 1989. Gestalt therapy. In *Current psychotherapies*, 4th ed., ed. R. J. Corsini and D. Wedding. Itasca, Ill.: Peacock.

Index of Persons

Index of Subjects

Index of Scripture

12–14—172
12:3—67
13—66, 102
14:9—104
15:12-57—47
15:39—45
15:42-53—52

2 Corinthians
1:15-17—55
3:18—59
5:1-8—47
5:1-10—52
5:14-21—46
5:17—58, 91
10:5—155

Galatians
1-10—172
4:4—48
5:22—102
5:22-23—67
6:1-10—172

Ephesians
2:3—55
4:1-6:9—172
4:1—172
4:23—45, 58

4:29—104
6:4—148
6:9—172
6:11-12—76

Philippians
1:21-23—47
2:1-4—172
4:8—155

Colossians
1:15-17—41
1:28—148
3:1—91
3:1-4:1—172
3:16—149
3:21—148
4:6—104

1 Thessalonians
2:5-8—149
3:13-18—47
4:13-18—47
5:12-15—172
5:23—45, 91

Titus
3:4-7—91
3:5—58

Hebrews
13:5-6—123

James
3:1—13
3:1-12—104
3:13-18—105

1 Peter
1:23—91
5:14—109

2 Peter
2:14—76

1 John
3:9—91
4:7-8—56
4:8—56, 102
4:16—56

Revelation
19-20—48
20:11-15—47
21-22—48
21:1-7—47
21:8—47